SEVEN DISCIPLINES

DISCIPLINES

OF A

LEADER

How to Help Your People, Team,
and Organization Achieve
Maximum Effectiveness

JEFF WOLF

with Ken Shelton

WILEY

Published by John Wiley & Sons, Inc., Hoboken, New Jersey.
Published simultaneously in Canada.

For general information about our other products and services, please contact our Customer Care Department within the United States at (800) 762-2974, outside the United States at (317) 572-3993 or fax (317) 572-4002.

Wiley publishes in a variety of print and electronic formats and by print-on-demand. Some material included with standard print versions of this book may not be included in e-books or in print-on-demand. If this book refers to media such as a CD or DVD that is not included in the version you purchased, you may download this material at http://booksupport.wiley.com. For more information about Wiley products, visit www.wiley.com.

Library of Congress Cataloging-in-Publication Data:

Wolf, Jeff (Economist)
  Seven disciplines of a leader: How to help your people, team, and organization achieve maximum effectiveness/Jeff Wolf.
      pages cm
  Includes index.
    ISBN 978-1-119-00395-3 (hardback); ISBN 978-1-119-00396-0 (ebk);
ISBN 978-1-119-00409-7 (ebk)
  1. Leadership. I. Title.
    HD57.7.W6495 2015
    658.4'092—dc23
                                                                      2014027703

Printed in the United States of America.

10 9 8 7 6 5 4 3 2 1

*To my mom and dad who always believed in me,
taught me right from wrong, and provided unconditional
love and support in everything I ever did.*

Contents

Acknowledgments

First and foremost, my thanks go out to my family who puts up with me through thick and thin. My beautiful wife Maria who many years ago suggested I go into this wonderful business of leadership development. You were right! My daughter Melissa, who has grown into a very successful young leader, whom I'm very proud of. My stepsons Greg and Alex, my brother Earl, sister-in-law Jacky, and, last but not least, Charlie (man's best friend), who keeps me humble during our nightly walks together.

Martin Smith, an honest and caring man who took me under his wing and helped me get published.

Ken Shelton, who said my original title, *The Essence of Effective Leadership*, would not resonate with people—but *Seven Disciplines of a Leader* would . . . . I hope you are right!

All the leaders I've been privileged to coach and work with during the past 14 years; I'm sure I've learned more from you than you've learned from me.

My literary agent, Jill Marsal, for believing this book had merit.

John Wiley & Sons for investing and showing confidence in me.

My PR team: Jessica, Marcie, and Jennifer. You bring unlimited energy to work each day, and I truly appreciate all that you do.

Thanks also to the people who read this book. I hope it will help you on your leadership journey.

Introduction

What Makes Certain Leaders Highly Effective?

Christopher had recently been promoted from shift supervisor to department manager in an online retailer's large distribution center. Unfortunately, Max, his boss, the shift manager, who leaned toward the theoretical side, was not as helpful or supportive as he could be and Christopher floundered. The distribution center's general manager recognized Max's failing and transferred him into a staff job that required no supervision. He replaced him with Janelle, a leader of considerable accomplishments, who understood how to develop promising employees.

Within weeks, Christopher's performance improved significantly, and he went on to become an outstanding leader for his company. Although he didn't realize it at the time, this experience was invaluable. In essence, what he discovered was that the very best people to teach leadership are those who have "been there, done that, learned from it."

In this book I highlight similar observations to help you learn hard-earned leadership lessons. I call these *hands-on advice*. Regard them collectively as your own personal leadership adviser, the spirit hovering over your right shoulder, whispering in your ear.

Okay, let's get started with the first of these based on Christopher's experience.

> *Hands-On Advice: Find somebody to advise you who's "been there, done that, learned from it."*

Why? Because that's the person who can give you the most valuable advice on leadership—the person who has insights into the

> *Hands-On Advice: Find a mentor, regardless of your level in the company.*

job based on his practical real-world experience. This is what I mean by the term *hands-on*. It has a corollary:

You might be a first-line supervisor, a middle manager, a top executive, a specialist, an aspiring manager. You should have somebody in your corner, somebody you can turn to when you need advice, somebody who can provide an objective opinion. That person might be your boss, another employee who you respect, possibly an outsider. The point is you will *always* benefit from the association.

And that's what I bring to the table. I've been there, done that, learned from it—admittedly, sometimes the hard way. The point is I've worked my way up from the lower ranks of a company to its highest position. Along the way I acquired some priceless lessons on what works and what doesn't in leadership positions throughout the organization. And I founded my company based on teaching others those very same principles.

How Does This Book Address the Answer to Today's Leadership Challenges?

- The book is based upon 14 years of coaching and training leaders at all levels and in all types of industries. I developed and refined the Seven Disciplines through my coaching practice and observing how the Seven Disciplines and Eleven Practices took leaders I've coached and worked with from good to great performers.

- Because of the inordinate amount of pressure exerted on leaders today, coupled with the business necessity of continually doing more with less, leaders have little or no time to hone their leadership skills. This book takes you through the process, step by step, with succinct and descriptive steps, each with real-life examples, and a guide and practice application at the end of each chapter to help coach you through the journey.

- Regardless of what section you read, skills can be gleaned from every chapter to improve leadership functions and abilities.

- Before you can lead others, you must have fundamental and proven disciplines as a basis to rely on for success. The core disciplines described in this book are those that successful leaders I've coached have used to improve their job performances.

- Not only are you learning the seven disciplines, which have proven themselves with literally hundreds of leaders, but you will also learn from stories of success and failure. Additionally, the takeaway section provides action items to further the application of the disciplines and practices learned best by doing. It's almost like having your own personal coach.

- The seven disciplines not only bring to light successful business leadership ideals, but those same disciplines can be applied to improve everyday life.

- Since the ability of leaders to motivate and inspire others is critical, the book shows you how to communicate and interact to execute and lead effectively.

- Employee engagement in the workplace is at an all-time low. In most cases, poor leadership is the reason. This book provides answers. It lays out a platform of proven concepts and ideas that will, if followed, eliminate this burdensome problem in today's workforce.

- Leadership starts from within and manifests itself on the outside. This book provides you with the skills needed within and shows how to seamlessly transfer them into viable actionable steps.

- Many leaders today are promoted based on their technical skills without any consideration for what it takes to perform effectively as a leader. The fate of an organization depends on its leadership. My book provides a step-by-step plan that every company can use to develop its leaders and point to and say: "This is the right way to lead."

- Most important of all, *Seven Disciplines of a Leader* is a book from the trenches . . . not a theoretical hodgepodge of data and ideas. These concepts and ideas are practical and easy to apply. They have constituted the basis of my pragmatic and highly regarded coaching sessions for years.

I've been a janitor who worked in a sweltering furnace room all day, sorting garbage by hand, tearing apart each and every bag and separating the garbage that would burn from the metal and aerosol cans that wouldn't. I always hoped I would be able to pick out all the aerosol cans so they wouldn't explode in the raging furnace and pop my eardrums. Yet every day I came to work motivated because I had a leader who inspired me to be the best that I could be and take pride in my work.

Early in my career I was a high school basketball coach and sought out great college coaches like John Wooden, Bobby Knight, and Al McGuire to see what made them successful and how to incorporate some of their methods of success and leadership practices into my own program. I had a thirst for knowledge that kept me seeking to improve my leadership skills every single day. I learned to motivate the young men on my team by challenging them to achieve peak performance, teamwork, and personal goals.

As an executive, I took the principles and lessons learned from those early experiences and realized that leadership is focusing on the people side of business. It's helping your people perform beyond their own level of expectations. It's bringing out the best in people, teams, and organizations, allowing them to quickly clarify their purpose and vision, set goals, and stay focused and committed.

Fourteen years ago, at the pinnacle of my corporate career, I completed a stint as a CEO and felt it was time to move on to a new career. After engaging numerous consulting firms, I imagined creating a single firm capable of providing truly innovative solutions to a multifaceted range of organizational problems.

I envisioned a unique team of highly experienced senior practitioners who could deliver unprecedented client satisfaction, improve performance, and exceed expectations in three critical areas: consulting, coaching, and training. This pivotal focus would allow us to develop long-term strategic partnerships that could effectively address every level of clients' changing needs.

Over the last decade, despite economic downturns, we've experienced dramatic growth, and I've been very fortunate to coach and provide leadership training to CEOs, presidents, corporate executives, as well as managers, supervisors, and business owners. We've worked with some of the largest and most well-known companies in the world such as Sony, Samsung, Qualcomm, Abbott Labs, Pfizer, CVS, Baxter, Monsanto, General Mills, Tupperware, and hundreds of others.

Having coached hundreds of leaders through thousands of coaching sessions, I've been able to narrow down the essence of leadership success to Seven Disciplines and Eleven Practices that I'll share with you in this book. I'm going to describe leadership skills I've applied in a common sense, easy-to-understand fashion to help leaders at every level of an organization make a real difference in the workplace. The strategies and techniques can be immediately applied to improve your leadership ability.

Over the past 10 years I've worked with people, teams, and organizations who were seeking to:

- Improve individual performance and productivity.
- Address leadership development and succession planning.
- Make a significant impact on their long-term success.
- Sharpen the leadership skills of high potential individuals.
- Change behavior of leaders to make a long-term positive impact on organizational performance.
- Develop the skill set of current and future leaders.
- Build more effective teams.
- Address specific workplace problems.
- Build job-critical competencies.
- Achieve individual performance objectives aligned with organizational goals.
- Raise employee engagement.
- Address the biggest problems facing leaders today.
- Improve employee retention rates and be an employer of choice.

My job is to provide a catalyst for change and equip leaders with the tools, knowledge, and opportunities they need to help them focus on the specific goals they want to achieve.

What makes this book different from others on the market is the fact that I've been there, done that, and learned from it, while so many authors of books on leadership have not. Without that crucial hands-on experience, it's impossible to separate the meaningful from the insignificant in teaching effective leadership principles.

This book is an extrapolation of the future of leadership based upon a varied business career and coaching and working with leaders at every level of organizations for the past 14 years. *Seven Disciplines* is up-to-date with what's happening in today's fast-moving and quickly changing business environment.

A New Generation of Highly Effective Leaders

Today's competitive global marketplace and the high number of retiring senior leaders is driving a great demand for a new generation of highly effective leaders. Where will they come from? How can they be developed? What makes certain leaders highly effective? Are leaders born or made? These questions have been hotly debated for decades.

As an executive coach, I've come to realize that while some people seem to be natural leaders, most great leaders aren't born highly effective with extraordinary skills; rather, they develop skills and become highly effective through instruction, experience, and practice of core disciplines.

Just as competitive athletes train to win, leaders must work hard, adopt a positive attitude, and demonstrate a desire to continuously improve. Effective leaders inspire people to do great things. They're visionaries who serve as role models. They also understand that their unique leadership style will change over time as circumstances dictate, so they must remain flexible and adaptable.

Leadership isn't about who's in charge; it's about those they lead and the paths they take. Larry Bossidy, former CEO of Allied Signal and coauthor of *Execution*, said, "At the end of the day you bet on people, not strategies." Leaders are needed at every level, and the success of their organizations depends on how well they're developed.

This Book Is Designed to Boost Your Leadership Effectiveness

I intend your experience to be, as my colleague Susan Spalc wrote:

- Thought provoking! It will cause you to think about your role in new ways.
- Challenging! It will stretch you to achieve higher performance.
- Meaningful! It is relevant to enhance your value on the team.
- Interactive! It challenges you to own your learning process.
- Rewarding! You feel that it's a great investment of your time.
- Inspiring! It moves you to take action.
- Practical! It provides easy transfer to your work.

This book will also deliver four major benefits: (1) Build and sharpen your core leadership skills; (2) Enhance your market position and reputation by attracting and retaining the best talent, leading to healthy revenue growth; (3) Improve your decision making, interpersonal relations, and teamwork; and (4) Assist you in becoming a highly effective and dynamic leader, leading to increased employee engagement, enhanced customer service, and a strong bottom line.

In my work, I address leadership development as a means of improving performance and productivity, empowerment and engagement, retention and succession, and making a long-term impact on teams and organizations.

Astute leaders today turn to coaches as catalysts to accelerate change and achieve desired results. Why? Because there is just so much time in the day, and leaders and their staffs are so overburdened there's rarely enough time to step back and examine the big picture.

The best executive coaching delivers dramatic results, expressly because its practitioners realize that coaching is not about them. They understand that people have the answers and solutions they need to make a positive behavioral change. They simply provide the discipline and resources for them to identify and implement their own solutions.

They are both coach and catalyst for change, helping clients focus on specific goals and providing them with the tools, knowledge, and opportunities they need.

I feel that most management education and leadership development fails top leaders because the discipline and resources are missing. I've seen it, and it is tragic: throwing younger supervisors of the company into the fray without them having any understanding of what it takes to lead and motivate their people, allowing them to make profound mistakes, and then relieving them of their responsibilities when they don't perform. The result: damaged careers and a loss of potential leaders for the company. Doesn't make sense.

During the last recession, which has been a new experience for many leaders, the focus has been on survival, with little attention on growing leaders or providing current leaders with the skillsets to lead in an uncertain economic environment.

When there were leadership development efforts, they were usually for the mid-level and senior level, provided mostly through training classes consisting of full-day or week-long sessions, but lacking a coaching component to reinforce the skills learned in these classes. Why is coaching so important? Because personal coaching not only changes the behavior of participants, but aids them in real-time on-the-job situations.

Additionally, organizations need to look at developing high-potential individuals and frontline leaders of managers and supervisors to provide them with the skillsets needed to hone their craft. This element has been absent for years, and now that the economy seems to be getting on track, hopefully this all-important group will be developed.

This demerit needs to be offset by a different mindset, skillset, and style. Leadership effectiveness is the result of a regimen of Seven Disciplines that culminate in the realization of a compelling vision of service to others, using the tools at your disposal, with a clear vision of what you want to accomplish with the resources at hand. Effective leaders create a synergy of interdependent functions to make the business run as a singular, unique, integrated, and open system. Nearly all executive decisions for solving any single problem cut across the organization, with consequences for multiple divisions. Hence, we see many examples of well intended decisions with unintended consequences that undermine profitability and sustainability.

The real test of leadership effectiveness happens during turbulent economic times and when changing strategic direction. You know that it's time for change when routine activities are not delivering the intended results. Since Dr. W. Edwards Deming, a celebrated statistician, engineer, and management consultant, proved that 94 percent of all results are systemic in nature, any successful leader must demonstrate effectiveness at leading and managing the entire value chain or entire system. Ultimate responsibility over the entire value chain is what sets the leader's position apart from other executive roles.

The responsibility for the value chain carries through to all levels of the company, including that of the first-line supervisor, the leader who is responsible for executing orders that originated at the top. As costs out of his control escalate (such as the price of purchased material and the hourly labor rate in a manufacturing operation), he has the burden of finding enough cost reductions to offset the increases. Oftentimes, the P&L of the company rests on his shoulders.

Leaders need not always learn by hard or bad experience or be left to their own devices. My development system, which I describe in this book, provides leaders with disciplines that help them organize and execute to get desired results.

Proven Process for Developing Highly Effective Leaders

In this book, I've integrated our Leadership Development Program Design with the Seven Disciplines. Thus, by reading this book, you experience a simulation of our leadership development program, perhaps even receive 80 percent of the benefit! To achieve this high standard, we've added a new feature: each section and chapter has applications and exercises to help you learn and practice the aim of the chapter.

There's also Section III. The Eleven Practices described there aren't tied specifically to any of the Seven Disciplines but affect them all. For example, Practice 1: Hire People Like a Casting Director is a precondition that underlies achievement of the Seven Disciplines. If you hire the wrong people you simply will be unable to get the most from any of the Seven Disciplines. So while the Eleven Practices are described independently, they all are prerequisites to successful leadership.

Given this developmental design feature, you use this book best when you use it for personal, team, and organizational leadership development, either alone or with a formal leadership development program (LDP). You'll find that our paradigm doesn't compete with, but rather complements, any other LDP or process you may now be using.

Leadership development should be practical, interactive, incremental (modular), and experiential to develop mindsets and skillsets that can be transferred and applied at work. It should be aimed at all levels of the organization, and especially at the lower levels, where less experienced employees need the most guidance. (You can read the 12 components in Chapter 13.)

Seven Disciplines of a Leader is organized into three sections: (1) The first offers an overview of effective leadership; (2) the second introduces the Seven Disciplines of highly effective leaders; (3) the third focuses on Eleven Practices that sustain the Seven Disciplines.

Takeaway Exercises

At the conclusion of each chapter you'll read a section titled "Takeaway." This section allows you the opportunity to evaluate your own leadership style through an exercise that will drive home one or more of the chapter's main points. It's designed to sharpen your leadership skills in a practical way. It doesn't attempt to cover each and every major point in the chapter. But, the benefit of performing these exercises is that you can apply the very same methodology to an entire range of issues at work.

If you do these exercises faithfully, by the time you finish this book you will have improved your leadership skills many times over.

The Nature of Highly Effective Leadership

I n organizations worldwide, people are promoted to management and leadership positions each day. Through no fault of their own, they seldom have a clue as to how to manage or lead effectively. Their companies, while demanding much of them, fail to provide them with the necessary skills, coaching, training, and tools to lead successfully.

This first section includes four chapters:

Chapter 1: Welcome to Leadership—Nature of the Job
Chapter 2: Who Said It Would Be Easy?—Scope of the Job
Chapter 3: Principles of Effective Leadership—Essence of the Job
Chapter 4: Disciplines and Practices of Highly Effective Leaders

1

Welcome to Leadership

Nature of the Job

Today, there's an unprecedented demand for highly effective leaders. As organizations strive to stay competitive in the tough global marketplace, the ability to develop effective leaders has become increasingly difficult. Organizations are facing—or must face—the reality that effective leaders, at every level, can make or break them.

An aging workforce and retiring baby boomers compound the challenge. Where will tomorrow's leaders come from? Smart organizations must identify and train their talent to meet rigorous leadership demands, or they risk failure.

The Need for Leadership Is Greater Now Than Ever Before

The *Gallup Business Journal* had it right in its March 25, 2014, article, "Why Great Managers Are So Rare." According to authors Randall Beck and Jim Harter, "Companies place the wrong leadership candidates in the job 82 percent of the time."

Think about that number for a moment: *82 percent?* Is it any wonder that so many companies fall by the wayside? As Beck and Harter put it, "Bad managers cost businesses billions of dollars each year, and having too many of them can bring down a company. The only defense against this problem is a good offense, because when companies get these decisions wrong, nothing fixes it. Businesses that get it right, however, and hire managers based on talent, will thrive and gain a significant competitive advantage."

The lack of effective leadership is further evidenced by the staggering number of employees who aren't working to their full potential. In another *Gallup Business Journal* article, "How to Tackle U.S. Employees' Stagnating Engagement," dated June 11, 2013, authors Susan Sorenson and Keri Garman claim that only 30 percent of American workers ". . . were engaged, or involved in, enthusiastic about, and committed to their workplace."

They go on to say, "An alarming 70 percent of American workers are not showing up to work committed to delivering their best performance, and this has serious implications for the bottom line of individual companies and the U.S. economy as a whole."

Mike Myatt, author of the book *Leadership Matters . . . The CEO Survival Manual* (Outskirts Press, 2007), writing in *Forbes* says, "Why do businesses fail? If you're willing to strip away all the excuses, explanations, rationalizations, and justifications for business failures, and be really honest in your analysis, you'll find only one plausible reason—poor leadership. I've often said real leaders refuse to take the credit for success, but they will always accept responsibility for failures. Harsh? Yes; but it goes with the territory."

Steve Tobak of *Fox Business News* puts it this way in an article he wrote for foxbusiness.com on January 20, 2013, "Why Good Companies Fail": "When you cut through all the BS [of a failing business] it always comes down to one thing. People. If you observe the people in charge, ask some good questions, and poke around a bit, you can usually figure out what's really going on. And what's really going wrong."

Steve continues: "At the core of every company in trouble is usually a management team that's not as competent as it needs to be, more complacent than it should be, and more dysfunctional than it can get away with."

In such an environment is there any basis for questioning the need for more capable leaders, or as I like to say, *highly effective leaders*?

Real Life, Real Lessons

I wrote this book after being prodded by thousands of people who have attended my speeches and workshops, the hundreds of executives I've coached, and the countless organizations I've worked with in consulting and training. I designed the book to address and answer a critical question: *What can you do to improve your leadership?*

This book provides you with simple, pragmatic principles, as well as stories and exercises that can make you a more effective leader as you read and apply the book's lessons.

Leadership is not rocket science. It comes down to living and leading by the golden rule: Do unto others as you want them to do unto you.

Through real-life stories and examples, I provide a window into the lessons gleaned in hundreds of coaching sessions. Certain names and details have been omitted to protect clients' identity. I confess that coaching alone wasn't responsible for their successes.

Leadership requires common sense, knowledge, and honesty with people. It's talking and walking the talk. Effective leaders learn about the people they lead, they communicate well, they offer relevant feedback and praise, and they give credit to those who deserve it. They are a positive force at work (where people spend most of their time), and create a welcoming, productive environment where people can enjoy their jobs.

Secret Ingredient: People

"You can dream, create, and design the most wonderful place in the world . . . but it takes people to make the dream a reality."

—*Walt Disney*

When Walt Disney made this statement some 55 years ago, he likely never imagined that it would be applied to the workplace and become a core management tenet.

It doesn't matter what business you're in—manufacturing, accounting, legal, high tech, biotech, blue collar, or white collar—nor the size or nature of your organization: *It's people who are your most vital resource*. Without highly motivated employees, your organization will struggle to survive.

Motivated people give you a competitive advantage. As a leader, you can make the difference between those who care deeply about their roles versus those who simply show up for work every day (if you're lucky), and go through the motions while collecting a paycheck. An effective leader motivates employees to work together and achieve greatness, instilling confidence and trust as they go about their everyday business.

Of the 70 percent mentioned in the previous Gallup article, 52 percent are not engaged, and another 18 percent are actively disengaged. These employees are emotionally disconnected from their companies and may actually be working against their employers' interests. That's a frightening number! What does this say about the state of leadership today?

People make companies. As leaders, we often spend most of our time on strategy and improving bottom-line results, but what about our people? It's our job as leaders to guide them, help them develop more skills, and increase productivity.

I've often questioned why so few MBA programs include essential people skills (often called "soft skills" in their curricula). I was therefore happy to read a recent *Wall Street Journal* article describing how top MBA programs are starting to incorporate soft skills into their course studies. It's about time! In today's workplaces, these soft skills can make or break a leader. Let me give you an example.

Jim Gets It Done the Right Way

Jim, an engineer at a pharmaceutical plant, was loved by everyone he worked with. When people in production had a problem, they would seek him instead of their manager for help. Jim was outgoing, pleasant, and well-grounded in the technical components of his job. He always had a smile on his face, a kind word for everyone, and a positive attitude. He went out of his way to show people how to do things correctly. And when anything extra needed to be done, Jim always volunteered. He was the first person in his department to arrive each morning and usually the last person to leave. With 15 years of industry experience under his belt, he knew what it took to be successful. He had all of the basic traits and talents to be an effective leader, yet no one ever considered him leadership material.

One day, the process engineering department manager suddenly left without giving notice, and the company was hard-pressed to find a replacement. Executives didn't believe anyone inside the company could step up, so they planned to recruit from outside.

One employee asked the obvious: How about considering Jim for the job? After much debate, the execs decided to take a chance on him, with the condition that he receive leadership training to enhance his skills. They called Jim into the conference room and asked him if he was interested. He initially stated he wasn't interested, saying he enjoyed doing what he had always done and didn't want to make a change. Besides, he told them, he had never been a manager or leader, and he didn't know what to do.

The executives asked him to reconsider, as the new job repre sented a major step up in his career, as well as an opportunity to share his knowledge with others. After giving the promotion much thought, Jim changed his mind and decided to accept the position. The management team was pleased, and they began a highly structured program through which Jim could develop his leadership skills. They sent him to seminars outside of the company and provided a coach to work with him. Company executives understood that they needed to provide Jim with the right tools if they wanted him to succeed.

After a few months of intensive training, a once-reluctant Jim was eager and ready for his first day of leadership. He felt both excited and nervous as he arrived early Monday morning and proceeded to stand at the entryway to his department. He greeted everyone by their first names as they walked through the door and asked about their weekend, family, and children. He made a concerted effort to learn about his employees' outside activities and personal interests.

Jim had worked over the weekend to learn something about each employee, and he came through the door prepared. His ability to demonstrate that he cared about his staff and that he viewed each member as an individual started him off on the right foot with his department. Jim's leadership training and coaching paid off on the first day of his new job, creating a buzz among employees about the newly promoted manager's genuine interest in his staff's personal and professional lives.

During his first week, Jim held one-on-one meetings with each team member, followed by weekly team meetings. Each session had a specific agenda, and he enthusiastically solicited input from team members. The group was excited and motivated because Jim demonstrated a basic leadership principle: *People make an organization, and engaging them creates loyalty.*

Over time, Jim's department developed a reputation for highly motivated, energized, and productive people. Company employees jumped at the chance to transfer into Jim's department. One of Jim's secrets of success is that he understood what his people wanted, not just what he wanted, and he acted accordingly. He proactively asked his staff for feedback about his leadership style and effectiveness. He quickly learned that what was important to him wasn't necessarily important to them.

Jim asked questions: What can I do to make you happier here? What do you find challenging about your work? What's energizing about your work? How can I be a better leader for you to be successful? What resources do you need that you currently don't have? What motivates you to work hard? Do you feel appreciated and receive the praise and recognition you feel you deserve?

Over time, Jim was deemed one of the best managers in his company, a designation that continues to this day. He continually works to improve his leadership skills and understands the premise that Walt Disney espoused 55 years ago: *It takes people to make the dream a reality.*

The Inevitable Result of Failing to Take Responsibility

Unlike Jim, many managers and leaders fail to take responsibility. They are quick to point their fingers at others for failures. Looking in the mirror proves to be too difficult for them, and they are more than happy to abdicate personal responsibility.

This concept was put to the test when J. Tyler Leverty, PhD, an assistant professor of finance at the University of Iowa's Tippie College of Business, studied failed executives, including:

- Lehman Brothers Chairman and CEO Richard S. Fuld Jr., (aka the Gorilla on Wall Street), named one of Portfolio.com's Worst American CEOs of All Time.
- The duo of Enron Chairman Kenneth Lay and CEO Jeffrey Skilling, whose illegal business exploits led to indictments, trials, and criminal convictions. According to Dr. Leverty, the pair blamed an angry short seller in Florida for the company's demise, the largest bankruptcy in U.S. history when it was filed in 2001.
- A coterie of CEOs at General Motors, who consistently blamed the economy and outside pressures for the automaker's failure and reorganization in 2009.

None of these leaders cited poor management or a corrupt culture as reasons for their companies' downfalls, but as Leverty notes, their highly deficient decision-making skills were to blame. "We found that managers of failed firms are less skilled than their peers, and the consequences of their incompetence are economically significant." Dr. Leverty and his coauthor studied 12,000 insurance companies to determine how the decisions of their chief executives over a 12-month period affected firm performance. They asked: Were costs minimized? Were revenues maximized? Did the company operate efficiently? Did the company use technology effectively? How did the quality of leadership affect solvency? Ultimately, "inefficiency is a manager's fault," Leverty notes. Leaders are charged with identifying and remedying every problem area.

Finger-Pointing

Manny was shipping manager for a regional delivery company . . . and he was *not* respected by his peers. He was quick to point fingers when shipments fell below plan, blaming his problems on others.

This situation persisted for years because Manny had the ear of the company founder. Unfortunately for Manny, the founder died and his son, who succeeded him, didn't appreciate Manny's finger-pointing. He fired him.

Hands-On Advice: Failing to take responsibility for the performance of your job is a losing proposition. Face your own problems and correct them.

It's easy to unconsciously slip into the routine of blaming others when things go wrong. And it may work for a time, but eventually you will be exposed. In the meantime, you risk alienating the people whose cooperation you rely on. Not a smart move.

Leading in Uncertain Times

The role of leaders in uncertain times transcends managing the bottom line. It requires remembering that their first priority is employees. Great leaders never forget that their employees are the keys to success.

As an executive coach, consultant, and former CEO, I've worked with hundreds of leaders who perpetuate the growth of their companies, departments, or teams. I find that successful leaders practice four simple leadership skills, all based on developing people. Implementing these skills keeps people focused, reduces anxieties and fears, reduces turnover, and makes employees feel loyal and positive about the company.

1. ***Communication.*** The late Sam Walton, founder of Walmart, said, "Communicate everything to your associates; the more they know the more they care. Once they care, there is no stopping them." Because of the downturn in the economy, people feel vulnerable and overwhelmed. They are also worried about cutbacks and layoffs. Communicate everything to them by letting

them know what is happening in your company, team, or department. Open the lines of communication with everyone and let them know that you care not only about their involvement in the workplace, but in their personal lives as well. A leader places a high value on human capital.

2. *Praise.* When you praise people you inspire loyalty and encourage them to perform great work. Praising also creates positive energy in companies when people are continually being praised for doing good work. Great leaders go out of their way to praise people; they catch people doing something right! When praising people, do it in a timely fashion, make it specific, and try to do it in front of their peer group. Use such statements as: Thanks for getting that report in so quickly. You handled that situation nicely. That was an interesting point you brought up. We couldn't have done it without your help. I can see you're improving in that area; keep up the good work. Your contribution is making a difference on this project. Praising your people will keep them motivated, inspired, and full of positive energy.

3. *Empowerment.* Great leaders know that they need to create more leaders at all levels. Empower your people; nurture their development as leaders. Don't just delegate work; delegate decision-making powers to people. When people have the authority to make important decisions, they feel part of the organization, and they're more likely to remain part of it. By empowering your people, you enable them to reach their potential. When you fail to empower people, barriers are created that people can't overcome. If these barriers remain long enough people give up and leave. Many of those people go on to become great leaders at other organizations.

4. *Coaching.* Coaching boosts productivity, builds teamwork, motivates employees to elevate performance levels, and helps people overcome obstacles to their success. A great leader spends time working with individuals to see the blocks in their performance. A successful leader and effective coach are one in the same. People won't change until they see the need to. Good coaches listen to

people to find ways to break down the barriers that keep people from reaching their full potential. They then work with their people to outline a plan of action that clearly states the goals for improvement and accountability. Coaching helps people learn, grow, and change. It provides a powerful structure through which people can focus on specific outcomes, become more effective, and stay on track.

Uncertainty calls for strong leaders who guide people through troubling and turbulent times. Inspire and motivate your people to help them adjust and be productive employees. By utilizing these four leadership skills, you can change attitudes and create a positive and nurturing environment.

Helen Gets It Right

When the board of directors of a failing company appointed Helen as CEO she brought with her all the requisite skills from her previous position with a competitor. She practiced the four techniques just described: communication, praise, empowerment, and coaching. Those skills enabled her to turn around the company.

> *Hands-On Advice: Bear this in mind—you can succeed where others have failed if you do the right things, have faith in yourself, and have the courage to persevere.*

Helen did it as thousands of others have before her, and at all levels of the organization. It's not easy, but it can be done, and it is those character traits that separate thriving leaders from mediocre performers.

Takeaway from Chapter 1

Define the traits, duties, and competencies of highly effective leaders you have known. Compare them to highly ineffective leaders you may have had the good fortune to work with. I say good fortune because watching leaders fail enables you to evaluate *why* they failed. Now contrast them with leaders who have had great success and determine *why* they succeeded.

I suggest you write this information, listing the traits, duties, and competencies in the left-hand column, and the names of the contrasting managers in the next two columns, then evaluate them one attribute at a time. In the third column, write your name, and have a coach or mentor evaluate you compared with the other two leaders, attribute by attribute.

Why write it? Because the act of writing assures that you won't skim over the information but instead give each of the traits, duties, and competencies the thought they deserve. This method will also help guide your thinking, organizing how you analyze an issue (whatever that issue might be), then let you come to rational conclusions in a systematic way.

There is no better school than this. Use the takeaway from this chapter, and each succeeding chapter, to improve your leadership qualities.

2

Who Said It Would Be Easy?

Scope of the Leader's Job

Leadership is a tough job, one that places you in difficult positions, facing vexing dilemmas. Regardless of your level—supervisor, manager, general manager, president, or CEO—leadership is challenging.

Five Fundamental Goals of Highly Effective Leaders

Let's examine those five goals:

1. ***Bring people together to work as a team.*** You guide your team, department, or group, and it's not easy leading a group of diverse people. The workplace today is more diverse than at any time in history: Greatest Generation, baby boomers, Gen X, and Gen Y. Each group has its ideas, values, and thoughts regarding what should be done and how to do it. Effective leaders work hard to build strong teams that accomplish great things. People who work together cohesively offer a competitive advantage.

2. ***Motivate people to perform.*** You can't lead without inspiring people to do great things. They must be willing to take that

next step, the one that allows them to reach beyond their perceived capabilities and step out of the proverbial box. Each employee has distinct values and needs, wants and desires. Effective leaders spend time coaching people one-on-one to find out what makes them tick, which challenges confront them, and which types of motivation will spur them to perform at a higher level.

People are motivated in two ways: intrinsically and extrinsically. Extrinsic motivation involves outside factors: money, power, or position. Intrinsic motivation comes from within: the desire for pride, a passion for one's work, and the desire to do a great job.

3. *Take responsibility for bottom-line results.* Regardless of your organization's size or type (public or private), much of your behavior is driven by the bottom line. If you are in a leadership role, you've got to work with people to produce and achieve the results necessary to be profitable. Leaders are measured by their results, as are the people who work for them. Every organization has financial goals. If they're unmet, the consequences may be severe.

4. *Make difficult decisions.* It's your responsibility to hire the right people, terminate the wrong people, and call people on the carpet to take corrective measures. It's also within your purview to change the direction of your department, team, or organization as the landscape changes in your business environment.

You may also have to decide whether friends or former colleagues are doing their job. You may find yourself in the unenviable position of having to reprimand, issue warnings, and occasionally terminate staff. The people who report to you must be in the right job for their abilities. You may have the right people, but the positions they're in may not be the correct fit, so you'll need to make the necessary changes.

5. *Create positive energy.* Team and company success depend on having highly motivated individuals who are excited about their work. Of course, no workforce operates in a vacuum. Employees need a strong leader with a positive attitude and enthusiasm. *Employees work for people (leaders), not for companies.* Conversely,

employees don't leave companies—they leave ineffective leaders. An employee's relationship with a manager/supervisor largely determines the length of an employee's stay. The main reason people quit is the manager's behavior. A quality leader is the key factor in attracting and retaining top talent.

There is no shortage of good employees today; however, there is a shortage of inspirational leaders and inspiring places to work. Leaders are seldom energy neutral. They either energize their employees, or they act as energy vampires, sapping workers' motivation and enthusiasm and contributing to low morale.

What's Wrong with Being Right?

Ego can serve as a powerful tool in regulating your personal and professional behavior. In Freud's psychological schematic, the ego maintains balance between our primitive emotions (the id) and our conscience (the superego). "The ego represents what may be called reason and common sense, in contrast to the id, which contains the passions," Freud explained in *The Ego and the Id*. The ego's job as referee may therefore prove difficult, as the id (think of it as your brain's inner toddler) strives for pleasure and instant gratification. Meanwhile, the superego (your brain's parent) may simultaneously demand perfectionism. These diametrical and concomitant objectives can get you into a heap of trouble if your ego fails to step in and play mediator.

At first glance, the superego's drive for perfection may sound like a positive leadership trait, but the opposite holds true. Let your bossy superego rule the roost, and you'll always find yourself frustrated. That's because perfection is unquestionably impossible to attain. Let me be clear: Any pride that you take in achieving what you perceive to be perfection is misplaced, in essence, a fantasy or delusion.

How, then, do you measure success? Instead of seeking perfection, aim for excellence. It's completely attainable with hard work, but be prepared to make your share of mistakes across a long career. While leadership requires you to be at the top of your game, you also must allow yourself the luxury of making a mistake from time to time. And to survive these career speed bumps, you must build and continually fortify the emotional resilience required to change directions and correct your course.

Zoe Learns an Important Lesson from Her Boss, Stan

At 27, Zoe was a hotshot art director for a large, multistate HMO. She had previously worked as a senior graphic designer for a well-known national advertising agency. Zoe decided to change jobs after a five-year stint at the agency so she would have the opportunity to earn more money and embark on a management career. Moving from a highly creative and informal workplace to a more rigid corporate setting was her first challenge, but she found herself settling in nicely.

She enjoyed supervising and mentoring two junior graphic artists, even though she had never received any formal management training. Thanks to her personality and excellent people skills, Zoe formed meaningful bonds with her staff and colleagues. She likened her new job to changing TV channels and graduating from *Mad Men* to *House*.

About three months into her tenure, Jack, one of Zoe's direct reports, failed to spell-check a document that Stan, the HMO's director of communications, had given him before placing the text into a brochure layout. Zoe caught the typos, pointed them out to Jack, and counseled him on how he could avoid the problem in the future.

This kind of interaction came easily to Zoe, who was known for being patient. But what her staff didn't know was that Zoe couldn't tolerate any personal mistakes, and she held herself to a higher, and unrealistic, standard. As a child, she had grown up with two college-professor parents, and scoring an A on a test was often greeted with the question, "Why didn't you get an A+?" The experience had a long-lasting effect, which continued well into Zoe's adulthood and work life.

Similarly, Zoe's prior stint at the ad agency exposed her to three partners who viewed any error as a potential loss of revenue. Mistakes amounted to the equivalent of criminal felonies that damaged the agency's credibility, and every copywriter and designer operated in a state of high alert and hypervigilance. Employees knew that presenting edgier, more eye-catching designs had the potential to offend certain clients, even though the agency's partners knew that stodgy clients required image upgrades to succeed.

In her new job, Zoe had to learn a new vocabulary and complex industry. It was easy to confuse terminology and often difficult to discern the nuances of the health care system. With perseverance, she was mastering her responsibilities and enthusiastically embracing the challenges each day presented.

When Zoe submitted her second brochure layout to Stan, she learned that one of her graphic designers had horizontally flipped a photo, and she hadn't caught it. Stan told her the doctor in the picture was reversed, which meant his lab coat and stethoscope appeared backward. Even though Stan spoke to her without a hint of anger, Zoe had turned beet red and was mortified.

After the conversation with Stan, Zoe tossed and turned in bed. Mistakes were anathema to her, and she felt ill: nauseous and short of breath. She shared the incident with some of her former colleagues at the ad agency, and they told her that she was being too hard on herself. Her closest friend advised her to let go and move on, but Zoe's conscience (superego) continued to berate her: How could you let this happen?

Zoe's embarrassment persisted, and she asked Stan to meet with her. She told him she was horrified by the error and was willing to resign.

Stan was shocked. "What do you mean, resign?" he asked.

"I screwed up that photo," she reminded him. "I feel terrible."

"So, you want to resign because a photo was flipped?" he asked. "A photo that has since been corrected, in a brochure that was first class?"

"Yes," Zoe confirmed, continuing to believe that any error on her part, no matter how large or small, warranted falling on one's sword in an act of misguided nobility.

"I appreciate that you take your work so seriously," Stan said, "but you're new at the job, and you didn't catch a mistake. Working here is a team sport. We have multiple reviews so we can prevent errors from making it to press, and I have your back."

"But I should have caught it," Zoe persisted.

"Do you want me to punish you?" Stan asked. "I don't think anything I could say would matter because you're doing an excellent job of beating yourself up. Did it occur to you that I've made mistakes along the way?"

"I suppose," Zoe mumbled.

"And if I made a mistake, would you think less of me?" he asked.

"No, Zoe said. "I'd think you simply made a mistake."

"So, why are you so special?" Stan asked. "Are you a computer? A robot? What makes you think you're any different from the rest of us?"

Zoe had no answer. She realized Stan was right, but she felt awful.

"You're still in your 20s," said Stan, who was almost twice her age. "You'll make many mistakes in the future: with your staff, with me and other bosses, and in your personal life. You need to prepare yourself for the curves life throws your way and accept the fact that you're not perfect."

Stan, Zoe realized, was a great mentor, and had taught her a life-changing lesson: Mistakes, in most cases, are not life-and-death affairs. Over the next few years, Zoe remained diligent and careful, but she ultimately accepted the gift Stan had given her.

Fear of Failure Is Dangerous to Your Job Health

Fear of making a mistake can cripple even the most talented leader's efforts to succeed. It stifles creativity and discourages risk-taking, while upping the stress ante and creating a tense work environment for everyone within a department or team.

Imagine how many inventions and technological innovations would never have become realities if the people who came up with them had been afraid to fail!

Anyone who ever did anything truly great failed first. Failure is part of trying. *It will happen.* What matters is how you deal with it. Famous failures include Abraham Lincoln, Thomas Edison, and Michael Jordan. They prove that failure can be a powerful teacher that leads to success.

Similarly, corporate trainer Ramesh Menon reminds us: "Worry can kill—no wonder the word comes from the Anglo Saxon word *weirgan*, which means to strangle, to choke until there is no life left."

Worrying about making mistakes is counterproductive, zaps your energy, and leads to a self-fulfilling prophecy. You may irrationally fear that you'll never be good enough and that you'll face the disapproval of others or other negative feelings if you're less than perfect. This can cripple you, especially as you move up the career ladder and take on new responsibilities that are outside your comfort zone.

Hara Estroff Marano, editor-at-large for *Psychology Today* and author of *A Nation of Wimps* (Crown Archetype; First edition, April 15, 2008) describes perfectionism as "a steady source of negative emotions." She explores how our performance should not be a measure of our self-worth. "Rather than reaching toward something positive, those in perfectionism's grip are focused on the very thing they most want to avoid—negative evaluation," she writes. "Perfectionism, then, is an endless report card; it keeps people completely self-absorbed, engaged in perpetual self-evaluation, reaping relentless frustration and doomed to anxiety and depression."

I encourage managers and leaders to write down their fears. This forces them to acknowledge these anxieties and dissect the faulty logic that may paralyze them. Consider keeping a journal that tracks what's bothering you and how you react to missteps. Does one type of error bother you more than another? Are you better able to recover from a mistake when you're having a good day? What, exactly, are you feeling? Humiliation? Embarrassment? Depression? A sense of even greater fear? How can you use reality checks to weaken the hold these feelings have on you?

You need to practice being unafraid. Perform at 100 percent of your capacity, and recognize that mistakes will still occur in rare circumstances, despite your best efforts to prevent them. Needless to say, if you make huge errors regularly, you may be in way over your head.

If you're a leader or manager who is plagued with chronic anxiety and unrealistic perfectionism, you must learn to defuse the fear time bomb so you can succeed at the work you love. You'll need to fire your inner critic, says productivity consultant Julie Morgenstern, as well as discover whose critical voice is really living inside your head.

Avoid looking at errors as black-and-white or all-or-nothing-at-all scenarios, she advises. A recovering perfectionist, she confessed her own fears and doubts in *O, The Oprah Magazine*. "When I first started speaking professionally, I knew when I had given a bull's-eye performance. I felt that I was 'hanging ten,' riding the waves of the audience's emotions. When I didn't hit that mark, I was disappointed and mad at myself."

Audience feedback was never as harsh as Morgenstern's personal assessment of her performance; in fact, her scores were always high, but she thought attendees were just being nice. See how we torture ourselves?

When Morgenstern sought counsel from a highly experienced speaker, he told her that hitting at least a 7 out of 10 with audiences would suffice, and that no one hits the mark every time. If you continue to struggle with severe anxiety, consider seeing a psychotherapist or setting up sessions with a qualified and objective executive coach.

Bob's Short and Unhappy Career

Instead of expecting himself to be perfect, Bob simply assumed he was, an attitude that drove his boss, coworkers, and direct reports crazy (not to mention his long-suffering wife). Bob never owned up to a mistake, even a minor one. As operations manager for a large sporting-goods manufacturer, he supervised 12 worker bees, each of whom he would throw under the bus in a New York minute to cover for one of his mistakes.

When the CEO confronted Bob about a mistake he made, Bob invariably blamed the gaffe on one of his staffers, even if the staffer had never laid eyes on the project. And when Bob's ideas were challenged in staff meetings or team projects, he fought to the death to prove his strategy was the best and only viable one.

Bob's arrogance ultimately led to his demise. His lack of respect for, and occasional verbal abuse of, his staff resulted in high turnover.

His colleagues were tired of his insistence that he was always right, and his boss had given up arguing with him. Bob was ultimately told that it would be best for all concerned if he found a new position at another company.

Leaders like Bob exhibit numerous flaws, according to consultant Loretta Malandro, PhD, author of *Fearless Leadership*. Their blind spots include: engaging in either/or thinking; ignoring evidence that challenges or disproves their beliefs; confusing their perceptions and assumptions with truth; listening automatically (distorting what they hear to fit their agenda); playing the victim and refusing to accept responsibility or accountability; being insensitive to the needs of those around them; diminishing others' viewpoints and opinions (sarcasm or rudeness); placing blame on others whenever convenient; treating their commitments casually; sabotaging others to make themselves look good; and insisting they're right and refusing to budge from their position without any evidence to back it up.

"If you want to play big and ensure that your organization survives and moves to the next level of success," Malandro writes, "then protecting yourself from making mistakes or being wrong is an ineffective strategy. You must learn how to include your imperfections in how you unite and motivate others and to do what fearless leaders do: Be transparent, authentic, and accountable."

While Bob's brand of arrogance is something every leader should avoid, employees will likely be stuck with the Bobs of the world if their departments remain productive and deliver results. When performance outcomes are high, abusive behaviors tend to be overlooked unless steps are taken to ensure that abusive managers are called on their behavior in performance evaluations. CEOs may need to redesign evaluation policy to include how a manager treats employees. Otherwise, problems are never resolved, the entire organization becomes contaminated and hostile, and people must work around, not with, their managers and leaders.

To determine whether you have any Bob-like qualities, answer these questions: Do you beat a dead horse in discussions, insisting that you know the *only* truth (one that seems to elude everyone else)? Are you always intent on having the last word? Do you reject opinions, facts, and research that suggest or prove you're wrong? Do you dominate conversations or meetings in an attempt to bully people into accepting your truths? Do you sacrifice others to escape the consequences of being wrong? Are you terrified of being wrong? If you're guilty, perhaps it's time to reevaluate the way you conduct yourself and seek professional guidance.

Takeaway from Chapter 2

What kind of leader are you? I'll assume you're like Jim, the engineer from Chapter 1 whose promotion into management ranks was justified by the foundation of trust and respect he established with his team.

If you have one or a few of the problematic qualities Bob exhibits, I encourage you to honestly compare the way you do business with the way Bob does business, and identify those relatively few poor practices you have that need changing. Perhaps, for example, you're driven to achieve your goals and objectives regardless of the cost in human turmoil. Or you're so obsessed with unimportant details that you're frustrating your employees' attempts to work effectively.

Objectively analyzing your personal shortcomings is vital to your success. If necessary, get a coach and don't allow your ego to stand in the way. *Write them down to fortify your conclusions.*

Well, wouldn't it be to your advantage now, today, here . . . to pick out just one foible of yours, admit your shortcoming, correct it, and incorporate the improvement into your daily routine? Select just one, and watch how the change inspires the people you work with.

Principles of Effective Leadership

Essence of the Leader's Job

In my work, I see three types of leaders:

1. ***Those who make things happen.*** These are the dynamic, get-things-done leaders who are driven to success. They use their drive and ambition to make a great difference every single day in the workplace. They're excited about their role, always seeking ways to improve, motivate, and inspire their people and teams or organizations to greatness. These leaders come in all shapes and sizes, all personalities and temperaments. There is no mold for them, only the desire to expand their repertoire of leadership skills and a thirst for knowledge. These leaders have a make-things-happen reputation.

2. ***Those who watch things happen.*** These leaders sit back and let the world pass them by. They're stuck in old ways and habits, and they refuse to stay abreast of new ideas to enrich their skills. They often aren't in touch with their people and are essentially running on autopilot.

3. ***Those who wonder what happened.*** These leaders sit back and say, "Hmm . . . I wonder what's going on out there." They don't have

a clue about leadership and are a detriment to those who report to them. They're the fake leaders who would never read this book. Worse, they contaminate others, especially those who report to them, by setting a poor example of leadership.

How to Make Things Happen

To be a leader who makes things happen, you need to develop and maintain a positive belief system. You must have four basic beliefs:

1. Your company is the best. You're proud to work for the best company in your profession or industry.
2. Your services, people, and training are the best. The services or products your company provides are prevailing in its industry. The training people receive and deliver should be equally strong.
3. You're the best. If you don't feel this way, no one will believe in you. Effective leaders develop a strong sense of self-confidence and believe they excel at their work.
4. Your customers or clients are better off using you and your company. You must know, without a doubt, that you can provide all or most of the solutions they need.

These beliefs are necessary if you want to take that next step toward effective leadership. I endorse the adage, "Those who say it can't be done should get out of the way of those who are doing it." Many leaders just give lip service. Effective leadership is about getting things done.

Grumbling George

George was transmission engineering supervisor for an electrical utility provider, a position he had held for 18 years. From a technical perspective, George had more knowledge than anybody else in the utility. But over the years he had started losing his enthusiasm. He spent so much time grumbling with the design engineers reporting to him that they avoided him whenever possible, despite his technical prowess. It got to the point that his performance was eroding, and the utility manager began to wonder if George had outlived his usefulness.

Hands-On Advice: Avoid negativity.

Negativity can damage your ability to work with other people. So, unless you work in isolation without the need to interact with fellow employees, remember that people like and respect positive people and absolutely dislike a Grumbling George. If you are a complainer you will not make it as a leader.

Attitude Is Everything

As you can discern from the three types of leaders, the successful ones are ambitious and self-motivated. They wake up each morning with a positive attitude that carries them through the rest of the day.

Each of us has a similar choice. We can either wake up with a positive attitude or grumble and groan (like Grumbling George) with a negative attitude. I look at it this way: If I wake up above ground in the morning and can see myself in the mirror, I'm positive. Positive attitudes can take us a long way; leaders with positive attitudes can take everybody else around them on the same journey. They're the pied pipers of business.

Success requires a whatever-it-takes attitude—whatever it takes to get the job done, within ethical business constraints. There are no shortcuts. Ethical business constraints is a key term because we've witnessed, over the last few years, despicable behavior, with the fall of Andersen, Enron, and many other companies.

Show Vulnerability

When you make a list of valuable leadership traits, vulnerability may not appear anywhere near the top, but at least one business expert believes that leadership happens because of vulnerability.

According to Ronald L. Dufresne, PhD, an assistant professor of management at Saint Joseph's University, the 33 heroes trapped 2,300 feet underground during the August 2010 Chilean mine collapse are perfect examples. Stranded for 10 weeks, as the world witnessed their plight, the trapped miners depended on teamwork and what Dr. Dufresne calls democratic leadership to survive. They divided themselves into groups, each of which had an elected leader who was charged with communicating with above-ground rescuers. The other team members had their own delegated responsibilities, including spiritual support, work-schedule maintenance, and food-rationing.

"Corporate America has a lot to learn from the Chilean miners," says Dr. Dufresne, who cites five lessons from the disaster: (1) Every member of your team has the ability to contribute to leadership practices. (2) Each of us can learn from the other members of our team. (3) Top leaders never have all of the answers. They depend on team members for advice, experience, and skilled guidance. (4) Training is critical to prepare your team for a crisis. (5) Be willing to listen. It takes a strong leader to practice humility and seek advice from bosses, peers, employees, and clients.

What I Learned from the Father of Professional Speaking

At the start of my career as a speaker, I sought training so I could take my skills to a higher level. I attended the Bill Gove Training Academy in Florida. Bill was in his 90s at the time and was viewed by many as the father of the professional speaking industry.

I was talking to him during one of the breaks, and something he said has stayed with me throughout my career. "As a speaker," he said, "you may not have all the answers or cover all of the planned material. But if you're passionate about what you're saying, the audience will remember that passion long before they remember the words you're saying."

According to a study conducted by the Gallup Organization and Hay Group, 50 to 70 percent of the way employees perceive their corporate culture can be traced to their leaders' actions. The more positive a leader's mood, the better the company's bottom-line results.

These are startling conclusions. What do they tell you about leadership, positive attitudes, and being passionate about your work? Think about what makes you feel excited and positive about coming to work each day. What makes you feel good about your job? Take a few minutes to write your answers.

Now, keep this page handy. Refer to it when things aren't going well for you. It will help boost your morale.

I've posted these questions to thousands of people in presentations and workshops over the years and asked them to turn to the person next to them and share their thoughts. You should see the smiles on their faces and the excitement in their voices as they share their narratives with strangers sitting next to them. I sometimes have trouble stopping them from talking after 5 or 10 minutes. It's wonderful to see, and I often wonder why they can't take this enthusiasm back to their jobs and apply it regularly.

Using the same page you just started writing on, answer the following questions: What has been your experience working with/ for leaders? List some of best leaders you've ever worked for/with. Be specific about the things that contributed to a positive, successful experience. Which characteristics made them effective leaders?

Now think about worst leaders you've ever worked for/with and answer the following questions and write them on the same paper: What made the experience negative and unsuccessful? Which characteristics made these individuals ineffective leaders?

When you make this comparison between leadership types, the differences are stark and compelling.

Highly Effective Leaders Build on a Foundation of Honesty and Integrity

In their book *The Leadership Challenge*, James M. Kouzes and Barry Z. Posner argue that the top trait of the best leaders is honesty. An honest leader tells the truth and knows right from wrong. Many leaders have failed their companies, shareholders, and customers because they either lied or didn't know right from wrong. They manipulated numbers and facts to fit their own agendas.

Each day, more business headlines indict so-called leaders: business-people, politicians, investment titans, people whose dishonesty has been catastrophic. Many companies have shut down, and innocent employees and shareholders have suffered greatly. In many cases, people's life savings have been wiped out, and careers have been sabotaged.

The minute you're dishonest and bend the truth, the minute you fail to tell it like it is, you lose your credibility. This applies to issues great and small. I've seen many leaders lose the trust of their employees, peers, and bosses when they compromise the truth, play loose with the facts, and fail to keep their word. Unethical behavior can taint an entire industry. The corrupt leaders at Enron, for example, polluted our views of accounting practitioners—a profession that seemingly lost its ability to self-regulate.

It's the little things that matter most to people. If, for example, you tell someone you're going to get back to her the next day, do it. If you tell your team that a project needs to be completed in a specific way, you'd better adhere to your own standards and requirements. *Double standards don't cut it in leadership*. You must do what you say and say what you mean, to paraphrase a Dr. Seuss morality lesson. If you expect your staff to be truthful, you must be the role model or you'll lose their respect.

As soon as an employee, peer, or boss senses you're being dishonest, you lose the first chance to make a great impression, and word will spread. Nothing sullies reputations quicker. A white lie may seem inconsequential to you, but people look up to their leaders and expect to take their word at face value. And, if you speak, it's like putting your comments in writing.

I once supervised Jack, a man who had major follow-up and time-management issues. He would regularly tell his staff that he'd promptly get back to them with answers to questions. Weeks and months would go by, and Jack would never follow up with them because he couldn't manage his time effectively. Things reached a tipping point when his staff became frustrated and refused to believe a word he said. His credibility was gone, and you can guess what happened next.

If your staff is waiting for answers and you fail to respond within the time you promised, you're actively destroying relationships you worked hard to build. I've observed leaders who believe they're so busy they can afford to ignore questions they deem to be inconsequential . . . and later pay the ultimate price for their dismissive attitude. That so-called inconsequential issue may be extremely important to the staff member who needs answers to do his job properly. Writing off an employee's questions translates to writing off the employee.

I recently coached Charles, an executive who was alienated by his boss. The boss kept Charles out of the loop on major decisions and refused to share information about important issues that directly affected Charles and his team. At one point, Charles learned his boss had lied to him. From that day forward, he never trusted anything his boss told him, and the boss's credibility vanished. From that day forward the performance of both Charles and his boss suffered, with the result that Charles, an outstanding performer, transferred to another position within the same company.

In the news, we read countless stories of rampant political corruption, financial mismanagement, government bailouts, pandemic layoffs, investment fraud, and unadulterated corporate greed. As leaders, we must avoid potential pitfalls, making a concerted effort to keep people motivated and productive, while building teams.

To maintain a healthy, disciplined work force, flaunt your honesty. Workers want their leaders to be role models whose allegiances and priorities are beyond reproach. Team leaders must have a strong character and integrity, walking the walk and talking the talk. The moment they bend the truth, they lose their credibility . . . and they'll never get it back.

Correct negative habits and behaviors. Again, people leave organizations because of the boss. Poor leaders create a climate of negativity, coupled with little or no praise and recognition. Not keeping your word, treating people poorly, taking credit for others' successes, and blaming somebody else to cover up your mistakes are behaviors that result in high turnover and a lack of engagement by those who remain. By failing to delegate or empower employees, poor leaders find it necessary to micromanage their work. Their inability or refusal to develop a culture of trust deprives people of opportunities to grow. If this behavior goes unchecked, there may be a point of no return that destroys a once-productive company. Poor leadership is often correctable, but only if swift corrective action is taken.

Seven Deadly Leadership Sins

Professor Wayne Hochwarter at Florida State University found that anger at work has reached record levels, and hostilities are compromising the manager/employee relationship. He surveyed more than 750 mid-level employees to determine how often they experienced one or more of their direct supervisors' seven deadly sins at work: (1) wrath/anger, (2) greed, (3) sloth/laziness, (4) pride, (5) lust, (6) envy, and (7) gluttony. Hochwarter says, "We chose these behaviors because they have an established history, are familiar to people in both religious and secular settings, and are documented to strain interpersonal relationships at work."

The results proved unsettling: 26 percent of employees said their bosses struggle to control their anger (wrath); 27 percent of employees said their managers vigorously pursue undeserved rewards (greed); 41 percent cited laziness, in the form of habitually pushing work onto others (sloth); 31 percent complained that their bosses regularly seek undeserved admiration (pride); 33 percent said their bosses force others to stroke their egos on a daily basis (lust); 19 percent said they could count on their bosses to act enviously toward others who succeed (envy); and 23 percent said their bosses intentionally hoard resources that could benefit others (gluttony).

Christian Ponder of Florida State University says, "Employees with leaders who committed these sins contributed less effort (40 percent less), felt overloaded as a result of forced responsibility for their supervisor's work (33 percent more), were less likely to make creative suggestions (66 percent less), and received fewer resources to effectively perform their jobs (60 percent less) than those without this negative type of leadership. Those who witnessed their bosses' self-serving behaviors also spent 75 percent more time searching for new jobs.

"Workers whose bosses were guilty of one or more sins also reported deteriorating health, more daily anxiety, less overall happiness, greater physical and emotional exhaustion, and more depression while on the job.

"It is interesting to see how people react when they feel that their backs are against the wall. Some leaders try to rally the troops, while others decide to go it alone to safeguard what they feel they have. Perhaps when the cloud of recession fully lifts and job environments become more stable, leaders will focus on employee development rather than self-preservation."

Pride and Envy Bring Millie Down

Of the seven deadly sins described in the section before this, Millie was guilty of two: excessive pride and envy. In the back-office operations of an investment brokerage house where she worked as a manager she was well known for defending her decisions regardless of how wrong they were. She was also insanely jealous of her peers' accomplishments. Millie got away with this for years because in other aspects of her job—especially getting the work out—she was a strong performer. Eventually her sins caught up with her when her peers wouldn't work with her any longer.

> *Hands-On Advice: Avoid any one of the seven deadly leadership sins; they'll bring you down over time. Having more than one will bring you down even faster.*

At the very least, any one of the seven deadly sins will certainly attract unwanted attention from your boss and peers. If you are guilty of any of them you really need to seek professional help.

Takeaway from Chapter 3

Do you have the courage to forsake substituting what's right for your career for what's best for your employees when those two sometimes disparate goals clash? If you don't, you're in danger of losing the support of those people most important to achieving your personal career success.

Take a few minutes to evaluate how you rate against the seven deadly sins described in this chapter. Sure, it's difficult to be objective, but perhaps you have a close friend or associate who can be more objective about who you *really* are. Oftentimes, friends who are truly interested in your well-being will tell you the way it is.

Again, write it down, and compare what you have written with what the objective friend finds. Surprised at the differences? You shouldn't be. All of us find it difficult to examine ourselves objectively. Doesn't it point the way toward how we must seek help evaluating our experiences?

An experience like this (I compare it to an intervention where friends come together to help one of their group who is struggling with a personal problem such as an addiction) can be an eye-opener. Call it a personal intervention, if you will, but try it, and I firmly believe you will more likely than not get an understanding about certain aspects of your behavior that can stand improvement.

Disciplines and Practices of Highly Effective Leaders

As shown in the following chapters, highly effective leaders practice the Seven Disciplines to first achieve personal and professional greatness and then to lead teams and organizations.

These Seven Disciplines, developed, maintained, and practiced on both a personal and organizational level, lead to and sustain high performance. Indeed, these seven disciplines are keys to sustainability—meaning, sustained high performance over time.

In your roles and relationships, you need to gain the power to influence people and then exercise and expand your influence over time in your own circles to gain and sustain desired results in personal, team, and organizational contexts.

New Paradigm of Discipline: Intrinsic and Extrinsic Motivation

As with motivation, there is both intrinsic (self- or internal) discipline and extrinsic (imposed, invited, social, cultural, environmental, or external) discipline. In most organizations and societies, discipline tends to be developed using extrinsic motivations and rewards (carrots and sticks). *A dedicated and loyal follower tends to rely more on extrinsic discipline. A capable and competitive leader relies more on intrinsic discipline.*

Dedicated discipline is practiced by people:

1. Who are being coached or mentored or taught.
2. Who belong to a team, club, or organization.
3. Who are united (perhaps even wear a uniform, often with their name on it).
4. Whose performance is measured and reported.
5. Who compete with other disciplined individuals or teams for something meaningful to them.

People who meet one or more of these five criteria tend to discipline themselves more.

We tend to be highly disciplined when we experience a rich combination of both intrinsic and extrinsic discipline. When we opt in or exercise choice, and when we also are being coached as members of a competitive, high-performance team, we enjoy the kind of dedicated discipline that leads to a high degree of leadership effectiveness.

The Necessary Foundation of Discipline

What are the origins of these seven disciplines, or for that matter, of any discipline? What engenders restraint, wisdom, moderation, discipleship, dedication, loyalty, and fidelity, all of which result in health, fitness, positive relationships, trust, high performance, and results?

The origins of personal discipline include desire, drive, goals, willpower, beliefs, faith, visualization, affirmation, diet, exercise, renewal, sleep, maintenance, fitness, organizing, and prioritizing.

The origins of professional, team, and organizational disciplines include: vision, mission, structure, system, process, supervision, job descriptions, measurements, incentives, and accountability for results.

Tap into the power of positivity, since positivity has 3 to 10 times more influence power than negativity, and the power of affirmation.

"I have the discipline power to produce 10 times expectation"—and visualization—"I see myself having influence and see in detail the desired outcomes of my discipline power."

You might also remember how your mentors affected you. Who has influenced you most? How? Create and tell stories of the power of positivity: the times when you or others exercised it and gained exponential results.

I believe that the Seven Disciplines of a leader develop character on a personal and professional level and develop culture on the team and organizational level. It's simple: highly disciplined people become highly effective leaders.

Daily Discipline Activities

Think of your daily discipline activities (DDAs) as your top priorities and schedule time for them each week until they become habits. *Select DDAs that align with your personal sources of discipline power*. Select your top discipline activity and schedule 30 minutes for it each day. Doing this activity daily for at least 30 days will make it a habit, and it will make a big difference in your relationships and results.

Why Be Disciplined?

Many people today are incapable of consistently working a 40-hour week, largely due to their inability to wisely manage themselves during their off-work hours. They are plagued by injuries, illnesses, addictions, disputes, divorce, litigation, disruptions, insomnia, stress, financial concerns, mental disorders, emotional eruptions, social break-ups, obesity, and immorality, often accompanied by dishonesty and denial.

One lie we sometimes tell ourselves that rationalizes our behavior is this old standard: "This personal indiscretion, weakness, or indulgence won't affect my work; whatever happens in my personal life won't impact my job performance."

A more reasonable and realistic line is this: like it or not, for better or for worse, I bring my home to work and my work home. My personal and professional lives are inextricably connected and undeniably intertwined. What happens in my personal life inevitably affects my work.

The personal coaching and mentoring craze, along with myriad training and transition programs, outplacement and recovery services, all witness the need for us to attend to basic physical and moral disciplines.

Pick up any major city newspaper, any day of the week, and you'll find one or two stories of people whose careers and reputations were damaged, if not ruined, by some action in their personal lives. Often these private, personal, secret, or hidden behaviors weren't meant to be public.

Jimmy Corrects a Problem

In his zeal to excel, Jimmy, customer service manager in a large electronics distributorship, drove his people relentlessly. When they complained he pointed to his 16-hour-a-day schedule as a model for each of them.

But Jimmy was a young, single guy without the family responsibilities his people had. While most of them tried to emulate Jimmy, it became obvious they couldn't keep up. Absenteeism increased as did mistakes on the job. The human resources manager of the company noticed the problem and helped Jimmy receive the corrective leadership training he needed. The training helped Jimmy realize the damaging effect of his actions. He eased back on the throttle enough to keep department performance high but without the strain his forcefulness had once produced.

> *Hands-On Advice: Be aware of the effect your interaction has on people you supervise.*

If you keep in mind that effective leadership means balance on the job and equitable treatment of employees, you will locate that happy medium ground where contented employees are also productive employees.

Talent or Hard Work?

Many high-performing executives will tell you they don't rely on their innate talents as much as their hard-earned skills. CEOs like A.G. Lafley of P&G and GE's Immelt have said that being forced to manage through crises early in their careers enhanced their abilities in ways that were critical to becoming leaders.

Certain practices can make our experiences especially productive: Coaching helps. Receiving feedback allows us to fine-tune our skills. Working in a safe learning environment is essential. Workplaces encourage practice and development, where mistakes should be viewed as learning opportunities. You also need to clearly define and develop a plan for achieving the abilities you wish to hone, including a measurable time frame.

Deliberate Practice: 10,000 Hours or 10 Years

In his book *Outliers* (Back Bay Books; Reprint edition, 2011), Malcolm Gladwell makes the case for 10,000 hours of practice to attain expertise. Almost all child prodigies in music, sports, chess, and the arts seem to put in 10,000 hours before they attain expertise and produce significant results.

In this sense, talent is highly overrated. Expert performers, whether in memory or surgery, ballet or computer programming, are nearly always made, not born. Many of us have already put in more than a decade of doing what we do. The question is whether we are practicing the right things in the right way.

Anders Ericsson, Professor of Psychology at Florida State University who is widely recognized as one of the world's leading theoretical and experimental researchers on expertise and his colleagues emphasize the importance of deliberate practice, characterized by several elements: It's an activity designed specifically to improve performance, often with the help of a teacher, coach, or expert; it can be repeated frequently; feedback on results is continuously available; it's highly demanding mentally; and it isn't much fun and entails hard work.

If you think you've outgrown the need for a teacher or coach, challenge this assumption. Without a clear, unbiased view of your performance, you cannot choose the best practice activities. Hire a coach who can stretch you beyond your current abilities and help you move out of your comfort zones. Otherwise, human nature dictates that you're likely to spend your time practicing what you already know how to do.

According to professor Noel Tichy, PhD, at the University of Michigan School of Business, our progress depends on leaving our comfort zone to enter the learning zone, where skills and abilities are just out of reach.

Three Disciplines of Highly Effective Leaders

Recognizing unsatisfactory elements of performance is difficult and uncomfortable. When you try your hardest to perform better, you place enormous strain on your mental abilities. Obviously, if the activities that require practice were easy and fun, everyone would do them. But in reality, most people won't practice or persist long enough to improve. This is good news if you're willing to do what most people won't. It's the reason you're more likely to keep your job and thrive in difficult times.

Highly effective leaders develop three disciplines of clarity.

Discipline 1: Take time to reflect. Take time to think, muse, and reflect, to process all that has happened, to sift through the clutter, to run ideas up the proverbial flagpole, and then to draw conclusions and project clarity.

Discipline 2: Select your heroes with great care. Effective leaders carefully select their heroes—people they choose to recognize and reward; employees whose performance they choose to celebrate.

Discipline 3: Practice. The best leaders practice the words, images, and stories to help people perceive the future clearly. Having refined their speech, they seek new and bigger audiences and then give the same speech.

Effective leaders don't have to be passionate, charming, brilliant, or great speakers. What they must be is clear. Our need for clarity, when met, engenders in us confidence, persistence, resilience, and creativity. So, show us clearly whom we should serve, where our core strength lies, which score we should focus on, and which actions must be taken today. We will reward you by working our hearts out to make our better future come true.

Deliberate Practice

In his book *Talent Is Overrated, Fortune* magazine editor Geoff Colvin notes that great performance is usually the result of *deliberate practice*, a rigorous discipline that produces desired results. More of it leads to better, if not great, performance.

What exactly needs to be practiced? Precisely how? Which specific skills or other assets must be acquired? What factors account for top performance? What is the chief constraint? The chief constraint is mental, even in sports, where we might think the physical demands are the hardest. The required concentration is so intense that it's exhausting. If deliberate practice is so hard, if in most cases it's not inherently enjoyable, why do some people put themselves through it day after day for decades, while most do not? Where does the necessary passion come from?

Colvin notes that deliberate practice is characterized by five elements:

1. It's designed to improve performance. It's vital for a teacher, coach, or mentor to design the activity best suited to improve performance. You may think that you can design your own practice, but you never outgrow the need for a teacher's guidance. Becoming great at anything is difficult without the help of a teacher or coach. Without a clear, unbiased view of your performance, you can't choose the best practice activity. Even if you could make an honest assessment of your own performance, you

can't design the best practice activity for that moment in your development—the type of practice that would put you on the road to achieving at the highest levels. You likely lack extensive knowledge of the latest and best methods for developing people in your chosen field. The best methods of development stretch people beyond their current abilities. Deliberate practice requires that you identify certain elements of performance that need to be improved, and then work intently on them. Only by choosing activities in the learning zone, the location of skills and abilities that are just out of reach, can you make progress. You can't make progress in the comfort zone because you can already do those activities easily, while panic-zone activities are so hard that you don't know how to approach them. Identifying the learning zone and then staying in it as it changes are keys to deliberate practice.

2. It can be repeated. A high rate of repetition is the most important difference between deliberate practice of a task and performing the task for real when it counts. Two points distinguish deliberate practice from what most of us actually do. One is the choice of a properly demanding activity in the learning zone. The other is the amount of repetition. Top performers repeat their practice activities to a stultifying extent. As our teachers so long ago told us, practice makes perfect.

3. Feedback on results is continuously available. You can work on technique all you like, but if you can't see the effects, two things will happen: You won't get any better, and you'll stop caring. In many situations a teacher, coach, or mentor is vital for providing crucial feedback.

4. It's highly demanding mentally. Deliberate practice is, above all, an effort of focus and concentration. That is what makes it deliberate. Continually seeking exactly those elements of performance that are unsatisfactory and then trying your hardest to make them better places enormous strains on your mental abilities. The work is so arduous that you can't sustain it for very long. Four or five hours a day seems to be the upper limit of deliberate

practice, and this is done in sessions lasting no more than 60 to 90 minutes.

5. It isn't much fun. Doing things you know how to do well is enjoyable, but that's the opposite of what deliberate practice demands. Instead of doing what you're good at, you seek out what you're not good at. Then you identify the painful, difficult activities that will make you better and do those things over and over. After each repetition, you force yourself to see, or get others to tell you, exactly what still isn't right so you can repeat the most painful and difficult parts of what you've just done. You continue that process until you are mentally exhausted.

If the activities that lead to greatness were easy and fun, everyone would do them, and they would not distinguish the best of us from the rest.

Tom Receives Feedback

Tom, merchandising manager for a large retailer, had been criticized by his boss for zipping from one thing to the next without regard to priorities, and in the process being curt with his staff. Tom took his boss's criticism to heart. He attended a course at the local college that helped him prioritize his work.

He then sought the help of his people. Tom was shocked to learn how his curt behavior had turned off his staff and how their work had suffered as a result.

Tom slowed down, was more careful to prioritize work, and deliberately practiced positive interactions with his employees. Improvement didn't come overnight but eventually it did.

> *Hands-On Advice: Focus on eliminating your negatives.*

It won't come without strain, but it will come with time, and both your job performance and personal satisfaction will improve.

Takeaway from Chapter 4

Deliberate practice will substantially improve your performance. As stated before, deliberate practice is a rigorous discipline that produces desired results. More of it leads to better, if not great, performance.

Deliberate practice is not easily achieved because, more than most elements of leadership style, this one demands a rigorous and unbiased look at habits you have developed over the years, habits that most probably were ingrained in you early in your career. You need an impartial outside observer with commensurate experience in helping leaders understand why they (and you) do the things they do.

You may need a professional coach to help you design a program that follows the tenets of deliberate practice. For this exercise focus on one major aspect of your performance you want to improve. Carry through the program for that one specific task, and you will soon find yourself applying the same technique for other tasks. Before you realize it, deliberate practice will become an essential component of your daily life.

Seven Disciplines

Having reviewed the role and responsibility of leaders, in this second section we introduce the seven disciplines of a leader:

Discipline 1: Initiative and Influence

Seize the Reins and Set an Example for Others

When you have vision and purpose, you can imagine a new course of action, and pursue it. Your conscience monitors all that you imagine, envision, and engineer. Your model behavior will activate the conscience of others and allow the desired results to happen. When you exercise imagination, you rely less on memory. Memory ties you to your limits and past. Imagination points you to your potential and future.

From an early age, we're taught to break apart problems to make complex tasks and subjects easier to deal with. But this creates a bigger problem: we lose the ability to see the consequences of our actions, and we lose a sense of connection to a larger whole. Systems thinking helps us see patterns and learn to reinforce or change them effectively to gain and sustain a competitive advantage. Systems thinking is a framework for seeing patterns and interrelationships. It's especially important to see the world as a whole as it grows more and more complex. Complexity can overwhelm and undermine: it's the system. I have no control. Systems thinking makes these realities more manageable; it's the antidote for feelings of helplessness. By seeing the patterns that lie behind events and details, we can actually simplify life and take initiative to solve problems.

The discipline of personal mastery includes three important practices and principles: personal vision, creative tension, and commitment to truth.

Personal vision. Most people have goals and objectives, but no sense of a real vision. Maybe you'd like a nicer house, or a better job, or a larger market share for one of your products. These are examples of focusing on the means, not the result. For instance, perhaps you want a bigger market share to be more profitable to keep your company independent to be true to your purpose in starting it. The last goal has the most value, while the others are means to an end, means that might change over time. The ability to focus on ultimate desires is a cornerstone of personal mastery. Vision is a definite picture of a desired future, while purpose is more abstract. But vision without a sense of purpose is equally futile.

Creative tension. There are unavoidable gaps between one's vision and current reality. You may want to start a company but lack the capital, for instance. Gaps discourage us, but the gap is itself the source of creative energy. It provides creative tension. There are only two ways to resolve the tension between reality and vision. Either vision pulls reality toward it or reality pulls vision downward. Individuals and companies often choose the latter, since it's easy to declare victory and walk away from a problem. That releases the tension. But these are the dynamics of compromise and mediocrity. Creative people use the gap between what they want and what is to generate energy for change. They remain true to their vision.

Commitment to truth. A relentless willingness to uncover the ways we limit and deceive ourselves and a willingness to challenge the ways things are characterize those with a high degree of mastery. Their quest for truth leads to a deepening awareness of the structures that underlie and generate events, and this awareness leads to the ability to change the structure to produce the results they seek.

Simply No Substitute for Honesty

Today's leaders must be honest, forthright, and ooze integrity. People want their leaders to be role models whose allegiances and priorities are beyond reproach. Sadly, we see far too many leaders who lie and manipulate people, finances, and processes to fit their needs. When we read headlines or surf the web, we learn about politicians, businesses, and executives who have been incredibly dishonest . . . and the results have been catastrophic. Leaders must have a strong character and integrity, which means walking the walk and talking the talk. The moment leaders bend the truth, they lose their credibility.

Mary Ellen and Jane Part Company

Mary Ellen and Jane were buddies. They graduated college together and started working for a national TV broadcasting company in New York as interns. Both worked hard, but while Mary Ellen was honest and forthright in her dealings with fellow employees, Jane spent too much of her time attempting to flatter her boss and other influential executives. I say attempted because her obsequious manner damaged her reputation, and while Mary Ellen was offered a full-time position with the broadcasting company, Jane wasn't, and she resigned.

> *Hands-On Advice: Flattery is phony and easily detected. It will damage your reputation irreparably.*

Reread the first two sentences of the section titled "Simply No Substitute for Honesty." They tell the story.

We understand the world and take action in it based on notions and assumptions that may reside deeply in the psyche. We may not be aware of the effect these models have on our perception and behavior, yet they have the power to move us forward or hold us back.

Why do good, new ideas rarely get put into practice? Often because they conflict with deep-seated internal images of how the world or the company works. These mental models limit us to familiar ways of thinking and acting, much to our detriment. That's why managing mental models, discovering them, testing their validity, and improving them, can be a breakthrough concept for learning organizations. Mental models govern how we make sense of the world and how we take action in it. An easy example is the generalization "people are untrustworthy." Such a sentiment shapes how we act and how we perceive the acts of others.

Innovation

"Are you crazy? Stick my face on the label of salad dressing?"
—Actor Paul Newman, founder of Newman's Own
$370 million earned for charity over 30 years

Innovation has become a buzzword in leadership circles, overused to the point of losing all meaning. Every job candidate's resume boasts some stale permutation of self-described brilliance that, when dissected, amounts to a healthy dose of creativity and common sense.

Should this assessment of innovation be viewed negatively? Absolutely not! Let's break it down to the nitty-gritty: innovation, as defined by the good folks at Merriam-Webster, is simply "the introduction of something new." The ancient Greeks were innovators when they introduced standard coins for early commerce in 600 B.C., as was Christopher Latham Sholes when he invented the first practical mechanical typewriter in 1867. You can thank great inventors like Emperor Shen Nung for tea (2737 B.C.), Benjamin Franklin for bifocal glasses (1784), Ruth Handler for the Barbie doll (1959), and the two amazing Steves (Jobs and Wozniak) for the personal computer (1976).

But not everyone is destined to be the next Pearle B. Wait (Jell-O, 1897). I certainly have no desire to quash your sense of serendipity and industriousness, but I do want to demystify the world of innovation, a word that's not always synonymous with invention.

"People have come to the erroneous conclusion that if they're not willing to start something separate, world-changing and risky, they have no business starting anything," notes Squidoo.com founder Seth Godin in *Poke the Box: When Was the Last Time You Did Something for the First Time?* (Do You Zoom, Inc., 2011). "Somehow, we've fooled ourselves into believing that the project has to have a name, a building, and a stock ticker symbol to matter."

Dipak C. Jain, PhD, former dean of Northwestern University's Kellogg School of Management, defines innovation as "a response to an unsolved problem or unexploited opportunity." Praveen Gupta, MS, director of the Center for Innovation Science and Applications at the Illinois Institute of Technology in Wheaton, calls it the "oldest known process" and "an extension of a person's creativity."

"Contrary to conventional wisdom, innovation isn't a genetic endowment magically given to some and not others," adds Jeffrey H. Dyer, PhD, a professor of organizational leadership and strategy at Brigham Young University's Marriott School of Management in Provo, Utah. "It's a set of skills that can be developed with practice. If you want to be one of the really successful people that make a mark in business, you want to be the person that comes up with the idea, not just the person who carries out others' ideas."

Meet Clarice Turner, Innovator

Pretend, for a moment, that you're senior vice president of U.S. operations at the Starbucks Coffee Co., and you want to find innovative ways to boost store traffic, particularly at night. That's when even the most dedicated caffeine addicts are slowing their coffee consumption, and they haven't historically perceived your stores to be dinner or cocktail venues.

If you're Clarice Turner, MBA, you introduce the Starbucks Evenings program, which offers small plates, desserts, beer, and wine to customers who want to wind down at their favorite coffeehouse.

Turner tested the program in major markets like Seattle, Los Angeles, and Chicago, recognizing that "innovation is critical to keeping ahead of the game." As she told *Nation's Restaurant News* Associate Editor Mark Brandau in May 2013: "We're a very innovative company, so customers expect us to evolve."

This particular evolution was inspired by Turner's knowledge of European coffee culture. The overseas coffeehouse "evolves as the day goes on," she noticed. "Maybe the music changes and small plates are served, and it becomes more of a gathering place."

For Turner, the road to leadership success has been clearly paved: "You have got to listen to customers and innovate, or you're dead."

More Lessons from the Restaurant Industry

As any highly energetic leader in the restaurant industry will lament, business has been extremely volatile as budget-conscious consumers choose to dine at home. While restaurateurs bring in $1.8 billion a day in the United States, industry insiders find that guest traffic is waning and customers are choosing cheaper menu options. In late 2012, even McDonald's experienced its first monthly sales decline in nine years (a drop of 1.8 percent), which experts attributed to increased competition from other fast-food chains (Burger King, in particular).

So, this question naturally arises: How do smart, highly effective leaders respond to this challenge? Here are examples of innovators at work in the restaurant industry:

- They expand their existing product lineup without diluting their brand. Customers used to head to profit-challenged Red Lobster strictly for the surf, but now they're also ordering the turf. The seafood-centric chain is serving wood-grilled sirloin steaks, pork chops, and chicken, a "natural progression of how we're trying to grow our business," senior executive chef Michael LaDuke told *Nation's Restaurant News* in April 2013. "We're listening to customers. We want to give them more opportunities and more reason to come into the restaurant."

- They study demographics and reach out to new markets. America's melting pot has never been more diverse. Highly effective leaders review their company's products and services, finding new ways to appeal to a wider customer base. Chipotle has introduced Asian-inspired entrees, while Carl's Jr. is topping burgers with teriyaki sauce and guacamole.

- They understand, and cater to, customers' special needs. Many restaurant-industry leaders have decided to appeal to the 1 percent of the population that suffers from celiac disease, an autoimmune disorder characterized by the inability to digest gluten. Even non-gluten-intolerant consumers, as many as 28 percent of today's diners, according to the consumer market research consultants at NPD Group, are snubbing wheat, barley, and rye. Leaders at restaurant chains like Chick-fil-A, Soup Plantation, and Chipotle have rallied by introducing gluten-free menu options.

- They follow industry trends. Conscious that Americans' waistlines are growing ever-thicker, approximately one-third of today's restaurant leaders have added small-plate desserts, even one-bite options, to their menus. Early adapters include fast-food behemoths like Dunkin' Donuts, Dairy Queen, and Baskin-Robbins. In addition, almost 80 percent of fine-dining restaurants have jumped on the bandwagon. "We noticed, in our business, people tend to not eat larger portions of desserts," Dennis Turcinovic, owner and managing partner of New York City-based Delmonico's Restaurant Group, told *Nation's Restaurant News* in May 2013.

- They're innovative promotion pros. New ideas, when effectively promoted, will drive consumers to your business, as Seattle-based market-research firm Placed Insights confirmed with its 2012 survey of 70,000 restaurant customers, "Dining Out in America: The Impact of New Menu Items." Researchers asked customers: "After seeing or hearing an advertisement for a new fast-food item, did you purchase that item in the next 30 days?" The results were impressive: When offered the opportunity (an important concept) to buy a limited-time special item, 36.5 percent of consumers polled said they had tried it.

- They put their money where their ideas are. Heavy advertising campaigns and value strategies allowed Domino's Pizza to experience a 66 percent increase in net income for the first quarter of 2013. The chain's innovation leaders introduced a new pan pizza and weekday carryout specials, which allowed local stores to enjoy high rates of repeat business.

- They reward customer loyalty. Panera Bread developed the MyPanera loyalty card in November 2010 and has enrolled more than 9.5 million members. When customers make purchases, their cards are swiped and choices logged into Panera's database. Collected data is used to analyze customers' needs and buying habits. And, as Panera collects email addresses, the company sends special offers (buy one, get one) to its customer base.

- They develop online platforms and resources. Domino's has led the pack in innovative online ordering systems. Customers can follow their pizza's progress via a visual meter, with alerts to indicate when their food is being prepped, put into the oven, sliced, and boxed. The company's highly effective leaders have been rewarded with double-digit growth, and they plan to introduce more sophisticated online user tools.

- They improve the overall customer experience. In almost every televised restaurant-makeover show, dingy walls are gutted, parking lots are repaved, signage is modernized, and the physical space is transformed from ugly stepsister to Cinderella. In 2012, innovative leaders at Wendy's remodeled 50 restaurants and launched 20 new ones with a contemporary feel. Digital signage/menu boards, faster service lines and Wi-Fi bars appealed to new and existing customers.

Ultimately, "innovation is the process of getting from A to B to create and deliver new customer value in the marketplace," conclude Curtis R. Carlson, PhD, and William W. Wilmot, PhD, in *Innovation: The Five Disciplines for Creating What Customers Want*. "This new customer value should also enable a sufficient profit for the company to grow."

Never confuse customers' needs with product features that appeal to your ego or specific tastes. Features become innovative benefits "only when they address the needs of customers," Drs. Carlson and Wilmot caution. Also remember that price is only one value that motivates customers. Evaluate their tangible (mobility, communication, hunger) and intangible (prestige, fear, security, love) needs.

Make an Emotional Connection

Gary Erickson, founder and co-chief visionary officer of Emeryville, California—based Clif Bar & Co., is a highly admired innovator in the world of natural and organic energy bars.

Exhausted and ravenous after a one-day, 175-mile bicycle ride in 1990, he couldn't stomach another unappetizing energy bar, so he came up with his own recipe, launching the Clif Bar two years later. Named after his father, Clifford, the bars brought Erickson his first $1 million within a year.

But Erickson found that while women enjoyed the innovative flavor choices, they were unhappy with the bars' calorie count. To cater to his female customer base, Erickson introduced the Luna Bar in 1999, and another industry hit was born.

Erickson practiced one of the most effective marketing strategies when attempting innovation: he made an emotional connection with his customers. Instead of pushing his values on them, he listened to their needs and came up with a highly profitable solution.

As Kevin Roberts, CEO of advertising agency Saatchi & Saatchi, wrote in a 2011 *Advertising Age* article: "The Age of Now is all about the mastery of emotional communication; not manipulation, but of having relationship. . . . In the Era of New marketing, it was all about your product. In the Age of Now, it's all about the single question consumers have of you: 'How will you improve my life?' Answering this is to deliver priceless value."

Borrow from Your Competitors

Plagiarism is frowned upon in college, but it can herald increased profits in the rough-and-tumble business world. McDonald's McRib sandwich, a seasonal mainstay since the 1980s, finally faced competition from chains like Burger King, which "got its pork on" in 2013. Instead of copping to copying a successful rival, Burger King reps say they decided to launch the BK Rib Sandwich after participating in a 2012 barbecue event.

Some critics argued that Burger King's product, which features roughly the same ingredients as its McDonald's counterpart, had ripped off a competitor's concept. Others saw the move from a different perspective: While the new sandwich is surely competitive, so are both companies' entire menu boards. "They've been competing against each other for decades," said one analyst.

Mark Thomas Kennedy, PhD, MBA, an assistant professor of management and organization at the University of Southern California's Marshall School of Business, has found that drawing parallels with your competitors can actually boost your business. "From business schools and marketing consultants, entrepreneurs are mostly taught that talking about the competition is a dangerous no-no," he says. "But in the early stages of new markets, talking just about yourself is even more dangerous. In fact, it actually hurts innovators' chances of success by increasing the odds they'll be overlooked or ignored as 'lone voices.'

"You have to dignify the competition to create the market—otherwise you are distinct, but irrelevant," he adds. "If you can be first in the market along with others, cocreating something new, you can get much more attention than by trying to go it alone."

Involve Staff and Customers

As customer demands mandate innovation at every level, innovation becomes everyone's job. Hence, more leaders are creating cultures where ideas are visibly promoted at all levels; risk-tasking and entrepreneurial behavior are encouraged; growth through innovation is deemed as important as managing costs; and failure is tolerated if people learn from it.

HR executives report that 60 percent of their companies have a formal process for gathering employee ideas. As a result, they have enjoyed significant growth in employee-generated ideas, many of which have been implemented. About 40 percent say their company has an executive in a chief innovation officer (or similarly described) role.

"Given the continuing globalization of companies and the expanding array of available sources for innovation," says Kathryn Troy, former director of The Conference Board's Performance Excellence research program, "it is not surprising that the need to align innovation activity across the organization is listed as a top challenge."

Case in point: LEGO Group has grown from a small, family-owned Danish business founded in 1932 to a global leader in the toy market some 80 years later. Upon being named one of the Top 10 Reputable Companies in the world by the Reputation Institute, Chief Executive Vice President and CFO John Goodwin stated: "We want children of all ages to experience joy and pride when exploring their creative potential. We want to leave a positive impact on the world. We want to deliver a world-class service to our customers. And not least do we want our employees to experience the strong sense of purpose and spirit that characterize the LEGO Group."

But LEGO has not always been at the top of its game (apologies for the pun). Paal Smith-Meyer, head of the LEGO New Business Group, and a self-described innovation nomad, recalls a time in the late 1990s when the company's expansion into theme parks took leaders' focus off its primary goal: the design of super-cool toys. Only when LEGO's highly effective leaders told design staffers to go wild and come up with imaginative new toys did the company experience a major turnaround.

LEGO enjoyed another wave of profits when it brought customers into the innovation fold. Highly effective leaders realized that the company's most loyal users could help with future toy designs. Effective leaders help team members establish trust through social activities that encourage collective thinking. As employees develop healthy relationships, they regularly exchange information and knowledge through email, phone calls, or informal conversations. Innovation requires diverse ideas and perspectives—not a culture of sameness.

Takeaway from Chapter 5

Mastery includes a series of practices and principles. Its three essential elements are vision, creative tension, and commitment to truth, and they add up to how disciplined your approach is to business.

Assume you are the founder of a company. Your personal vision is to create and perpetuate the business. To achieve your vision you have individual goals that build and sustain your dream: a unique product wanted by consumers, a dedicated team to run the business, the physical property and equipment to make it happen, and selected goals along the way to keep the business profitable, such as increasing shareholder value.

Now, using that example, answer this question: What is your own personal vision, and how have you made it a reality? Next, examine the goals you set to achieve your vision. This exercise will help you see the difference between goals and objectives and personal vision. The ability to focus on ultimate desires is a corner-stone of personal mastery.

Describe how reality is threatening to deter achievement of your personal vision. Then answer this question: Do you accept reality or do you use your imagination to think of new ways to knock down roadblocks and achieve personal vision? This is creative tension, and you have to accept the fact that you either defeat it or it defeats you. Answer it in specific terms, addressing explicit things you did to improve the current reality.

Finally, do you have the courage to challenge self-imposed limitations when faced with seemingly intractable problems? This is the cornerstone of your commitment to truth: the ability to *not* fool yourself into thinking that it can't be done when it can. Cite specific instances.

For this exercise I suggest that you contract an impartial observer skilled in leadership evaluation—either a trained outsider or somebody from within (such as an HR manager skilled in coaching). Either way, this observer needs to be familiar with your background.

Discipline 2: Vision, Strategy, and Alignment

The Progression from Plans to Accomplishments Marks a True Leader

Highly effective leaders engage others in creating a clear, compelling, and inspiring vision, and communicate it in such a way that everyone understands it and in a way that motivates and inspires people to work as a team toward common goals. Only then will people be motivated. Leaders must clearly define and paint an exciting path to the future, while providing ethical and logical reasons as to why they're moving in a specific direction. They must articulate a clear framework and provide a cogent message that delineates each individual's role in realizing the vision. This builds support and enthusiasm, creating a culture where people are aligned and eager to participate in achieving company goals.

Leaders must also create excitement and spark people's imaginations regarding what the future holds. When strategies, objectives, and paths to success are clearly defined, individuals, teams, and organizations will be motivated, inspired, and energized.

Bruce, the CEO of a large corporation, had been in his position for about 18 months, and he had never communicated his vision of where he wanted to take the company. Employees were performing their roles and working hard, but they received no direction and had no idea of what to expect or the direction in which the company was going.

Through coaching, Bruce was instructed to articulate his vision for the future. He was reminded that he was the leader and people looked to him for leadership and vision. Bruce, however, simply wouldn't—or couldn't—do it, and he was promptly replaced. The board brought in a new CEO. Within 60 days, she laid out a clear vision for the company's future with specifics: how it was going to get there and what every employee's role would be. The company is now thriving because its new leader effectively communicated her vision so that everyone, from the top to the bottom of the organization, understood it.

Shared vision. No organization becomes great without a shared vision, goals, and values. Relying on a vision statement or the leader's charisma is not enough. A genuine vision breeds excellence and learning because people in the organization want to pursue these goals.

Melvin Takes Over as Hospital Purchasing Manager

Melvin's predecessor didn't understand the difference between acting as a purchasing agent and his role as a purchasing manager. When the hospital administrator discovered that purchasing agents were ignoring established purchasing procedures resulting in a huge increase in rejected purchased parts and material, she took action. The incumbent was demoted to purchasing agent (a job he did well), and Melvin took his place.

> *Hands-On Advice: Engage your employees by having them participate in establishing department goals and the working procedures needed to achieve those goals.*

With the aid and support of his purchasing agents, Melvin set clear goals and expectations for the purchasing department, and rejections of purchased parts and materials dropped significantly.

Involving employees in establishing goals unifies your team and makes it easier for everybody to focus on what's important for the organization.

What do we want to create? The answer to that question is the vision you and your people come together to articulate, build, and share. Unlike a vision that emanates from one person or a small group and is imposed on the corporation, shared visions create a commonality that gives a sense of purpose and coherence to all the activities the organization carries out. Few forces in life and the business world are as powerful as shared vision.

Shared vision is vital for learning organizations that want to encourage focus and energy in their employees. People learn best when they strive to accomplish things that matter to them. In fact, you can't have a learning organization without shared vision. The overarching goal that the vision establishes brings about not just commitment but new ways of thinking and acting. It fosters risk-taking and experimenting. It also encourages a commitment to the long term.

How to Share Vision

New leadership roles require new leadership disciplines. Three of the most critical disciplines are building shared vision, surfacing and challenging mental models, and engaging in systems thinking. These disciplines can only be developed through a lifelong commitment. And in learning organizations, these disciplines must be distributed widely, because they embody the principles and practices of effective leadership.

How do individual visions become shared visions? A useful metaphor is the hologram, the three-dimensional image created by interacting light sources. If you cut a photograph in half, each half shows only part of the whole image. But if you divide a hologram, each part, no matter how small, shows the whole image intact.

Likewise, when a group of people comes together to share a vision, each person sees an individual picture of the organization at its best. Each shares responsibility for the whole, not just for one piece. But the component pieces of the holograms are not identical. Each represents the whole image from a different point of view. It's something like poking holes in a window shade; each hole offers a unique angle for viewing the whole image. So, too, is each individual's vision unique.

When you add up the pieces of a hologram, the image becomes more intense, more lifelike. When more people share a vision, the vision becomes a mental reality that people can truly imagine achieving. They now have partners, cocreators; the vision no longer rests on their shoulders alone. Early on, people may claim it as their vision. But, as the shared vision develops, it becomes everybody's vision.

Five Useful Skills

Building shared vision involves these five useful skills:

1. *Encouraging personal vision.* Shared visions emerge from personal visions. It is not that people only care about their own self-interest; in fact, people's values usually include dimensions that concern family, organization, community, and even the world. Rather, it is that people's capacity for caring is personal.

2. *Communicating and asking for support.* Leaders must share their own vision continually, rather than being the official representative of the corporate vision. They also must ask: Is this vision worthy of your commitment? This is hard for people used to setting goals and presuming compliance.

3. *Visioning as an ongoing process.* Many managers want to dispense with the vision business by writing the official vision statement. Such statements often lack the vitality, freshness, and excitement of a genuine vision that comes from people asking: What do we really want to achieve?

4. *Blending extrinsic and intrinsic visions.* Many energizing visions are extrinsic, focusing on achieving something relative to a competitor. But a goal that is limited to defeating an opponent can, once the vision is achieved, easily become a defensive posture. In contrast, intrinsic goals, such as creating a new product, taking an old product to a new level, or setting a new standard for customer satisfaction, elicit more creativity and innovation. Intrinsic and extrinsic visions need to coexist; a vision solely predicated on defeating an adversary will weaken an organization.

5. ***Distinguishing positive from negative visions.*** Many organizations only pull together when their survival is threatened. Similarly, most social movements aim to eliminate what people don't want; thus, we see antidrugs, antismoking, or antinuclear arms movements. Negative visions tend to be short-term and carry a message of powerlessness.

Two sources of energy motivate organizations: fear and aspiration. Fear, the energy source behind negative visions, can produce extraordinary changes in short periods, but aspiration endures as a source of learning and growth over time.

Strategy. Decide what's important (and what's not important) so you can aim the allocation of resources—time, money, and creativity— toward this end. In this annual discipline, leaders systematically and regularly review and renew their mission, values, strategic position, vision, their few most vital objectives, and agree what to stop doing.

The effective leader must articulate five means: (1) here's where we're going, (2) here's why we're going there, (3) here's how we're going to get there, (4) here's your role in getting us there, and (5) here's how we're going to work together to get there.

Your team must be inspired and understand what the present and future hold for them. Everyone on your team, department, and organization listens to radio station WIIFM (What's In It For Me?). Employees must understand their particular roles in achieving the vision, along with: What's in it for me if I work hard to achieve these goals?

Inspirational leadership. If you want people to do great things, then your leadership style must be inspirational. Inspirational leaders have a positive attitude, and they can help ordinary people do extraordinary things. When a leader is not inspiring, people will do just enough to get by. Workers usually have more potential than they show. It's up to the leader to provide the guidance and inspiration to do better.

How do you measure up as a leader? Do you dedicate time to working one-on-one with your people? Do you train and give them the tools necessary to become better at their jobs? Do you set goals and help employees attain them? Do you empower people to make decisions (not delegate mundane tasks)?

Empowering people allows them to grow, and they appreciate that you believe in them. They know you trust them to make important decisions that directly affect the department, team, or organization. Empowered people feel valued and respected, which inspires them to improve and come to work energized.

Align People and Systems behind Your Vision

Align systems. The systems—policies, processes, technologies, measures, and people—are often at cross-purposes with the stated priorities because most leaders lack an organized approach to keep their systems aligned with their strategy. This discipline taps the knowledge of the entire workforce to identify the areas where the company will get the best return on investment in policies, processes, measures, technologies, and people.

Leaders need to ensure each person shares a commitment to a common vision, purpose, and principles. Leaders give people a sense of direction and constantly model values to build trust; pathfinding to create clarity and commitment; aligning structures, systems, and processes; and empowering people to translate strategy into action plans and disciplines.

The key to enhanced performance is having mutual vision, mission, values, and focus, and then aligning and creatively cooperating to execute the solution. We then think win-win; we seek to understand first; we create a spirit of synergy; we focus on execution; we know what we are about; we're all on the same page (alignment).

Alignment: Highly effective leaders align their motive and mission, purpose and passion, with a market need and business strategy. To check alignment, seek feedback on how your behavior affects your boss, peers, and direct reports to learn how others perceive you. Such feedback can highlight areas for improving your relationships. Since perception is reality, to lead well, you must manage perceptions. By asking questions and seeking feedback, you open up a dialogue so you can receive feedback on your behavior. You also show humility and gain credibility as you ask: What can we do to make the organization, team, group, or department better?

Vision/Strategy and Alignment

"Know who you are, and understand where you want to go."
—Sharlonda Buckman, CEO, Detroit Parent Network

Meet Mollie Katzen, Cookbook Maven

A child of the 1950s, Mollie Katzen grew up in a fairly traditional Jewish home, with a grandmother who lovingly baked homemade challah (a braided egg bread) and prepared her own phyllo dough from scratch.

Katzen's mother, however, was another story. She wasn't blessed with the cooking gene and routinely relied on highly processed convenience foods to feed her family. In fact, Katzen had never eaten a fresh green vegetable until reaching the age of 12, when she dined at a friend's house. How, then, did Mollie Katzen become one of *Health* magazine's "Five Women Who Changed the Way We Eat?"

In the early1970s, the artistically and musically gifted 20-something finished putting herself through college by working in a San Francisco restaurant. While pursuing a graduate degree in 1972 and enjoying the local food scene, Katzen's vision coalesced: establish a vegetarian collective and restaurant dedicated to sustainable living. She and seven friends subsequently launched the famed Moosewood in Ithaca, New York, several decades before tofu and vegetarianism went mainstream.

Moosewood's mission statement was straightforward: "spread the notion that protein and aesthetics need not be sacrificed when you leave meat out of a meal," Katzen noted in the first of her 16 best-selling books, *The Moosewood Cookbook: Recipes from Moosewood Restaurant* (Ten Speed Press, 1977). The collective soon grew to include 20 members, with profits channeled back into the restaurant.

A highly motivated Katzen sold 800 copies of her hand-lettered cookbook before receiving a huge book deal. By then, Moosewood was garnering glowing national reviews and was thriving against the cynical backdrop of the Watergate era, during "a time of passion and conviction, of high ideals and unconventional ideas," noted writer Nancy Harmon Jenkins in the *New York Times*.

But in 1978, Katzen decided to part company with Moosewood, and a lengthy, painful legal battle ensued. While she lost the use of the Moosewood name, she was awarded the rights and royalties to the cookbook.

Katzen was now on her own. She needed to figure out her next step. Like many undeterred visionaries, she opted to shape her own future by following five critical rules:

1. *Capitalize on your reputation and previous successes.* Katzen published her second best-selling book in 1982: *The New Enchanted Broccoli Forest* (Ten Speed Press; Revised edition, 2000). She dedicated it to her parents and grandparents.

2. *Read the marketplace.* By the late 1980s, Katzen realized that most working families were struggling with time constraints. Busy parents didn't want to spend hours in the kitchen. Her *Still Life with Menu* (Ten Speed Press; First printing edition, 1988), featured recipes for harried on-the-go families.

3. *Attract new clients/customers.* Studies revealed that children are more willing to eat vegetables if they have a hand in growing and preparing them. Katzen decided to write two children's cookbooks: *Pretend Soup and Other Real Recipes* and *Honest Pretzels*.

4. *Follow trends.* By 2000, Katzen recognized that cholesterol-conscious consumers wanted to cut fat from their diets. She revised the recipes in her original *Moosewood Cookbook* and promoted the new edition as a heart-healthy alternative.

5. *Seize opportunities for strategic alliances.* Katzen's hard work paid off yet again in 1998, when the Harvard School of Public Health hired her to design more healthful meals for student and faculty dining facilities. She also co-created the university's respected Food Literacy Project.

Searching Your Leadership Soul

Like Katzen, Deepak Chopra, MD, and founder of the Chopra Center, believes vision originates from deep in a leader's soul. Highly effective leaders must answer three questions: Who am I? Why am I here? How can I tune into the soft-spoken urgings of my soul to fulfill my life's purpose and make a difference?

In his book *The Soul of Leadership*, Dr. Chopra explains that answering these questions requires you to take full responsibility for your personal and professional life in two ways: first, accept the premise that you alone are accountable for your values and vision; and second, take ownership of the ways you communicate these values and visions to the people around you.

Only then, Dr. Chopra notes, can the "invisible seeds planted in the silence of your deepest awareness" become tangible realities. "As they unfold, you will manage their growth with passion and energy. Your purpose will be apparent to all. The results you achieve will benefit everyone—you, the group you lead, and the world at large."

Sharing Your Vision

"A leader has the vision and conviction that a dream can be achieved. He inspires the power and energy to get it done."
—Ralph Nader, political activist/former Green Party presidential candidate

Sharing your vision involves three core components, according to Michael Lee Stallard, cofounder and president of E Pluribus Partners. In *Fired Up or Burned Out* (Thomas Nelson First edition, 2009), he emphasizes that staff members must be: (1) motivated by the organization's vision; (2) united by its values; and (3) proud of its reputation.

These three requirements cannot be achieved without proper training and development. At McDonald's, which now boasts more than 34,000 restaurants in 118 countries, serviced by 1.8 million employees, top-performing restaurant franchisees take full advantage of the company's training resources. Corporate-sponsored studies show that training-focused franchises enjoy:

- Better alignment with corporate values and goals.
- Lower employee turnover (managerial and rank-and-file staff).
- Increased employee engagement.
- A fast track for employees who seek promotions.
- Higher customer satisfaction, with fewer complaints.
- Greater profitability.

John T. Eggers, PhD, a correctional program specialist for the Federal Bureau of Prisons, wants highly effective leaders to know that execution of one's vision cannot be accomplished without psychological safety, a concept that social scientists define as the ability to trust one's peers, subordinates, and bosses. As a leader, your words and actions must be in alignment, and transparency is critical when you want to share your feelings and values.

Transparency "promotes increased participation in decision-making and greater trust in the leader," Dr. Eggers noted in the February/March 2011 issue of *Corrections Today*. "When leaders act with transparency, followers perceive psychological safety, which may result in higher employee engagement on the job. When individuals are engaged, they may exhibit extra effort and assume more responsibility for outcomes."

Col. Tom Guthrie and Maj. Matt Dennis, veterans who served in Afghanistan, propose "4 E's" for ensuring that staff members can execute the vision:

1. *Equipment:* Provide team members with the equipment they require, teach them how to use it properly, and allow them to improvise or make changes when they discover potential improvements.
2. *Each other:* As team members work with their peers and leaders, trust begins to form. Team members quickly learn each other's

strengths and weaknesses. Bonds form, and team members are committed to helping each other. They also hold each other accountable and establish standards that peer pressure helps enforce.

3. *Environment:* Team members must report important observations to the appropriate leaders, "who must be empowered to recognize when their action or inaction can lead to an advantage, and be confident enough to make decisions accordingly," noted Guthrie and Dennis in the April/May 2011 issue of *Infantry*.

4. *End state:* Is everyone on the same page? Has the goal, or end state, been adequately defined? Is it truly attainable?

"Alignment is a prerequisite for mission command," note Guthrie and Dennis. "Without alignment, empowered and decentralized sub-units can drive in different directions. Alignment is the responsibility of the commander."

Candid Communication

As a highly effective leader, you must share your vision candidly and authentically. Notice my use of the word "share." Don't dictate, tell, or instruct when you want to communicate your vision. Sharing allows you to be honest yet still confident and assertive. It shows that you care about your subordinates and remain committed to boosting morale.

Leaders who lack candor run the risk of alienating their teams by:

- Appearing too busy to communicate well, rushing through their presentation to save time.
- Being sarcastic, insensitive, or tactless and confusing these communication styles with candor.
- Being manipulative (pretending to care about what others think, while lying to get what you want).
- Refusing to share information because they irrationally fear it will make them look weak.

Candor is the antithesis of arrogance, one of the most egregious leadership sins. Never assume or communicate that you know everything. As Lord Ian MacLaurin, former chairman of British supermarket giant Tesco, warned 450 retail executives at a 1997 conference in London: "There are classic examples of people who have taken an arrogant attitude, thought they knew it all in head office, and suddenly found they had a problem."

If you're in middle management and work for a CEO who hoards information, don't use this as an excuse for being cagey or secretive with your department or team. I can't think of a faster way to create anxiety, estrangement, and ill will.

Positively Negative

"I'll always use the negativity as more motivation to work even harder and become even stronger."
—Award-winning quarterback Tim Tebow

There will always be naysayers whose personalities, behaviors, self-interests, and narcissistic tendencies interfere with your desire to create a visionary team. The jealous, overly pessimistic, or drama-addicted members of your department or organization undoubtedly relish their reputations for sucking the energy and joy out of every endeavor. Virtually all organizations seem to have one (or more) of these malcontents, and their CEOs obliviously allow them to sabotage team efforts.

In their book, *The Drama-Free Office* (OnCourse Publishing, 2012), executive coaches Jim Warner and Kaley Klemp divide these difficult team members into four categories:

1. *Complainers.* Complainers specialize in whining, waffling, and resignation. They always manage to be the injured parties who are unwilling to find viable solutions to team challenges. They moan, groan, and phone in their contributions, with the ultimate goal of blaming others when group efforts head south. They may start projects, but their attitudes and behaviors ensure they'll never

complete them. Highly effective leaders must beat them at their own game by killing them with kindness, providing frequent feedback, offering guidance when they're overwhelmed, and refusing to take no for an answer. Praise positive behaviors whenever possible.

2. *Cynics.* Cynics specialize in discounting, sniping, and withdrawing. "This will never work" is their personal motto, and they'll go to extremes to defend their indefensible positions. In meetings, they're the class clowns who divert the group's attention with superfluous objections and snide remarks. But their self-righteousness, bluster, and sarcasm mask an extreme sense of vulnerability and poor self-image. Smart, highly effective leaders manage them by keeping group discussions on point, steering dialogue in a positive direction and focusing on constructive problem-solving. Effective leaders also recognize that cynics are often extremely bright and creative; if you can appropriately channel their energies, you may discover innovative ways to tap into their intellectual curiosity.

3. *Controllers.* These employees specialize in steamrolling, micromanaging, and impatience. They're the archetypical playground bullies who cannot play well with others unless they get their way. Controllers take a "my way or the highway" approach to business, believing their ideas and methods are always better than their peers', and even their boss's, suggestions. While controllers may be extremely effective and efficient, their inability to conform to suitable group dynamics may mean they're more trouble than they're worth; highly effective leaders need to evaluate this prospect. Once again, you can reward them for positive efforts and recognize their unique abilities, but you must "guide them toward becoming empowering rather than domineering," note Warner and Klemp. Praise them for taking initiative, but reprimand them quietly and firmly when they ruffle too many feathers.

4. *Caretakers.* Caretakers specialize in overcommitment, conflict avoidance, and rescuing the situation. Their favorite mantra is, "Don't worry; I'll take care of it." And, indeed, caretakers are

responsible, efficient, and highly productive, however, they have a tendency to jump in and rescue their peers, even when their help isn't wanted or needed. They're the ultimate volunteers, with unbridled energy and seemingly empty schedules. They're also part-time controllers who crave attention and recognition for their efforts. Fail to praise them, and they'll likely become martyrs. Highly effective leaders can teach them how to avoid overpromising and embrace cooperative efforts. Show them how their desire to take over the world stunts their peers' professional growth. "Your greatest coaching challenge will probably center on helping caretakers set and uphold limits," Warner and Klemp advise.

Make the Mentoring Commitment

"When a young person, even a gifted one, grows up without proximate living examples of what she may aspire to become, whether lawyer, scientist, artist or leader in any realm, her goal remains abstract. Such models as appear in books or on the news, however inspiring or revered, are ultimately too remote to be real, let alone influential. But a role model in the flesh provides more than inspiration; his or her very existence is confirmation of possibilities one may have every reason to doubt, saying, 'Yes, someone like me can do this.' "

—U.S. Supreme Court Justice Sonia Sotomayor

Starting Off on the Right Foot

Effective leadership spells the difference between success and failure for both employees and the organization. Ineffective leadership spells disaster.

Pauline found that out when she was hired as assistant supervisor in the information analysis department of a payroll company. Through example, her boss, a slacker, showed Pauline how to goof off on the job, how to take extended lunch breaks, how to pad the productivity report, and a host of other time-killing and destructive techniques.

After a couple of years on the job, Pauline's modus operandi was set in stone. What once had been an ambitious new employee had transformed into a jaded slacker.

> *Hands-On Advice: Be careful where you place new employees and newly appointed supervisors.*

As a mentor, you should provide two levels of support: career growth and psychosocial enhancement, according to Kathy E. Kram, PhD, a professor of organizational behavior at Boston University School of Management in Massachusetts.

Dr. Kram defines three critical phases of an effective mentoring relationship in her widely read text, *Mentoring at Work: Developmental Relationships in Organizational Life* (University Press of America, 1988):

1. *Initiation:* A relationship forms. The protégé develops respect for the mentor's knowledge and abilities. In turn, the mentor must believe that the protégé deserves the benefits of this special relationship.

2. *Cultivation:* The mentor and protégé take time to learn about each other's strengths and weaknesses. Each recognizes and accepts the benefits of the relationship. Dr. Kram cites the cultivation phase as the most beneficial to the protégé.

3. *Redefinition:* The mentor and protégé work toward separation. The protégé becomes more independent and works autonomously, seeking to become a visionary in his or her own right. The mentor becomes more of a coach with less frequent contact. The protégé may now be in a position to assist his or her former mentor, as each party is on a more equal footing.

Through each of these mentoring phases, be sure to listen to your protégé. A 2009 study of aerospace professionals found that "30 percent of mentors and 35 percent of those mentored responded that listening and communication skills were the most valuable aspects of mentoring" the next generation of visionaries.

Takeaway from Chapter 6

Having a personal vision, the creative energy to spot new opportunities, and a commitment to yourself and to your organization to see it like it is and tell it like it is, is simply a beginning.

How you communicate your vision to the organization is another matter entirely. Take this opportunity, away from the daily fray of work, where demands for your time are incessant, to sit quietly and reflect on your ability to be heard by your customers and employees. Ask yourself how you communicate with them and how effective your method is. Some executives communicate best through the written word, but that preference might be a barrier detracting from their vision reaching every level of the organization if it's not frequently accompanied by constant staff contact.

There's a reason highly effective leaders regularly visit the firing lines of their businesses and customers in their habitat: It gives them the opportunity to find out if their message is getting through. Ask yourself how frequently you visit the firing line of your company, how often you visit customers, and how effective you are at communicating your message when you do.

Discipline 3: Priorities, Planning, and Execution

Execution Cannot Succeed without the Team's Acceptance and Endorsement

We have a greater need now to be highly effective through clear focus on purpose, centered on principles, and execution around priorities. If there is little agreement on purpose and direction, the culture is characterized by control, contention, and confusion. The reason for this tragic ineffectiveness is a lack of focus and execution.

Priorities. Focusing on priorities unleashes talent and energy and creates a culture where each person shares a common focus and executes around priorities. When change accelerates, formerly successful processes and practices don't work. Nothing fails like past successes. Today everyone must have the same purpose, principles, and focus; they must know who they are, what they are trying to do, where they are trying to go, why they need to get there, and how they will cooperate. It must be internalized. Leaders get people on the same page, executing around priorities, which releases talent and energy.

Planning. Set goals that lead. Well-defined goals are among the most effective tools available to any leader, yet most leaders don't set goals that lead their people in the right direction. The purpose of this discipline is to produce clear and measurable annual goals. Pursuing these goals will lead people to align their daily activities with the few vital objectives set in the strategy. The result is a brief goals statement that every team member can support.

Execution. Work the plan. One of the best learning tools is the individual quarterly plan. In this discipline, every person works with the team leader to develop individual plans for the coming quarter. These goals are reviewed and aligned with company goals. This plan serves as a time-saving template for a weekly status report. Every person knows how to set goals, understand priorities, take responsibility for those goals, become accountable, report progress, and solve problems.

Let's examine the previous three points in more detail. We put first things first; we're proactive and responsible; we're a product of our decisions, not our conditions; and we regularly renew our focus and execution.

1. *Planning.* Through this discipline, a plan, is born. The plan depicts the desired end or aim and specifies the best means for achieving it.

2. *Organizing.* This discipline seeks to optimally organize resources to achieve the plan. This requires identifying all actions and activities and organizing them to maximize resources and results.

3. *Measuring performance.* This practice recognizes that what gets measured gets managed and gets done. This discipline measures how well activities are performed and signals management when they are poorly performed.

4. *Executing.* This means assigning all of the plan's activities to employees to perform (nothing is left to chance). This leads to attaining the plan. Executing expectantly engages and empowers employees to ideally perform their assigned activities and holds them accountable when they don't.

5. *Following up.* This practice generates actionable feedback, aligns expected outcomes with actual performance, instills cooperation and accountability, and reinforces making right things happen.

6. *Real-time reporting.* This takes collected feedback (timely, reliable, and accurate performance data), shares it, and makes it readily available so managers can take action to address problems.

7. *Problem-solving.* This occurs when problems are identified, understood, addressed, and monitored. This requires a system that provides quantitative and qualitative feedback with which to resolve problems and improve performance. This system ensures the constant use of the seven learned disciplines. Systems drive action, and these actions produce certain outcomes.

You can replace ineffective habits of coasting, avoiding responsibility, taking the easy way out, and exercising little initiative or will-power with the discipline to focus on the important but not necessarily urgent matters of your life, thereby gaining leverage and influence. You go from victim to creative resource, from futility to hope, from having can't and won't power to being focused and having can and will power and the discipline to realize your top priorities.

Judy Sees the Light

Judy, a highly regarded young executive, had worked for a major corporation for six years. When promoted to a managerial position, she appeared to have the right stuff: technical know-how and a firm understanding of her industry's intricacies. Her clients loved her and her peers respected her. Her highly developed interpersonal skills made her indispensable when problems arose.

But Judy lacked certain key leadership traits. She procrastinated when making key decisions and didn't know how to instill confidence in her team. Her poor time-management skills forced her to work unnecessarily long hours, and her failure to delegate led team members to think she didn't trust them. Over time, they felt alienated.

In our coaching sessions we began addressing Judy's time-management skills. We assessed each team member's strengths and weaknesses, and Judy soon recognized she had a talented, capable staff that wanted to accept more responsibility. To reach her full potential, and to help team member reach theirs, Judy realized she had to stop micro-managing. The first time Judy delegated to Chris, she tossed and turned for several nights. She worried he'd miss his deadline, fail to meet the client's expectations, or that the client would disapprove of delegating the work to a subordinate. In terms of stress, Judy rated it as "agony."

But Judy's epiphany came at week's end, when the job was completed and the client was thrilled with the results. When talented staff members were given opportunities, Judy acknowledged, they could accomplish great things. The coaching had paid off, and an enthusiastic Judy celebrated her successes. She had learned to delegate responsibility and empower others. How wonderful, she said, to see another team member rise to the occasion and do an extraordinary job. After years of working hard and completing tasks by herself, Judy had finally learned an important lesson: Being an effective leader means letting go and empowering others to make decisions.

A week later, at our next coaching session, Judy told me how proud she was of her decision to delegate and about the wonderful job Chris had done. When she finished, I asked, "Did you tell Chris what a great job he did? Did you call him into your office and give him the praise and recognition he deserved?"

"No," Judy admitted, after a long pause. "In all the excitement, I never did. We always have so much work to do. I just moved on to the next project."

I asked Judy how she would have felt if she'd been in Chris's shoes. "Oh," she replied, a light going on in her eyes. "I see it now. I never took the time to give him the praise and recognition he deserved." In this aha moment, Judy acknowledged one of the most important tenets of effective leadership.

Priorities, Planning, and Execution

"I don't believe that it absolutely, positively, takes a disaster or a crisis to put a company culture back on the strategic rails. But sometimes it certainly seems that way."

—Evan M. Dudik, PhD, Strategic Renaissance

Disorder at Denny's. Back in 1993, 21 U.S. Secret Service agents, the law-enforcement professionals who help protect the president, entered a Denny's restaurant in Annapolis, Maryland, at around 7:30 A.M. to enjoy breakfast. The agents were seated at several tables within the same section of the restaurant. Six African-American agents chose to sit together at one specific table.

By 8:25 A.M., the agents had finished their meals and were getting up to leave. But there was one notable exception: The table of six African-Americans still had not been served, and the agents believed the slight was intentional.

"I thought the fight for the right to eat in a restaurant was a thing of the past," Agent Alfonso M. Dyson told *The Baltimore Sun* afterward. "I never thought any of this would happen to me. This is the 1990s."

The six agents slapped Denny's with a civil rights lawsuit, and it wasn't the first time the restaurant chain had found itself in the discrimination crosshairs. Two years earlier, 10 African-American high school and college students in San Jose, California, complained that a Denny's manager told them they would have to pay for their meals prior to being seated. A group of white students visiting the restaurant at the same time had been seated and hadn't been asked to prepay. When the African-American students refused to pay in advance, they were denied service. Sadly, numerous complaints were filed about similar incidents at other Denny's restaurants throughout California.

Denny's leaders defended the chain, citing isolated problems with "slow service," not racial intolerance. But the company was already facing a series of class-action lawsuits, which eventually led to a hefty payout of $54.4 million on more than 4,000 nationwide claims. The U.S. Department of Justice had substantiated an indefensible pattern of racial discrimination.

A year later, the six Maryland Secret Service agents received $35,000 each, and Denny's leaders were functioning in damage-control mode.

"It's bad sociology, immoral, and everything else. But, also, it's just lousy business," Christopher Muller, PhD, told a *Black Issues in Higher Education* writer in August 1994. The Cornell University School of Hotel Administration professor added: "If you are going to stay in business, customers are customers, regardless of their [race] or what they look like."

"Organizations have come to realize that it's a lot easier to do it right the first time," agreed Donald J. Walters, a former industry professional and a visiting professor at the William F. Harrah College of Hotel Administration at the University of Nevada–Las Vegas. "It's become extremely cost effective to have people trained in customer service."

Denny's hadn't done it right the first time. Minorities held 70 percent of the low-level, low-paying industry jobs and a disproportionate percentage of managerial positions. Many experts, including those in Cornell's hotel administration program, which prepares students for leadership roles in the hospitality arena, urge students, as well as the industry at large, to make meaningful efforts to promote cultural diversity.

Denny's executives were concerned that the negative publicity was discouraging African-Americans, who comprised 10 percent of the chain's customer base, from eating at any of its 1,500 restaurants. The company's strategic-planning efforts were being driven by despair.

C. Ronald Petty, former head of Burger King U.S.A., was hired to help repair Denny's public image. He worked with corporate executives to prioritize, plan, and execute several vital action steps:

- *Sensitivity training.* *Every* employee participated in company-mandated sensitivity training. The prospect of such training was often poorly received in some small towns, but no exceptions were granted.
- *Employee screening.* Petty wanted to prevent Denny's restaurant managers from hiring racist servers and supervisors. He instituted the use of H.R. Easy, a computer-based interviewing tool that screened potential hires for racial bias.
- *Clear priorities and directives.* CEO Jerry Richardson stepped down from his post. New CEO Jim Adamson told employees: "Anyone who doesn't like the direction this train is moving in had better jump off now . . . and I will fire you if you discriminate."

- *New standards for executive recruitment.* In 1993, there were no minority corporate officers or vice presidents at Denny's. By 1996, 11 percent of the company's executives were minorities. Adamson instructed his executive staff to "never miss an opportunity to preach the gospel of diversity."

- *Fast-track managerial program.* Denny's created a fast-track program to increase the number of minority restaurant managers and franchisees. By 2002, there were 64 minority-owned franchises (compared to only 1 in 1993), and 32 percent of the company's supervisors were minorities.

- *Culturally diverse alliances.* Denny's increased its contracts with minority suppliers ($0 in 1992, $100 million by 2002).

- *Targeted philanthropic endeavors.* Denny's increased its philanthropic efforts in key minority communities, pledging $1 million a year to human rights and civil rights organizations.

Denny's reinforced these plans by airing 60-second commercial spots that reaffirmed its leaders' commitment to bias-free customer service. Part of the broadcast script read: "Everyone who comes to our restaurants deserves to be treated with respect, with dignity, with fairness. . . . If there's a mix-up, we'll apologize, and we'll make it right. . . . All of us at Denny's want you to know that we care about your feelings. Which is why all 46,000 of us have signed this pledge and reaffirm our commitment to you."

The U.S. Department of Justice stated that while "Denny's discriminatory practices by some employees were clearly wrong," its leaders "should be commended for their actions" in accepting blame and employing forgiveness strategies, particularly nondiscrimination policies that terminate employees who engage in proscribed conduct.

"You will hear us all say here that the lawsuit was one of the best things to happen to Denny's," Chief Diversity Officer Ray Hood-Phillips told the Associated Press in 2002. "Although it was a historic low point, I think there were huge opportunities. We had no place to go but up."

There's another critical lesson to be learned from the Denny's case study: Don't wait for a crisis to begin prioritizing, planning, and executing.

Nancy Can't Find Her Way

Let's face it. Not everybody is cut out to be a leader. Nancy, for example, was a clerical leader for a large insurance office. Since the clerical workflow was progressive (work progressing from one station to the next in a daisy chain of stations), the balance of work moving from one station to the next was of paramount importance.

Nancy was highly intelligent, hard-working, and ambitious. But she had one glaring fault: she overemphasized the production (execution) aspect of her job, and underemphasized the planning function. That shortcoming produced holes in the flow of clerical work from one station to the next. Some workstations were flooded with backlog, others shut down waiting for work.

Since Nancy had trouble handling that aspect of her job, the company was forced to add an assistant supervisor to plan the workflow. That situation didn't last too long. The company found a supervisor capable of handling both functions.

> *Hands-On Advice: Your primary job as a leader is prioritizing, planning, and executing your area of responsibility.*

Neglect any one of those three crucial functions and your department's performance will suffer . . . and so will you. Companies need leaders who are generalists not specialists.

Identifying Priorities

"Organizations today are as filled as they ever were with managers who have the potential to be effective strategists, but that potential is going undeveloped. Organizational leaders must step in and fill this void by recognizing and rewarding big-picture thinking in the same way they do specific functional

achievements and by focusing on transferring their own conceptual thinking skills
to their peers and to the next managerial generation."
—Dr. John H. Humphreys, professor of management, Texas A&M
University, Commerce, *MIT Sloan Management Review*, Fall 2005

When the U.S. Department of Agriculture asked agricultural economist James J. Wadsworth to help the dairy industry with strategic planning, he began by asking managers across the nation's dairy herd improvement system to assess their organizations' strengths and weaknesses. Several key areas emerged, from financial stability and operational efficiency to innovation initiatives and facilities management.

Wadsworth followed up by asking managers whether they were optimistic about the future. A robust 95 percent said they were, indeed, optimistic about their ability to cope with industry changes and job pressures. Some had already conducted planning sessions on how to adapt to technological advances, while others felt they were making headway. The majority of these managers said they recognized that you have to adjust to change or be passed by, and Wadsworth knew that strategic planning would guide organizational adjustment and industry positioning.

The managers' self-identified strengths and weaknesses served as a framework for Wadsworth's 10 core priorities: (1) Expand membership; (2) Gain efficiencies; (3) Maintain financial strength; (4) Develop opportunities; (5) Be technologically innovative and progressive; (6) Be an industry leader by keeping up with professional counterparts; (7) Provide quality member services and products; (8) Supervise records/embrace rules and regulations; (9) Retain member loyalty; and (10) Remain competitive and viable.

Wadsworth worked with managers to develop strategic directions that included community education and promotion, aggressive solicitation of business, progressive programs and services, increased flexibility when working with individuals, improved coordination, efficiency measures, continued development of technological capabilities, and nontraditional ways to improve systems.

To survive in a changing market, Wadsworth recognized that organizations must provide affordable services and be resource-strong, and be headed by leaders who are ". . . progressive, open-minded, and involved. They must collectively brainstorm and listen to each other and the marketplace. Alternative strategies and directions must be explored in light of industry conditions and with a keen eye on system-wide goals."

Managers were asked to provide definitive *action steps* to meet the identified priorities, and they came up with these winners: Make functions faster, simpler, and less expensive. Operate in a more businesslike manner. Meet industry needs as they change. Incorporate financial management into the system. Weed out traditional thinkers. Invest more money to push technology and Internet services. Have less top-down direction and more reliance on stakeholders. Make systems less regimented. Continue to adapt to technological changes. Use the wealth of available data to prevent organizational decline. Develop marketing training for field forces. Develop more cooperation among the states. Build trust.

As Wadsworth noted at the time: "Although these commonsense concepts are well understood, they are not always well followed and are worth discussing from time to time. Indeed, such phrases emphasize focus, and leaders need to take them to heart and evaluate their organizations in regard [to them] on a regular basis."

Productive Planning Meets Effective Execution

"Being busy does not always mean real work. The object of all work is production or accomplishment, and to either of these ends there must be forethought, system, planning, intelligence, and honest purpose, as well as perspiration. Seeming to do is not doing."

—Thomas Alva Edison

Ray Attiyah, MBA, couldn't agree more with Thomas Edison. As founder and chief innovation officer of Definity Partners, a leadership-improvement firm, he has counseled many clients who measure results based on how much paperwork they generate as opposed to true progress or profits. "Success to these managers is measured by the number of printed pages contained in their plan," he wrote in *The Business Journal*. "Success is measured by the amount of trivial and useless information shared amongst their executive team."

Does any of this sound familiar?

Many leaders cannot resist the temptation to complicate their planning and execution efforts, turning an exercise in straightforwardness into a tortuous, labyrinthine affair.

Alan Siegel and Irene Etzkorn, officers at corporate-identity consulting firm Siegelvision, refer to this tendency as a "crisis of complexity"—a "thief that must be apprehended."

Just as credit card contracts (average: 31 pages), the U.S. tax code (3.8 million words), and virtually every legal contract can overwhelm our ability to understand their content, managerial planning can become an exercise in excess. More does not necessarily equal better when planning, and filling, your action plans with jargon-riddled buzzwords makes them less comprehensible . . . and a guaranteed way to lower your staff's morale.

In their most basic form, planning and execution can be summarized by answering six key questions:

1. Exactly where is our team, department, or organization right now?
2. What do we want to accomplish (goals and objectives)?
3. What must we do to achieve these priorities (action steps)?
4. Who will participate in planning and execution?
5. How will we budget and manage costs?
6. How will we know when we've successfully executed our plans (end point)?

In a nutshell, "where," "what," and "who" must lead to definitive "hows."

"Once you have a better understanding of needs, you can make informed decisions on behalf of others," note Siegel and Etzkorn in *Simple: Conquering the Crisis of Complexity*, (Twelve, April 2, 2013). "To simplify is to curate, edit, and lessen the options and choices that overwhelm."

Once you've discussed priorities with your team, it's time to devise a planning checklist and assign staff members to handle individual tasks:

- *Research and background.* What information do staffers need to begin planning? How will they obtain reliable information? How will this data be checked for accuracy?

- *Resource assessment.* What resources will they need to formulate and execute plans? Do you have a reality-based budget? Have you communicated budgetary limits to your staff? Have you budgeted for unforeseen events?

- *Delegation of action steps.* To whom will you assign key tasks? Will people work individually and/or in teams? How will you monitor their progress throughout the planning and execution process? (Don't be afraid to subject plans to regular "tune-ups" to ensure alignment with priorities.)

- *Strategy steps.* How will your staff carry out specific plans/action steps? Push for details.

- *Assessment.* How will you determine whether priorities and plans have been met? Which tools or techniques will you use? Have you and your team clearly defined an end point?

Execution cannot succeed unless your team is on board with your plans. Each team member must understand that his or her efforts can facilitate or derail planning efforts. Team members must share common goals, so it's important to weed out staff members who may thwart the group's efforts. You may be surprised to find that you've added too many staffers to your team. Can you simplify the execution process and improve efficiency by trimming the number of team members?

Throughout the planning process, remain in close communication with your team. Too many leaders and managers assume efforts are moving along, without taking time to ask for details. While you may have built a trustworthy team, it's all too easy for miscommunication and misunderstandings to occur.

Peter Schwartz, founder of Global Business Network, encourages leaders to hold informal conversations with staff members whenever possible. As he notes in *The Art of the Long View* (Crown Business; Reprint edition, February 8, 2012):

"Informal conversations take place everywhere: in the 'invisible' strategy sessions of the elevator ride, the lunchroom, or the carpool. In these 'nonthreatening' locales, ideas are developed and tested, and these ideas ultimately become part of the formal proposals or strategic plan."

When formal and informal conversations intersect, you have created an optimum environment for learning, creativity, and reality-testing. Team members can feed off each other's ideas and learn to brainstorm effectively.

Schwartz also reminds highly effective leaders that organizational culture can promote or inhibit planning efforts. "Start by doing what you can to make your organizational culture welcome diverse points of view and lively discussion," he emphasizes. "You should state, up front, that the group is open to new information. No one should be penalized for raising questions or ideas."

The Prophet versus Leader Paradigm

"The strategic planner, previously notoriously poor in people skills, now has to excel in dealing with people: energizing them, mobilizing them, holding them, stretching them, and providing the tensions and slack needed to get the difficult job of making and owning those plans done."
—Annabel Beerel, PhD, *Leadership & Organization Development Journal*

Dr. Annabel Beerel, a Sudbury, Massachusetts-based organizational consultant and founder/CEO of the New England Women's Leadership Institute, asserts that strategic planning has two primary roles: prophet and leader. She learned about these roles firsthand when heading strategic-planning efforts for The Weston Jesuit School of Theology, a Cambridge, Massachusetts-based Roman Catholic seminary.

The Weston Jesuit School of Theology faced radical demographic changes when it allowed female and international students to enroll in theological degree programs. Competition among graduate divinity programs was also on the rise, and students were shopping for institutions. An aging faculty, coupled with students' increasing demands for individual attention, created further challenges for Weston Jesuit, in particular, plummeting morale.

Dr. Beerel worked hard to understand both the macro and micro environments in which the school operated. Perhaps inspired by Weston Jesuit's religious focus, she devised the prophet/leader metaphor to demarcate business executives' distinct planning functions.

"Prophets are not just divinely inspired forecasters," she explained in her 1997 *Leadership & Organization Development Journal* case study. "Rather, they exhort others fully to see and face present-day realities in order to avert future harmful consequences."

The prophet role requires highly effective leaders to:

- Assess immediate and short-term future needs.
- Communicate how the organization will deal with these needs.
- Put plans into action.
- Prepare for expected and unexpected changes.
- Deal head-on with the consequences of these changes.
- Ensure, every step of the way, that leaders and staff operate with the highest ethical intentions.
- Assess trade-offs associated with any plan or decision.
- Balance competing agendas.
- Question staff when important issues arise.
- Carefully review the answers to these questions to ensure plan compliance and effectiveness.

In the leadership role, highly effective leaders must:

- Ensure that their vision is realistic, relevant, and attainable.
- Communicate this vision to all stakeholders.
- Mobilize all resources required to carry out priorities and plans.
- Create an *ownership culture* that rewards staff for carrying out priorities and plans in alignment with the organization's vision.
- Help employees master core competencies and reach their potential.
- Nurture the emotional and creative spirit within staff members.

- Encourage staffers to embrace change.
- Manage conflicts and enforce appropriate boundaries.
- Develop strategic alliances.

As both leader and prophet, recognize that many organizations fail to meet their goals because environmental factors interfere with team efforts. Employees quit. Emergencies occur. Organizational politics interfere with execution. Staff members display a lack of discipline. Despite these common nuisances, highly effective leaders must never put their planning efforts on the back burner or, worse, suspend the execution process.

Top 10 Ways to Sabotage Yourself and Your Company

Even the most impressive highly effective leaders can make critical errors when prioritizing, planning, and executing. Here's my Top 10 list of fatal leadership attitudes, beliefs, and actions:

1. I'm too busy "doing" to set priorities or plan.
2. I trust my team implicitly. I know my staff will complete the task because they've been assigned to it.
3. Everyone knows that businesses hold too many meetings. Why should I contribute to "meeting pollution"? My team will let me know when everything is done. I don't want to be bothered with progress reports.
4. My day-to-day activities keep me far too busy. I need to pay more attention to them, and planning can take a backseat.
5. I know my plan is a winner. I don't need to make adjustments or assess team members' progress.
6. I don't need to provide my team with costly resources. Just let them be creative with minimal support. So what if they get frustrated? It's no big deal.
7. I know there's one clear way to reach our planning goals. I don't need to involve my team in figuring out how we'll get there.

8. This chapter encourages me to embrace simplicity. Well, I'll make things really simple. I'll set a goal, but I'll let my team wing it!

9. I know everyone will support my ideas. There's no need to share them with my boss or organizational stakeholders.

10. I can plan once a year. That's what's expected of me.

Takeaway from Chapter 7

Describe your operating plan and execution schedule and list its major components. Next to each component, list the specific requirement(s) needed to implement those components along with the people responsible for achieving them. Describe components that you failed to achieve and reasons why. Write them down and be as completely candid as possible. Have a close friend or coach go over the individual failures to assure that they agree with your assessment.

By studying such individual failures and learning what you must do to improve, you will strengthen your performance. Chip away at it, year after year. Tom Seaver, the pitching staff mainstay of the New York Mets' amazing 1969 World Series champion team, always analyzed his failures after every game, win or lose. And he always ranked at the top of his game.

Discipline 4: Social/Emotional/Political Intelligence

The Tribulations of Leadership and Their Remedies

Diego had a hardscrabble start to life. He was born in the *favela* (slums) of São Paulo and abandoned by his parents. He was one of those nameless children left adrift to fend for themselves. But Diego had a fierce passion in life: he wanted to better himself. To escape the *favela* he worked 10 hours a day as a busboy in a popular São Paulo restaurant and 7 hours a day as a house servant until he had accumulated enough money to get his high school and college degrees in Brazil. As soon as he graduated he immigrated to the United States and found work with a multinational company in Miami that needed business professionals who spoke both Spanish and Portuguese. Diego was adroit at working with people. He was an avid listener, so much so that after people talked with him they didn't really know much about him, because the entire conversation centered on their interests, not Diego's.

You can see where this story is going. Diego rose quickly through the ranks from interpreter to salesman to sales executive to division general manager, then company CEO.

Hands-On Advice: Listen more, much more. Talk less, much less.

As you'll discover in the following paragraphs there are many good reasons for this beyond the knowledge you'll acquire. Read on.

When you face problems, you tend to think, "I understand you, but you don't understand me. So let me tell you my story first." But, when you show your home movies or tell some chapter of your autobiography, the other person tunes out. When you truly listen, you transform the relationship. You don't need to agree or disagree, just listen with empathy and capture how they see the world. This requires restraint, respect, and reverence. And making yourself understood requires courage and consideration. You go from fight and flight to two-way communication.

Most negotiation is positional bargaining and results in compromise at best. But when you get into synergistic communication, you understand basic needs and interests and find solutions to satisfy them both. If you get the spirit of teamwork, you start to build a powerful bond, an emotional bank account, and people subordinate their immediate wants for long-term relationships. Synergy means producing solutions that are far better than what either party originally proposed. You move from defensive communication to creative alternatives.

You listen with empathy and speak with honesty to gain and maintain trust with stakeholders. Make your communication count. Today, many people feel vulnerable. Open the lines of communication; let them know that you care about their personal lives as well as their work. Great leaders are great listeners who connect with people. Learn through listening. Listen openly, ready to learn, as opposed to listening defensively, ready to rebut.

But don't make this mistake. A new leader usually assumes a position of responsibility, and his first inclination is to become too friendly with people. After all, everyone wants to be liked. But by trying to become everyone's friend, leaders run the risk of losing respect and influence. If your staff considers you to be one of the group, they may not respect your judgment on important issues.

Additionally, they may lose their motivation to achieve goals, fail to work hard, and assume deadlines are soft when they believe their friend would never reprimand them. That's why leaders must avoid falling into the trap of becoming too friendly with their staff members. The bottom line? You're the boss, not a best friend! You cannot be objective and unbiased when staff members view you as a work pal.

Leaders with SEP intelligence exhibit self-control which allows them to rise to the occasion, stay cool under pressure, and provide a calmness which reassures others that they're in control no matter how difficult things may seem. It is having self-confidence in their abilities while holding themselves accountable for their actions and the performance of others.

As leaders, they are responsible for results and therefore they must be able to influence others to achieve desired results. Being aware of people's feelings, needs, and concerns provides the ability to work with others as they strive toward shared goals and objectives.

Here's the bottom line of social/emotional/political (SEP) intelligence: Successful leaders network regularly, socialize to maintain core relationships with key stakeholders, and guide people using social/emotional/political intelligence.

Always Seek Feedback

The higher your position in the company, the further you are from what's really happening on the firing line. It's just natural to assume that people who work for you, even under the best of conditions, are going to be reluctant to bring you bad news. This problem is exacerbated if your demeanor and the way you respond to people who work for you is inconsistent. They simply won't know what to expect and will choose not to let you know of problems.

A failure to realize the effect your behavior has on your boss, peers, or direct reports can ultimately destroy your leadership effectiveness.

More importantly, if you don't know how others perceive your actions, how can you become a more effective leader?

Prior to starting any coaching engagement, I perform an online 360-degree feedback assessment followed up with personal interviews with bosses, peers, and employees (called raters). These assessments and interviews allow me to review how others perceive the person I'm coaching, including core strengths and weaknesses. For people to develop to their full potential, they must understand their strengths and weaknesses. Personal insight is fine, but input from others will often provide a stark contrast to how we see ourselves or validate our beliefs.

The assessments and interviews are held in the strictest of confidence. The raters are told that their names will not be divulged; rather they will be lumped together in a composite report. Upon completion, I provide the person I'm coaching with a specific report of gaps, strengths, and challenges I've found. Together, we begin the process of discussing how she can leverage strengths and change negative behavior to become more effective.

This method has produced insights that have profound effects on the people I've coached. It provides a sense of self-awareness, which aids in their growth and development. It also provides more objectivity and accuracy about behavior, a critical adjunct to personal perceptions.

John Discovers that It's Never Too Late to Learn

Whenever I think about the impact of 360-degree feedback, I'm reminded of one of the shortest coaching assignments in my career. John, a 25-year company veteran, was the SVP at a publicly held company. He had risen from the bottom to his current position, and he had more knowledge of the company's inner workings than anyone, including the CEO. He was a valuable piece in the company puzzle and would be hard to replace.

But John had a major problem: poor people skills. Anytime employees needed help, John would degrade them, be condescending, and criticize everything they did. He'd often refuse to look up from his work to give them an answer, or he'd wave them away with his hand. On a scale of 1 to 10, John scored a *negative* 5 for building morale. He believed that people in certain positions had to figure everything out on their own, and that they shouldn't have to come to him for any help or answers. He was nasty, and while people respected his knowledge, they hated his demeanor and actions. Staff members were frustrated, and morale and productivity were rapidly declining. Many skilled and talented people were leaving the company, which pushed the CEO into acknowledging that something had to be done, and quickly.

The board of directors was going through a succession planning process, and John's name was mentioned repeatedly for the president's position, which would open up in a year. The problem was, how do you put a person like John, with all of his knowledge, but horrible people skills, into one of the most important positions?

The board explained to me that if he didn't change his behavior, one of two things would happen: (1) He would be let go, and a wealth of knowledge would be wasted as he walked out the door, or (2) He would be passed over for the president's position, and the company would bring in an outsider. John would see the handwriting on the wall, and he would leave on his own accord, taking valuable information with him.

Either scenario was a no-win proposition for the board. Pushed into a corner, its members called on me to meet with John and take on the coaching assignment. My first meeting with John was very cordial; in fact, I liked him right away. We seemed to have good chemistry. As we discussed the coaching process, he seemed reluctant to engage in it; he figured it would be a waste of time because he had been with the company for more than 25 years. He thought it was obvious that he didn't need any help to move into the president's chair. He did, however, realize that I had been brought in because of board pressure, so he acquiesced and provided the names of 10 people for his 360-degree assessment and interviews.

I completed the assessment and received the worst feedback I'd ever experienced. The online assessment and every person I interviewed had only one thing good to say about John: he had the most knowledge of anyone in the company. Other than that that, each person provided a long laundry list of negatives, from never praising people to yelling at them in meetings to driving several people to break down in tears.

They reported that former employees had left the company because they couldn't tolerate working with John. I was not looking forward to presenting these facts to John, and I mulled over the strategy I'd use to coach him. We met in his office, and I gave him the feedback reports, allowing him to read them firsthand. After 20 minutes, he stopped and turned as red as a freshly boiled lobster tail. Needless to say, I was expecting a major-league blowup and confrontation.

Much to my surprise, John took a deep breath and said, "Never in my wildest dreams could I ever imagine that people perceive my behavior this way. I'm shocked that this is the perception they have of me."

For the first time in my coaching career, I was in shock. The feedback had hit John over the head with full force. I asked John why he thought people perceived him in this way, and I read him a specific comment: "Whenever I come to him for help, he doesn't acknowledge my presence and provides a half-hearted answer, without looking up from his work.

John answered, "There is not enough time in the day for me to get things done, and if I stop to answer everyone's questions, I'd be here 24 hours a day!"

John had never been told his behavior was inappropriate, and he assumed it was okay, so it became his modus operandi. Armed with this new knowledge, John embarked on changing his behavior. During the first month, the board members who had hired me said others were coming to them to offer positive comments on the changes John was making. Sixty days later, John was still receiving great feedback; at the three-month mark, his metamorphosis was virtually complete. We reduced the number of sessions, and after four-and-a-half months, John felt he was ready to be on his own, without our regularly scheduled coaching appointments.

John made the necessary changes to become an effective leader. The feedback he received and his commitment to work on his behavior made the difference. Today, John is president of the company, which is exceeding all its goals and expectations. I can't take credit for his success; it was the 360-degree feedback he received that triggered his transformation.

This feedback assessment is worthwhile for all leaders. It improves their relationships with the people they work with, and it provides a valid measure of the areas that require work. It's imperative for leaders in all industries to understand how their behavior is perceived by others. In the business world, perception is reality, and to lead well, we must manage people's realities.

If your organization lacks the resources to hire a coach and conduct 360-degree feedback, or if you're just starting out as a leader, you can ask the people with whom you work for feedback to these 12 questions:

1. How would you describe our current working relationship?
2. What do you see as my key areas of strength?
3. What do you see as my key areas of weakness?
4. How do I work in a group?
5. What are some of the things I need to work on to enhance my effectiveness?
6. If I could change only one thing, what would make the biggest and greatest impact on my effectiveness?
7. Are my values, vision, mission, and plans being deployed?
8. Communication is very important to me. Am I communicating effectively or ineffectively, and can you provide examples?
9. How do you perceive my decision-making abilities?
10. Do I bring out the best in people by motivating and inspiring them; can you give me some examples?
11. What are your thoughts on my ability to drive change and innovation?
12. How would you describe my ability to do the right thing?

By asking these questions, you open up a dialogue with others so you can receive their feedback regarding how your behavior is perceived. Once you begin asking questions, people will feel comfortable answering you, and you will go a long way toward creating the communication needed to change for the better.

Emotional Intelligence/Resilience

Resilience is the ability to bounce back from a mistake or setback. Clinical psychologist Joan Borysenko, author of *It's Not the End of the World*, compares resilience to a rubber band: "When it's stretched out, there's stress on the rubber, but when you release that stress, it snaps back into shape." But when you stretch that rubber band mercilessly, or a protracted period, it will ultimately give out.

Self-awareness is the first step toward developing healthy resilience. It starts with becoming conscious of who you are (a hardworking, yet fallible, person) and how you respond to others (offering to resign versus recovering from a setback and enjoying a healthy self-esteem).

In addition to reading your staff's and coworkers' verbal and nonverbal cues, you must learn to decipher your own emotions, feelings, and preexisting attitudes. This begins with gaining insight into your behavior by internally processing why you felt, or reacted, a certain way. Leaders with greater self-awareness tend to trust themselves and are less dependent on other people's opinions. They're better able to take positive control over everyday situations and interactions.

The concept of emotional intelligence (EI) was first introduced by Charles Darwin in the nineteenth century, when he suggested that our emotional expressions are an adaptive response to our basic survival needs. More recently, psychologist Daniel Goleman resurrected the topic in his bestseller, *Emotional Intelligence*. Goleman compares EI with IQ (intellectual intelligence). His model includes:

- Self-awareness: the ability to sense and understand other people's reactions within a social setting.
- Self-management: controlling one's emotions and adapting to a situation.
- Social awareness: being aware of the social and political elements of culture.
- Relationship management: the ability to inspire or influence others, even in conflict situations.

All of these skills are critical for leaders and managers, but learning them may prove challenging. You first have to unlearn all of the previous assumptions that have caused you to doubt yourself.

Start by setting aside some time to think about your and others' feelings, as well as how you respond to others. Most leaders fail to develop this understanding, as it requires them to be completely honest with themselves and to explore alternative behaviors and reactions. Simply acknowledging your need to increase self-awareness will help you to become more self-aware, and you'll tune into your subconscious thoughts.

Psychologists encourage their patients to practice introspection, which may be achieved through meditation or yoga. By learning to relax and access your subconscious, you gain greater compassion and empathy for yourself and others. Meditation encourages you to become more comfortable with silence, which also stimulates self-awareness.

Reframing is another psychological tool. When faced with a mistake or failure, you can choose to beat yourself up ("I suck") or reframe the situation ("I'm disappointed with myself, but I'm going to focus on righting the problem and use it as a learning experience"). Such self-analysis is a huge step toward developing healthy self-awareness.

Headaches of Management

Have you seen an employee promoted for his technical know-how and high performance or perhaps because of attrition? Mr. Success moves to a corner office, from which the boss orders him to lead. As often happens, he receives no training in basic leadership skills. Why, then, are we surprised when he underperforms? We wouldn't expect a poorly trained physician to cure us. How can the business world expect ill-equipped managers and supervisors to lead without appropriate training?

The economic downturn has compounded the problem, and leadership training has gone the way of the Tyrannosaurus rex. In businesses, the negative impact of poorly trained leaders trickles down, creating a vicious cycle: new leaders fail because they are unprepared, and their hardworking employees may grow disenchanted and leave.

Larry was a great salesperson, an outgoing, happy-go-lucky guy who everyone loved. One day, the general manager told Larry that his boss of six years had accepted a position with another company. As top salesperson, Larry was asked to become the new sales manager.

This came as a surprise. Larry had never before assumed a leadership position. But the promotion meant more money, less time on the road, and the opportunity to lead 15 sales professionals. He and his family were thrilled, knowing Larry would be spending more time at home while embarking on a new career path. Nothing could stop him. His hard work had paid off, and he envisioned a remarkable future. Two weeks later, the company issued a formal announcement: One of the company's own had been promoted to a leadership role. He now had a private office, a secretary, and the accompanying perks.

On his first day as sales manager, Larry drove to work and, instead of fighting for a parking space, pulled into his newly reserved spot in front of the building. As he walked through the front door, he was greeted with smiles, high-fives, and congratulatory best wishes. He walked down the hall to his new office, with his name newly imprinted on the door, and settled into the oversized leather chair behind his polished cherrywood executive desk. Leaning forward, he looked at the freshly painted room and smiled. This was going to be great, he thought.

His secretary entered and asked if he wanted coffee. For the first time, an engraved china cup with the company logo replaced the standard Styrofoam cup Larry was accustomed to. As he was settling in, there was a knock at the door. Carol, a top salesperson who had been competitive with her new boss, wanted to discuss several issues. She and Larry had worked together for years, and they liked and respected each other.

Larry invited her in. The next two hours astonished him. Carol vented about problems relating to people, management situations, and customer issues. Larry listened politely and intently, but he slumped in his chair, somewhat dazed, when Carol left.

Only minutes later, the telephone rang. Rick had a problem. Fifteen minutes later, Sam called to find out when Larry was going to hold a staff meeting. By noon, Larry felt completely drained, with indecision and panic racing through his mind and body. He realized his former boss would have handled these situations with ease, confidence, and grace, but Larry had no idea what to do, much less how to do it.

After three months of constant bombardment, Larry's performance fizzled, and as it did, morale waned and sales were slipping. The company was concerned, and Larry's boss called me to request coaching services. The powers that be were questioning Larry's ability to lead, as well as their decision to promote him. They shared stories of poor managerial decisions, employee dissatisfaction, and unmet sales goals. If they couldn't turn the situation around quickly, top performers could resign. Bringing in a coach, the executives reasoned, would give Larry the skills and tools he needed to fulfill expectations and jumpstart his leadership career.

Larry Becomes a Leader

When I called Larry to set up an initial meeting, he sounded nervous and uncomfortable. I felt it was important to meet with him away from his office, so we decided to have lunch at a quiet restaurant where we could talk in confidence. I hoped getting him away from his everyday environment would put Larry at ease.

Larry showed up 20 minutes late for our lunch meeting, apologizing profusely. The morning had been hectic, he said, and he'd even thought he might have to cancel our meeting because of a few personnel issues. As we were led to our table, Larry's body language revealed tremendous stress. We ordered lunch and, for the next two hours, Larry talked nonstop about his frustrations, feelings of incompetence, and strong desire to do the right things, but nothing seemed to be working.

As I listened to this bright, young man, who only a few months earlier had been full of confidence as the company's leading salesperson, I sympathized with his plight. He'd been placed in a leadership position without receiving any training.

It's an all-too-common mistake. Leaders promote highly success-ful workers, failing to recognize that their past successes and current skill sets won't magically translate into leadership success. In Larry's case, colleagues he'd known for years had become disillusioned with him and were voicing their unhappiness. He was second-guessing every decision he made, was frustrated with his inability to fill his old boss's shoes, and had no one in whom to confide. Going to his new boss with problems, he believed, would be a sign of weakness, and asking other managers for help might lead them to think he was completely ineffectual. At home, his wife complained about how depressed he'd become and wondered where the man she had married had gone. Life was a mess.

When Larry finished talking, I asked him a few questions, trying to ferret out whether he really wanted to lead. Was it possible he wanted to go back into the field as a salesperson, where he excelled and was happy? Larry looked down, thought for a long time and told me he did, indeed, want to become a good leader. It was a good move for his career, but he had never realized how difficult things were going to be.

I then asked him if he was open to working with me as his coach to improve his leadership skills. He responded: "When do we start?"

Over the next few months, Larry and I formulated a plan that would allow him to develop effective leadership skills. Much to our delight, he began seeing immediate improvements. We started by analyzing what had made him a successful salesperson. We then took one of his strongest attributes, listening, and used it to determine each staff member's needs and wants. Larry worked diligently to form one-on-one relationships with each team member, and he set up SMART (specific, measurable, attainable, realistic, and time-based) goals to provide incentives. He also brought his team together regularly to keep lines of communication open so he could be more accessible, and he worked tirelessly to become a better communicator. Larry gained confidence daily, and others noticed a tremendous difference. Sales improved, his department was motivated and positive, and Larry began to believe in himself again. After basic leadership training through one-on-one coaching and months of practice, he had become the leader everyone hoped he'd be.

Takeaway from Chapter 8

Gaining and using the techniques of social/emotional/political (SEP) intelligence is of paramount importance if you expect to excel as a leader. Leaders who understand the power of SEP invariably perform with better results than those who neglect this crucial aspect of leadership.

Probably the best way to go about it is to find some quiet room in a relaxing environment (as we've discussed in previous Take-aways), where you can reflect without the distractions and pressures of everyday work.

Start by reviewing the 12 questions posed to the people you work with as shown on page 97. Reflect on their responses as objectively as possible, even when it hurts (and accept the fact that occasionally it will). You're not perfect but you must always strive for excellence.

Next, pick a leader you worked for that inspired you to achieve bigger and better results for your organization. Now, item by item as defined in the 12 questions, compare your performance as reported by your people to the performance that inspirational leader achieved. Do you measure up? Be ruthless; do not miss an opportunity to criticize your performance, because only in this way can you overcome the natural tendency to rationalize your failures.

This form of self-analysis will not only help you improve your performance, it will also help form your thinking patterns for analyzing future problems and opportunities.

Discipline 5: Reciprocation, Collaboration, and Service

Effective Leaders Must Influence and Inspire Others

When your security comes from principles, you see everything through principles. When your boss or colleagues make mistakes, you're not accusatory. Why? Your security does not come from them living up to your expectations; it comes from within you. You share recognition and power. You see an ever-enlarging pie. The assumption about limited resources is flawed. The abundance mentality produces more profit, power, and recognition for everybody. You go from a scarcity to an abundance mentality by desiring mutual benefit.

The Way It Was

Mark, a near-retirement executive who had worked for a large national company in the 1980s, told me this story as we waited out a storm delay at the airport in Dallas. I didn't know Mark, in fact, I had met him only in the airline lounge when the airline announced a two-hour delay. After commiserating with each other about the delay, we decided to pass the time over a couple of drinks. We were both anxious to return to our respective homes after a hectic week on the road, and we let down our hair a bit as we talked. He reminisced about his earlier years in business.

"It was the day of the conglomerates," he said, referring to the 1980s, "and companies were buying up other companies as fast as they could. It didn't seem to matter what business the acquiring companies were in. Companies bought telecommunication carriers, medical supply manufacturers, movie studios, hotels, technical schools, and insurance companies. The list goes on and on. Regardless of what business the original company was in, it expanded its wings to buy any kind of other business that had a potential for a higher stock price. Regardless of its products and services."

He paused for a moment and shook his head slowly. "There was a kind of arrogance about the executives of those companies, as if they could continue shareholder growth indefinitely. It was like a fever in the air. Now that I look back at it, the only thing these acquisitions appeared to have in common were financial yardsticks."

"Excuse me for interrupting," I said, "but how do you mean that was the only thing they had in common?"

"The typical conglomerate, headquartered for the most part in New York City, was really a holding company. The one I worked for, one of the most famous, started as a manufacturing company making mundane communication products and selling well under a billion in sales. It went on an acquiring spree and bought enough companies so that its revenues . . . now get this . . . exploded to over 15 billion in less than 10 years."

"I think I recognize the company you're referring to. But pardon me, that doesn't answer my question."

"Don't get snarky, Jeff, I'm getting to that," Mark said, the booze starting to take hold. "I just wanted you to understand the business environment. Those were heady times, I can tell you. I was in my late 20s and worked for the company's headquarters industrial engineering group and spent about 45 weeks a year traveling to many different companies in many different states and countries."

"If I'm not mistaken the company you worked for at the time made over 300 acquisitions in something like 75 countries."

He smiled. "Yeah, you're on to me, all right. Now let me tell you how these companies operated, and then I'll answer your question about the financial yardsticks. . . . Well, the small headquarters group responsible for spotting what we euphemistically called investment opportunities, pored over financial reports of companies with growth potential and then our company swooped down on them and acquired them, either with their approval or without their approval. And that's when the fun began."

I raised my eyebrows. "The fun?"

He nodded. "The fun. The headquarters financial people constructed operating and financial forecasts, not based on what the acquisitions could do, *but what headquarters said they should do*. Sales, costs, profits, ROI, shareholder price. And let me tell you, those reports were detailed! Dozens, if not hundreds, of pages of detailed plans. Executives of the acquired companies were seldom consulted. The entire future of acquisitions was planned by our corporate headquarters, mostly financial types."

"How in the world could they make operating plans without having the acquired company participate?"

"Call it hubris, but nobody cared. As long as our shareholder price continued to soar, the investors were happy, headquarters company employees were ecstatic, everybody involved was overjoyed . . . except the poor employees of the acquired companies, of course."

"I can see why, if their leaders had no say in how the company was run."

"Oh, they had their say, all right. Operating company presidents could do whatever they felt was necessary as long as they produced results. And when they didn't . . . well, I think you know what came next."

I shook my head in sympathy and wonderment. "Yes, I can imagine."

"Turnover was high in the management ranks of the acquired companies."

"That's certainly not surprising."

"Headquarters staff would invade the acquired companies periodically for operating reviews. Invade is not too strong a word. The atmosphere was toxic. Those meetings were a thing of pure horror. Imagine the president and his staff of one of our acquisitions gathered in a room awaiting virtual execution. Corporate would bring in a few dozen financial people and industrial engineers, as visitors examined every last facet of the company's financial and operating performance, so by the time the review started the president and his staff of the acquired company had better know every last detail that the invading hordes knew, or the corporate chairman and his henchmen would tear them to shreds. It was really humiliating, tearing down top executives right in front of a roomful of a few dozen people. Needless to say, those meetings were the precursor of beheadings. Many, many beheadings.

"During the reviews, our corporate CEO and his huge staff sat on one side of the room, the president and his half-dozen operating heads on the other side of the room in an adversarial position. As the old but true saying goes, the tension was so thick you could cut it with a knife."

"Yet, your company and the other conglomerates of that era, for that matter, were the darlings of Wall Street. The better ones topped sales and earnings quarter after quarter for a period of 10 years or so. Have to give them that."

Mark nodded. "Sure do, but once the era was over, the walls came tumbling down. Once our corporate CEO stepped down, there was nobody else to take his place, nor anybody else who wanted to. The driving force was gone. The company was eventually broken into parts and sold off. Little remains of it today . . . and over the years, thousands of managers lost their jobs. The same thing happened with most of the conglomerates of the time."

The Brutal Way of Old

Another airport acquaintance, a management consultant, told me this story:

"I work for a consulting company whose history dates back to shortly after World War II. Its specialty at the time was headcount reduction. No matter what the product or service, my company promised to cut payroll costs 25 to 30 percent, and it always kept its promise.

"Of course, once consultants completed their assignment and left, the program often fell apart and costs rose, although, in all honesty, seldom to the level they were before the consultants arrived.

"Some of the old-timers told me how they conducted headcount reductions. In one case, after the consultants completed their initial analysis, the company agreed to lay off about 150 employees. The way they did it was to have the department managers stand at the time clocks, and when the affected employees clocked out they were told they had been discharged and could pick up their final paychecks in a week.

> *Hands-On Advice: You can't treat people like cogs in a machine and expect them to perform well.*

"I don't have to tell you, if you tried that today there would be hell to pay. . . . It was bad business, all around."

Today, more than ever, employees need to be treated with the respect they deserve and the respect you take for granted as their leader.

The Need for Reciprocity

"Brutal styles of ruling the roost can get results in the short-term," says Cary Cooper, professor of organizational psychology and health at Lancaster Business School. "But in the medium to long term, you lose good people and even if they stay, they become less productive and there's every chance they'll burn out or become ill."

Occupational psychologist Paul Brewerton adds that many managers simply don't have people skills. "Time and again, I see people being promoted because they are technically very good at their jobs, but they have no training in considering their team's feelings or motivation."

A better way involves reciprocity. Saira Karim, PMP, in her article "Harnessing The Law of Reciprocity," says, "I have become an ardent advocate for 'the law of reciprocity'—the principle that when you do a favor for someone, he or she will have a deep-rooted psychological urge to do something nice in return. And I believe it should be consciously practiced within the work culture.

"Reciprocating to a goodwill gesture is one of the universal rules of good manners. It is a principle that comes naturally to many of us despite our culture. Organizations and businesses are now capitalizing on this principle to build relationships internally with their employees and externally with clients and customers."

Reciprocity exists in many ways. Building on Karim's study, it means:

- Offering help for persons in need, especially fellow employees.
- Recognizing an employee's contribution to his job or fellow employees.
- Making suggestions that improve the workplace environment.
- Rewarding employees for their personal or group achievements and successes.
- Sharing job leads or networking contacts.
- Developing free or near-free services for customers.
- Sending thank-you messages to people who have helped you.
- Acknowledging achievements of employees publicly.
- Rewarding superior work.

Collaboration: The Key Ingredient

Andrew S. Field, founder and CEO of PrintingForLess.com the nation's first e-commerce commercial printing company, built his company based on six collaborative principles:

1. Communicating company expectations, including defining specific, accountable roles and responsibilities within the team. "Our employees, from sales through manufacturing, have the power to stop any order to ensure accuracy and quality. Every member of our team knows they are equally accountable for customer satisfaction," Field said.

2. Setting team goals that are concise and measurable so that all team members know the team's goals and how effectively they have been accomplished. "Getting the team to focus on goals will keep individual efforts aligned with desired outcomes. Each quarter the outcome of each goal is also published. This keeps us focused and transparent."

3. Fostering a creative environment that allows team members to ask any questions they like and participate in an open, criticism-free environment. "One way we cultivate a creative atmosphere at my company is by providing leadership training that encourages character development."

4. Building cohesion, which means including all team members in the decision-making process. "This keeps everyone [reading from] the same playbook and enables team members to redirect their efforts as needed."

5. Learning about fellow team members, their skills, experiences, and their capabilities. "Different personality dynamics, skill sets, and experiences are present in every team. It is worth the effort to . . . openly discuss likes and dislikes with regard to communication, tasks, and personal focus."

6. Leveraging team member strengths. "The team makes every effort to assign tasks that play to each team member's respective capabilities, strengths, and desires."

Nicholas Christak, author of *Connected*, defines collaboration through six key principles: active participation; collective decision-making through consensus; open debates (transparency); encouraging independent thought as opposed to group-think; being persistent in obtaining your goals; and what he calls emergence, which he defines as the intense focus on the end result. "Remember that the point of mass collaboration is to achieve great results, so ensure you focus on the end goal rather than worrying about how that is achieved. You will need your collaborative community to set their own goals and objectives."

Humility Will Improve Your Performance

Effective leaders are humble. In his book *Good to Great*, Jim Collins talks about the best companies over time. Their leaders, he notes, were almost universally humble, were happy to give credit to others, and were willing to share ideas. The minute you begin to tout yourself, you lose your credibility and other people's respect. As stated earlier, it's not about you. No single individual is responsible for an organization's success. It's about us, a concept that requires humility.

Similarly, good leadership is not "my way or the highway" anymore. This may have worked in the old days, but it's an obsolete notion. Today, effective leaders must influence others, creating a culture where people want to do things. A thirst for power will lead to your downfall; striving to influence will put you at the top of your game.

Organizational goals should always be put above personal goals. We often read about leaders who pursue the latter, which does not serve the organization well. You always need to ask yourself: What can we do to make the organization, team, group, or department better? I've had to fire some of my best friends because the needs of the organization that employed me came first.

The Benefits of Community Service

Progressive companies encourage their leaders to take an active role in their communities. Most companies have values that include respect for the individual, good citizenship, and integrity. When company leaders also become leaders of charities, schools, and other nonprofits, they show their commitment to those values, encouraging and inspiring employees. Community leadership roles are opportunities for employees to practice skills that will be valuable at work.

There's no doubt that community service offers benefits for participating companies and their executives, including the following:

- An improved corporate image, always important especially in today's business environment where some groups such as the "99 percent" incite antagonism of the public against businesses.

- Better relations with the local city and state governments. The closer that business and government work together, the more likely it is for laws and ordinances favorable to the community at large to exist.
- Volunteerism that brings diverse people from all branches of the community together for the common good.
- A well-rounded executive who integrates his corporate performance with his community contributions.

Takeaway from Chapter 9

Things change. In his story, Mark described a management style that was brutal, condescending, unproductive, hard on employees, and a health hazard (who knows how many employees suffered heart attacks, ulcers, strokes, and other physical and emotional calamities). It was a management style that bred unhappiness and resulted in subpar performance and lower share prices (the very thing it was attempting to improve).

Recall an instance in your career when an abysmal manager's leadership style had a negative effect on your performance. We all, at one time or another, have had poor managers. Chances are those few instances are seared into your memory, because they simply go against all the decent impulses people have to be treated fairly and with respect, and we resent managers who either unthinkingly or uncaringly treat us like robots.

Next, remember the damage it did to your outlook and your perspective about your company. Terrible, wasn't it? That's what happens when an employee is manipulated by a lousy boss. Now project those same feelings onto your employees, any of them, and you can appreciate the damage poor managers can do to the very people they are depending to get the job done.

Discipline 6: Love and Leverage

There Is No Substitute for Passion about Work

If you enjoy your work, you will excel at it. And you, your company, employees, and stakeholders will benefit. Joy spreads.

Do What You Love, Love What You Do

If you love what you're doing, you'll never have to work a day in your life. I'm continually amazed at the number of leaders who don't like or enjoy what they're doing. When I speak at meetings, conventions, and conferences, I ask audiences: How many of you love your work? How many of you get excited about what you do?

Usually, a few hands go up. Everyone else sits very quietly and uncomfortably, looking with envy at those who have raised their hands.

I love what I'm doing. I can't think of anything else I'd rather do. I've coached, spoken to, consulted with, and trained people, teams, and organizations to increase their effectiveness. I'm up at 5:00 A.M. each day and in my office by 6:00 or 6:30, excited about starting my day. I'll often work until late in the evening, because I'm thoroughly enjoying what I do.

My wonderful and tolerant wife, Maria, understands my love and passion for work, but she often thinks I'm going to burn out. I've told her that my job doesn't qualify as work for me. I love the opportunity to meet with a wide variety of people every day, learn from them, communicate with them at various levels, and coach them to take their skills to a higher level. Going into an organization as a consultant and making it function better is not work to me. It's fun! Standing up and speaking in front of thousands of people, or making a difference in somebody's life, either professionally or personally, is not work. It's exciting, something I see myself doing for the rest of my life.

The gratification I get from effecting changes that help people and organizations is truly thrilling. When I coach executives and watch them grow into successful leaders, I feel great joy. Perhaps I'm the poster guy for those who adore their work.

Most people who experience such fulfillment are highly successful people who are following a creative path. As leaders, they're not only in touch with themselves, but also, more importantly, with the people who report to them. This kind of exhilaration becomes contagious, rubbing off on the people you lead. Without this passion, you cannot provide the direction and guidance your job requires.

A friend in the wine business once said, "Life is too short to drink bad wine." I say, life is too short to be doing something you don't love.

If you lack passion and enjoyment, people will see right through you. You'll never be able to inspire them to greatness or be effective. Life is too short to struggle at a job you hate. So, if leadership doesn't fulfill you, it's time to do something else.

What is your passion? How do you communicate it to others? How do you let people know what inspires you? While you needn't possess every skill that characterizes great leadership, you must be able to explain why you're passionate about your work. So do the people who work for you. They may not have every required technical skill when they're hired. These are areas for which you can provide training. What you cannot teach is passion. A person either has it or she doesn't.

Take 10 minutes to describe why you're passionate about your work. What is your passion and how do you communicate that passion to others? What do you do that lets people know what you're passionate about? Certainly, expertise in certain areas is essential for job performance. But that alone will not assure your effectiveness on the job. The excitement and enthusiasm and fervor you show is contagious and will help shape your new hire's attitude. Technical skills are important, yes, but their success will ultimately rest on intangible values such as those I just mentioned.

Sophie Mirman, England's Youngest Millionaire

Sophie Mirman grew up in a fashion-conscious London home. Her mother, a famous milliner, designed hats for Christian Dior and the Queen of England. Her father worked as a Dior vice president.

Mirman, now 57, never developed her parents' artistic talents. "My mother could fiddle with a hat and make it into an extraordinary creation. But if I touched it, it would turn into a complete disaster," she told British management professors Susan Vinnicombe and John Bank during an interview for their book, *Women with Attitude: Lessons for Career Management* (Routledge, 2003).

This only child nonetheless displayed a take-charge attitude and zeal for achievement. As a young girl, she delivered hats for her mother. By the age of 15, she wanted to earn her own spending money, so she offered French lessons for 50 pence an hour. By 17, she helped run the office at a bilingual secretarial agency.

Mirman's first job was in the typing pool at London's famed Marks & Spencer department store, a job she despised. She then floated among various departments, ultimately meeting Lord Sieff, the store's chairman. He became her mentor, exposing her to all facets of the retail business. At first, Mirman swept floors and assisted in the warehouse. As she gained experience, she was promoted to merchandiser and then manager. These assignments provided an invaluable overview of business operations.

Mirman eventually set her sights on the entrepreneurial life. In 1983, she and husband Richard Ross launched Sock Shop, an upscale retail hosiery emporium that grew into a chain of 140-plus boutiques. She became England's youngest millionaire, and her company eventually went public.

But several years later, the recession hit. Customers' buying patterns radically shifted, and Mirman's equity in her company tanked, becoming virtually worthless. Sock Shop went into administration (the British version of insolvency) and was purchased by a public accountancy firm, only to be sold again. (Acquired by textile giant Ruia Group in 2006, Sock Shop is now a British Internet business.)

Undeterred by her losses, Mirman came up with her next big idea when shopping with her young children. Son William needed a haircut, while daughter Natasha was on the lookout for a new pair of shoes, meaning that Mom was forced to travel to various locations. A cranky William howled during his haircut, and a frustrated Natasha couldn't find shoes to her liking. After a frustrating and exhausting day, Mirman wondered why children's retail products and services couldn't be housed in a single building.

This was her "eureka!" moment. Mirman launched Trotters Childrenswear Ltd. in 1990, a still-thriving chain of six London stores that sell clothing, accessories, and, of course, hairdressing services.

How does someone like Sophie Mirman climb out of debt and despair to rehabilitate a career? "It would have been much easier to have left and not do anything else but just bury myself in the countryside," she confessed to the *Times of London* in March 2008.

But Mirman persevered, and you may be surprised to learn that money was not her primary motivator. Her secret to success can be summed up in five simple words: "I love what I'm doing," she says.

Work Passion: A New Discipline

Many organizations rely on tangible benefits to motivate employees: salary increases, performance-based bonuses, stock options, paid vacations, health insurance, retirement packages, and time off. While psychologists agree that this approach offers short-term rewards, the most effective motivator is intrinsic: job satisfaction.

Innovative human resources professionals view work passion as a brand-new discipline, one that warrants its own field of study. Social scientists are formally defining the qualities that determine one's level of on-the-job passion:

- Having a "calling" that leads you to choose a specific career path (certainly helpful, but not always necessary).
- Enjoying a sense of personal fulfillment and meaningfulness at work.
- Experiencing *flow* (a term coined by Hungarian psychologist Mihaly Csikszentmihalyi to describe one's ability to concentrate and tune out all external stimuli when working).
- Feeling engaged at work.
- Enjoying quality relationships with peers, supervisors, and customers.
- Feeling self-confident and empowered.
- Being emotionally available.

The Troubling News

Gallup, Inc., conducts regular polls on employee engagement, and the organization's most recent effort reveals disheartening results.

According to Gallup's 2012 telephone interviews of 151,284 workers, only 36 percent of managers and executives are engaged at work, more specifically defined as "deeply involved in, and enthusiastic about, their work and actively contributing to their organization."

Unfortunately, the trickle-down theory applies all too well. The engagement levels for other job classifications are even worse:

- Professional workers: 31 percent.
- Clerical/office workers: 30 percent.
- Construction/mining workers: 30 percent.
- Sales workers: 29 percent.
- Installation/repair workers: 29 percent.
- Service workers: 29 percent.

- Transportation workers: 25 percent.
- Manufacturing/production workers: 24 percent.

Gallup cites a "proven strong relationship between employees' workplace engagement and their respective companies' overall performance," concluding that U.S. businesses (and the economy at large) are failing to maximize the workforce. And while there's "variation in engagement by occupation, there is a great deal of opportunity to improve workplace engagement in all jobs."

Any attempt to resuscitate organizational morale must start at the top. Dispassionate leaders pass their lack of engagement onto their staffs, and they set the stage for high employee turnover. Leaders who boost their own level of passion are "more likely to inject hope and stability" into their teams, resulting in improved workplace engagement and productivity, Gallup suggests.

Research conducted by iOpener, a business consulting firm, showed that the most passionate professionals: are 180 percent more energized; are 180 percent happier with life; are 155 percent happier in their jobs; are 108 percent more engaged at work; love their jobs 70 percent more; are 50 percent more motivated; have 40 percent more confidence; achieve their goals 30 percent more often; and contribute 25 percent more.

Passion's Nemesis

If you're like many of today's leaders, you may feel overworked and energy-depleted, especially in economic times that require you to do more with fewer resources. How can you preach the gospel of passion when you have trouble getting out of bed in the morning?

Job burnout takes three specific forms:

1. Emotional exhaustion and cynicism.
2. Depersonalization (feeling divorced from your body; watching yourself act without feeling any sense of control).
3. Diminished personal accomplishment.

Blend these three ingredients and you have a surefire recipe for workplace disaster: chronic absenteeism, low morale, high turnover, and health problems (depression, headaches, gastrointestinal problems, cardiovascular conditions, and the like).

Luckily, work passion is an achievable, do-it-yourself process. It must be self-initiated. No one at work has been tasked with the job of pleasing you. Passion "doesn't have to be a haphazard by-product of what you do, but something that you can get more of if you choose to," says iOpener CEO Jessica Pryce-Jones in *Happiness at Work* (Wiley, 2010).

Lessons from Industry Leaders

Highly effective leaders across industries share these suggestions for increasing workplace passion:

- Take care of yourself physically, mentally, emotionally, and spiritually. No leader, no matter how talented, can survive the daily onslaught of professional demands without fuel. "If you say that you value your health, but never set aside time to exercise and eat properly, you are creating inconsistency and guilt for yourself," warns Loret Carbone, president of Ozumo Concepts International, a northern California leader in Japanese fine dining. "That causes stress. It affects the way you feel about yourself. Feeling bad about yourself is not a place where leaders want to be. A depressed leader is not inspirational."

- Find nourishment in the best parts of your life. Special Agent Robin K. Dreeke, an instructor at the FBI's Counterintelligence Training Center and adjunct faculty member at the FBI Academy's Leadership Development Institute, recalls an eager rookie agent who became terribly frustrated with a project that was going nowhere fast. While reaching into his briefcase for a pen, the agent accidently grabbed a journal his children had given him for Father's Day. Looking through the photos, he had "an immediate boost of enthusiasm and morale," Dreeke writes in the August 2008 issue of the *FBI Law Enforcement Bulletin*. "He began inserting into the journal a few photographs of close family and friends, flattering and inspirational emails and letters, and any remarkable event that happened either at work or in his private life. His only rule for the journal was that all of the content must be motivational and inspiring. The journal became a repository of positive thoughts and experiences. Adding material and writings in the journal proved extremely self-motivating."

- Stay optimistic. Pessimists lack passion, while optimists find ways to create it. Researchers at the University of Tennessee, Chattanooga, surveyed 120 restaurant managers in the southeastern United States to determine levels of optimism, life satisfaction, stress, and job burnout. Not surprisingly, they discovered that the more optimistic managers could better adjust to, tolerate, and overcome stressful on-the-job situations. Their results, published in the November 2007 edition of the *Journal of Psychology*, concluded: "Managers who reduce their level of job burnout by approaching their work more optimistically may be more likely to stay in the job longer, therefore reducing turnover. Lowered turnover rates may lead to substantial savings because less time will be spent selecting and training new managers." Additional benefits include fewer sick days, decreased irritability, improved marital stability, fewer family problems, positive relationships with co-workers, feelings of accomplishment, and a greater willingness to pursue career development.

- Take control of your fears. Richie Norton, CEO of Honolulu-based Global Consulting Circle, describes fear as the "freaky troll" under the bridge that leads to achievement. Even the most passionate leaders can sabotage their best ideas by capitulating to crippling fears. Unresolved anxiety may cause you to "make decisions from an emotional, unreliable, and downright unhealthy state of mind, all significant roadblocks on our way to success," Norton says in *The Power of Starting Something Stupid* (Shadow Mountain, 2013). "If you choose not to manage your fear, in whatever form it takes for you individually, eventually your choice will equate to zero goal achievement."

- Branch out. Mark Opperman, a certified veterinary practice manager and consultant in Evergreen, Colorado, believes burnout can be extinguished by pursuing new responsibilities or services. Traditional veterinarians, for example, could branch out into dentistry, orthopedics, or alternative medicine, he advised in the January 2009 issue of *Veterinary Economics*. "Visible physical exhaustion, mental confusion and bad feelings, and frustration and anger can all be signs your flame is guttering," he says. "If you're struggling to muster any excitement about your work, it's time to rekindle the fires."

- Find a respected mentor, and expand your social network. Don't expect to feel passionate about your job if you lack guidance and social connections. Researchers at North Carolina State University in Raleigh surveyed women in the parks and recreation industry to determine their levels of work passion and job satisfaction. Their study of 1,214 respondents revealed that supportive networks and respected mentors are critically important to job satisfaction. As one respondent told them: "Find other women/mentors who are understanding and supportive of your personal and professional goals."

- Keep the focus on your team. Do you stress the "me" in manageMEnt? Reclaim your passion by remembering that work is a team sport, and it's up to you to model positive behaviors. "Many people have spent the majority of their careers pursuing a leadership position," says retired police supervisor/training officer Joseph Pangaro, now the CEO of Pangaro Training & Management. "When they get there, they lose perspective on what their main goal and focus must be: their people, not their own career track," he notes.

Phil Recharges His Batteries

Phil, treasurer for a software company, knows how to stay fit, alert, and intellectually engaged. He runs five miles every morning at 6:00 A.M., lifts weights three days a week at the gym after work, and builds remote-

> *Hands-On Advice: Keep some balance in your life.*

controlled model airplanes, cars, and helicopters on weekends. He is also on top of his game at work.

Workaholics are no longer looked upon with awe. Today's professional leads a balanced life, knowing that in doing so he is not only happier but also a better contributor at work.

The Dog Days of Work

You're probably familiar with Cesar Milan, more commonly known as the Dog Whisperer. This determined immigrant is not shy about sharing his past: He "jumped the border" (in his words) at age 21 and was homeless for two months before establishing himself as an expert in handling aggressive dogs. Enter actress Jada Pinkett Smith, Milan's first of many celebrity clients, and a business empire was born.

Milan draws parallels between his belligerent four-legged pupils and the folks who inhabit your workplace. As mammals, dogs and humans are often held hostage to the basic physiological fight-or-flight response. When a stressor triggers us, from horrible Friday-evening traffic to dealing with shareholder whims, we react, and not always in ways that serve our best interests. If our stress level escalates, we can make bad decisions . . . sometimes irreparable ones, at that.

To experience workplace passion, your reactions to life's stresses must be controlled. "Think before you act" may seem like a facile grade-school concept, but wiser words were perhaps never spoken. You want to avoid, at all costs, falling victim to a feedback loop in your brain that leaves you feeling out of control. You must reverse course quickly and refocus your priorities.

We're our own worst enemies when we're overly attentive to the micro aspects of our work and somehow manage to forsake macro thinking. "We create a lot of stress by focusing on the wrong things," Milan says in the August 2013 issue of his magazine, *Cesar's Way*. "We're so busy thinking about what we don't have that we can't enjoy what we do have. Learn from your dog—she is totally focused on what she has in that moment."

The Highly Effective Leader Passion Assessment Tool

Ask yourself the following questions to determine your level of engagement and passion:

1. Am I energetic and enthusiastic?
2. What do I like about my job?
3. Which areas require me to make an attitude adjustment so I can become more passionate?
4. Can I clearly define my organization's expectations and expectations of myself?
5. Have I created the opportunities required to achieve success (self-initiated passion)?
6. Have I surrounded myself with people who are passionate and committed to achieving organizational goals?
7. Do I believe my work is meaningful?
8. Is what I do important?
9. Even though I'm at the top of the organizational chart, have I taken advantage of training and development opportunities that would allow me to increase my level of passion?
10. Do I tap into my talents each day, or am I simply coasting?
11. Do I embrace innovation and new ideas, or do I tend to be complacent?
12. Am I emotionally committed to my job?
13. Do I have a good social network?
14. Do I lead by modeling high performance?
15. Do I allow fear to compromise my job satisfaction?

Takeaway from Chapter 10

Describe one specific aspect you like about your job and follow that by describing one specific aspect you dislike. Ask yourself what makes you like one aspect while shying away from the other.

For example, perhaps you're the type of person who enjoys crunching numbers but doesn't enjoy everyday give and take with fellow employees. You have always had the ability to work with numbers, and that led you to become an accountant and take a job with a CPA firm. Your performance reviews were always top drawer . . . until you were promoted to a managerial position. It was only then that you discovered how much you disliked supervising people.

But the company had faith in you and invested in a coach to help you make the adjustment. It was only then that you discovered that your problem was a result of your lack of understanding of the basics of managing people. With the proper training and direction, you overcame those problems and today you're a happily adjusted and effective manager.

In examining your likes and dislikes, you may find that your problem is one of education and direction. Therefore, the message is: Don't blindly accept that what you dislike you will always dislike. What you dislike today could readily turn into your passion tomorrow.

Discipline 7: Renewal and Sustainability

Those Who Practice Renewal and Sustainability Avoid Common Pitfalls

Kathryn was a woman wise beyond her 24 years. She understood that life itself is a state of flux where everything you're familiar with can change in a matter of moments, and often does. She was intimately familiar with the maxim that the only thing permanent in life is change. That knowledge had fueled her journey from a work farm in Ireland to the United States and her job as an agrarian specialist for the U.S. Department of Agriculture. She counted her blessings daily.

> *Hands-On Advice: Expect changes in your life and welcome them.*

If you fight them, you will lose and risk being left behind. But if you embrace them and shape them for your benefit and the benefit of your organization you will succeed.

I once watched and enjoyed a movie—a comedy called *Things Change*, starring Don Ameche and Joe Mantegna. It's the story of how a gangster on probation teams up with an old Italian-American shoeshine boy and creates havoc as circumstances (things) change. Without revealing too much of the plot, it demonstrates that the need for renewal and sustainability can be crucial, so much as to actually save lives (and careers).

The point of the movie is that nothing is truly permanent; things change and they can change for the best or they can change for the worst, but guaranteed they will change, and that renewal and sustainability are requirements to make positive changes last.

Janet, a former client, discovered this fact just in the nick of time.

Janet Transitions from Hard-Nosed Boss to Exceptional Leader

"My father was a career Marine," Janet told me. "When he was home, which wasn't too often, my three brothers and I fell in for inspection every day before breakfast and received our orders for the day. My job was to empty all the wastebaskets in the house, clean them, and take out the trash—every day. And I had to stand for surprise inspections when my father decided to check my work. Too many demerits and I lost my allowance or TV privileges."

I chuckled. "Looks like it hasn't really hurt you. You've done pretty darn well for yourself. Thirty-one years old and running the distribution center for a very large retailer."

Janet grinned. "The military upbringing did me a lot of good, I realize that. It gave me the discipline to face any number of challenges."

We were having a cup of coffee in the canteen of the warehouse and shipping center where Janet was headquartered. She had recently joined her present employer after a very successful nine years with an online retailer where she had progressed from management intern to director of order fulfillment, a three-shift operation employing about a thousand workers—a pretty astonishing achievement for such a young person.

Incredibly, she was failing at her new job, and I had been asked to find out why and help Janet regain her footing. The company's CEO thought the world of her and believed she had the capability to advance much further within the company. Her stumble had been quite an unpleasant surprise and a little embarrassing for the CEO, since he had championed her.

After spending some time with Janet, taking the rounds with her on her day-to-day duties, assessing her administrative capability, discussing her past with her, and checking her background, I believe I had an insight into what her problem was and, hopefully, how to correct it.

"Janet, one word that creeps into your dialogue every so often is 'control.' Tell me what it means to you."

Janet looked at me as if I had asked a foolish question. She cleared her throat and said, "It means exactly what you think it means: controlling operations, controlling costs, controlling labor performance, controlling overhead expenses, controlling capital expenditures . . . should I go on?"

"I understand what you're *saying*, but I'm not sure I understand what you *mean*."

She sat back and took a sip of her coffee as she thought about her answer. "Okay, let's talk about labor performance as an example, and let me start with my last job because that company had an exceptional labor control system for picking (retrieving customer orders from bins and shelves and storage areas), packaging customer orders, and loading the finished orders into shipping containers, all on schedule and under budget."

"Tell me about it."

"Every picker, packer, and shipper worked by the clock and . . ."

"By that you mean they had to pick, pack, and ship so many parts per hour, right?"

Janet raised a finger. "Not every hour, mind you, every 20 *minutes*."

"In other words, the performance of workers in your department was measured every 20 minutes, and they were expected to pick, pack, and ship the budgeted number of parts."

"That's right, and *always* within the budgeted time. The production work tickets contained both the number of parts that workers had to handle and also how long it should take to perform their tasks in standard minutes."

"By that you mean individual work schedules."

"Exactly. And the supervisors were expected to check on each worker every 20 minutes or so to see how he or she was performing to standard."

"That sounds almost impossible when you have 1,000 workers."

"You're making it sound hard. It wasn't. We worked by the rule of exception. Whenever workers picked, packed, or shipped completed customer orders, they punched their production tickets onto a work-station clock and their performance flashed real-time on an electronic board at the worker's station."

"For all to see—workers, supervisors, managers, everybody?"

Janet frowned. "The way you say that it's like I—and I mean the entire management team—committed a sin. The idea was to keep on schedule and when something went wrong to find out what happened and correct the worker's performance. You can't run a business any other way."

"Correct the *worker's* performance?"

"Sure, the worker. The man or woman doing the job."

"But what happened when a failure to meet expectations wasn't the fault of the worker? Say a material shortage, an equipment breakdown, or a broken tool or fixture, for example?"

Janet shrugged. "The system automatically rang a bell and the supervisor was required to go to that worker's station, find out what happened to cause the shortfall, and take corrective action."

"Okay, but was the supervisor's assessment always on target, or was there a tendency to make a fast—sometimes too fast—evaluation and pass the buck to the workers?"

Janet smirked. "Are you trying to knock holes in the system we used? Because if you are, you're heading down the wrong path. The system was spectacularly successful. Month after month, quarter after quarter, year after year, we met budgeted dollars and labor hours."

I clicked open my briefcase and took out a report. "Not really, Janet. At least not recently, and by recently I mean the last three years, two of which you managed."

Janet's face turned dark. "Like I said, Jeff, I never failed to meet budget. That's a fact."

"I'm not criticizing your performance, Janet. I'm just noting that your former boss told me that labor performance has been slipping the past three years. Not much, but noticeably enough to get their attention. He was emphatically stating that the system in place was antiquated and—"

Janet snorted. "Antiquated? He never told me that."

I held up my hand. "Let me finish. Whether or not you know it, your former company has recently embarked on a program to deemphasize labor control and instead place more emphasis on handing greater responsibility to workers on the line. Not a new or radical concept, I might add."

"You know, Jeff, I have to admit I could see some changes coming. There was a lot of grumbling in the workforce the last year or two I worked there, although things were going so good I tended to overlook it."

"It's a new day and age, Janet. Specialists, such as sociologists, who study behavior patterns for Millennials, the newest generation to join the labor force, suggest that overcontrol will have just the opposite effect. More so even than with Generation X. They're suggesting that the way companies treated previous generations is definitely not going to cut it anymore. The Marine drill instructor approach simply doesn't work anymore . . . if it ever did."

Janet shrugged. "I don't really have trouble accepting that. Actually, I'm beginning to see that for myself. I guess I have to shrug out of my own skin, examine my own upbringing."

"Good for you. Now tell me how workers responded to your former company's labor system? I mean the whole thing: the standard minutes, the pressure, the supervisors breathing down their necks?"

"I've got to admit, none too well. Turnover was high."

"Well, Janet, it's the same on your new job. You've been here almost a year now, and turnover is still high . . . no substantial improvements from the previous director, and there's a lot of unhappiness in the ranks. Complaints of supervisors figuratively beating up on workers for not meeting required standards, excessive pressure to get the work out while neglecting quality standards, that kind of thing. Something is obviously going wrong."

Janet slumped back against her chair. "I know," she whispered.

"Then can you accept the fact that we have some work to do? It's not too late. You still have the support of the chief executive, but that won't last forever."

Janet leaned forward, slapped her hand down on the table. Her frown turned to a look of determination, the determination of a courageous warrior ready for battle. The legacy of her Marine father shone through. That's one of Janet's attributes I had come to like and greatly admire: her ability to face an unpleasant truth, rethink her position, and correct her performance.

It wasn't long afterward that Janet, through coaching, began the process of changing her top-down, command-and-control approach toward employees. She established a plan that gradually turned over greater control of the workplace to workers. It took some time and a lot of training and reorientation, but the transformation worked. Janet blossomed into a highly effective leader, well regarded by her contemporaries and staff and respected by the top executives in her company. Today her organization is a model of worker efficiency.

The World Is Changing: Was It Ever Not So?

If you don't constantly improve and renew yourself, you'll fall into entropy, closed systems and styles, where everything breaks down. Sharpening requires continuous improvement, innovation, refinement, and renewal.

In this turbulent world, we face a new economy characterized by the globalization of markets and technology, the democratization of information and expectations, universal connectivity, an exponential increase in competition, and new wealth centered in people and social capital. This turbulent economy has virtually dissolved old lines of positional authority based on command and control and elevated moral authority based on character and competence.

Those who practice sustainability avoid common mistakes and sins that often derail other leaders. They may be promoted for their technical know-how and job performance, but once in a management or leadership position, they gain the soft people skills required to sustain high performance. They maintain credibility and avoid pitfalls by being honest, forthright, and open; their values, allegiances, and priorities are beyond reproach. Their strong character and integrity are manifest by their walking the walk and talking the talk. They create a climate of positivity, punctuated with frequent praise and recognition.

Takeaway from Chapter 11

Do you have the same potential for failure as Janet? Identify one time in your career when conditions changed sufficiently that it demanded a major change in response from you. How well did you do? Write it down. Use these row headings: The change. How you responded. The results. How long it took to make the change.

Make three columns: one where you answer, one where a respected member of your team expresses his opinion, and one where an outsider or coach expresses hers. Now, have the team member and outsider make their assessments of each other and you. Only when they complete their assessments should all three be combined on the same form.

The results will likely surprise you because it's difficult for us to assess our own strengths and weaknesses, and you never know how others will react to the changes. Evaluate your ability for renewal and sustainability.

Eleven Practices of Highly Effective Leaders

Practice makes perfect. It makes sense, doesn't it? Can you imagine Rafael Nadal or Serena Williams *not* practicing for their tennis matches? And how many grueling hours did Mike Tyson put in the ring, training for his championship bouts? How about baseball teams practicing in the Grapefruit League or Cactus League during late winter?

The same principle holds true for leaders and aspiring leaders. In this section, you will engage in 11 best practices to sharpen your leadership skills. Since you learn best by doing, practice effective behaviors (habits, actions, and patterns) and apply them in your real world.

Practice 1: Hire People Like a Casting Director

Highly effective leaders hire smart; they hire the right people and put them in the right positions. They choose people for key positions as carefully as a casting director. Recruit, hire, and promote people who fit the culture and brand and empower them to act their part well. Only the right people (talented individuals who do great work) are your greatest assets. Fire the job misfits, and take corrective measures with under-performers. Set high standards, and never compromise them in hiring. Hire slowly and fire fast. Leave a position open until you find the right person who is also the right fit for the job.

Roger Makes His First Hiring Decision

Roger, newly appointed supervisor of maintenance for a luxury hotel in Hawaii, was replacing a retiring HVAC mechanic. He was inundated with applications and, with the help of the hotel's administrative director, narrowed the selection to two job candidates. Both candidates had strong academic and technical credentials, both came highly recommended, and both had positive work attitudes. One of the candidates was an older more experienced man, the other a younger man about Roger's age.

Which candidate did Roger select?

He went with the older man because, frankly, he feared that the younger man would be a competitor for his own position, and that factor alone forced Roger's hand.

As it turned out, the older man was promoted into Roger's job before the year was out because the hotel's maintenance function had started to slide, and that was an intolerable condition in a luxury hotel. Roger was demoted.

> Hands-On Advice: Hire the very best people you can.

Their strength is your strength. Had Roger adhered to that position he might still be holding his supervisor's job.

Casting: Hire Smart

As a leader, surround yourself with the best and brightest people you can find. Don't be afraid to hire people who are stronger, smarter, and have better skills than you. Leadership is not about egos; it's about having people you can count on in a crunch. Believe me, crunch time happens all too frequently, the higher the caliber of the people you've hired, the better your chances for success.

So many companies suffer from a dearth of good people. There's a war for high performers, as there always has been and always will be. This means it's often difficult to fill many key positions. As a leader, you can never compromise. Set high standards, and never deviate from them. Once you compromise, you diminish the level of talent on your team, and morale will suffer.

With a shortage of talented people, many companies fall victim to the fog-the-mirror approach to hiring. They basically hold up a mirror, and if a job applicant can fog it by breathing, he's hired. This is no way to hire. Even in challenging times, you want to recruit and hire the best people out there. If you can't find a highly talented person to fill the job, leave the position unfilled. It's a far better solution than plugging a mediocre worker into an important slot.

Casting directors never deliberately compromise; a movie's key players often spell the difference between success and failure of the movie, and casting directors recognize that. For example, visualize George Clooney playing the role of Tony Soprano in HBO's hit series *The Sopranos*. Doesn't really hit home, does it?

Attract the Best People

Make your life easier, and make your company more successful. Smart leaders don't recruit the best people, they attract them. Why? Because it makes their lives easier and their companies more successful. How do they do it? They have a clear purpose for existing (PFE), and they live it and tell the world about it. . . . And the best people come to them.

The success of attraction is based on two principles. The first is a basic tenet of life: Like attracts like. In any animal or human culture, subgroups are composed of individuals with similar characteristics. A leader who defines his company's PFE is saying, in essence, "We are zebras. If you, too, are a zebra, come join us."

The second principle is that the best and the brightest people seek more than just a paycheck from a job; they seek fulfillment of their own PFE. They seek companies whose PFE supports their own. In certain industries, labor shortages will likely occur again later this year. The repercussions will be felt in lost opportunity costs as companies can't find qualified talent to serve their customers or to fill open positions. Total costs to replace a skilled manager can exceed 150 percent of the person's salary. With over 50 percent of salaried people planning on moving as jobs become available, this cost will be substantial for many companies. Thus, the opportunity to attract the best people, as well as keeping the right people, becomes more relevant.

Take Three Key Steps

To attract the best candidates, follow three key steps.

1. *Clarify your PFE.* What is your PFE? Why was the organization formed? What unique function does it serve? Make sure the PFE

is deeply imbedded in the culture, codified in writing, clearly articulated, and widely distributed. An example of a PFE that is clear and impactful is that of Merck & Co., a global pharmaceutical company. Its PFE is as follows: "Our business is preserving and improving human life. All of our actions must be measured by our success in achieving this goal."

2. *Tell the world your PFE.* When you have a clear PFE, articulate it. Place it conspicuously in all your marketing materials, internal documents, websites, and communications with buyers, suppliers, customers, placement offices, and partners. Make sure that when people hear the name of your company, they know what your PFE is. Your PFE will have an impact on the people who interact with you. Those who have a personal PFE that is similar to yours and who can fulfill their PFE by helping you fulfill your PFE will be attracted to you.

3. *Fulfill your PFE.* Ralph Waldo Emerson said, "What you do speaks so loudly that I cannot hear what you are saying." To attract the best people, you must live up to your PFE. Exhibiting actions incongruent with the PFE will damage your credibility and decrease the attraction. For organizations that live the PFE they create, every action makes the attraction that much stronger for potential candidates.

By following these three steps, you approach hiring in a new way. Creating awareness about your PFE and then interviewing people attracted to the company will become the norm. Once you start taking these three steps, if you have to work hard to recruit someone, you are likely trying to get the wrong person. Make your life easier, and make your company more successful. Don't recruit the best people . . . attract them.

Pat's Hiring Policy Fails

Pat was the VP of a successful pharmaceutical company. As the company grew, she continually sought to fill critical positions to keep up with staffing demands. Pat always had trouble finding good people to join her team. In fact, over two years, the company had a revolving door of staffers. Morale was low, turnover was high, and the CEO was at his wit's end with Pat. You see, Pat was hiring to fill vacancies, not hiring to find the best employees. We can compare her ineffective approach to sports, where players try not to lose, instead of playing to win—a terrible strategy. Pat thought that placing warm bodies in open positions was her main goal. What she didn't realize was that all she got was exactly that: bodies.

When I coached Pat, I explained that this was no way to run a business unit and that her company was paying a huge price for her mistakes. The hardworking employees who stayed suffered from low morale as colleagues came and went. As they witnessed high turnover, their psychological state was damaged, and their productivity dropped.

After I worked with Pat, she finally understood that warm bodies alone would never cut it. She needed to find the right people for each of the positions that needed to be filled.

Hire for Attitude

Why is hiring the right people with the right attitude so important? Ninety-five percent of a company's success is based on its workforce. Of course, finding those people can prove challenging. We often hire on the basis of an impressive resume or a recommendation from a friend or colleague. In doing so, we may forget *attitude*.

People with great attitudes make great workers, as long as they have the necessary skill set for the job. But just having great skills doesn't guarantee success. You need that winning combo of core skills and a positive attitude. Skills can always be taught. A negative attitude is unlikely to morph into a positive one, no matter how much prodding a leader does.

If you hire positive people, their attitude becomes contagious, lifting the skills and mindsets of all around them. Conversely, if you hire people with great skills and lousy attitudes, other team members will feel deflated.

In our current economic environment, be patient; wait until the right candidate, with the proper skills set and attitudes, comes along.

The cost of a bad hire can be steep, in terms of money wasted on salary and training, as well as the damage inflicted on morale.

The person you hire should also be a team player, as so much of the work performed in today's organizations involves teams. You want to ensure the person you bring on board is a *we* (not a *me*) performer. The wrong hire can break a formerly strong, cohesive group, one in which you've invested so much time and money.

To determine whether a potential hire is a team player, ask this open-ended question: "Give me an example of a team or collaborative project that brought you success." If candidates have trouble answering, or redirect their answers, this may indicate they're not team players.

Also pay attention to the questions job candidates ask during interviews. Are their questions me-focused? How attentive and interested are they in the prospect of team projects?

Be conscious of the two-way flow of information during interviews, and beware of candidates who have nothing to ask you. They either don't care about the job, or they feel lucky to have gotten this far in the process.

Once you've hired new team members, you must:

- Establish an orientation program to help acclimate recent hires to the company's culture, norms, and procedures.
- Make them feel welcome and valued, beginning on their first day on the job.
- Schedule monthly performance reviews during their first six months on the job.
- Encourage them to provide insights and suggestions to gain a fresh perspective.
- Find out what motivates them.
- Ask about what's important to them along with conditions that will keep them in the job. Invite them to a monthly breakfast or lunch. Don't talk business! Ask about their families, interests, and lives. Learn what matters to them.

When you do fill a position, make sure it's the right fit. So often, leaders hire people and then place them in jobs for which they're not right. A good fit is vital.

Santiago Succeeds Despite an Early Failure

Santiago was a young MBA who wanted to become a salesperson. He convinced the company executives to give him a try. The company that hired him acquiesced and put him out in the field. For a year, he never came close to landing a client. He was outgoing, personable, and intelligent, but he just didn't know how to sell, let alone close. The situation reached a point where they were going to fire him, but I told management that his apparent failure wasn't his failure alone and possibly not his failure at all.

Yes, he aspired to be a salesperson; he asked to be placed in sales. But did his bosses ever stop to consider whether they had put him in the wrong position? I didn't think so.

I told them they were taking this passionate young man, who loved his work and the company, and were about to make a huge mistake. Why terminate him because he wasn't working out in sales? There had to be other positions for which he was highly qualified.

Santiago's managers eventually moved him to a supervisory position in the financial side of the business and provided the necessary technical and leadership training to help him succeed. Soon, he began to flourish. Within five years, he was promoted to vice president. Three years after that he became a senior vice president and one of the key players in the company's growth and expansion. Yet, in the beginning, he had been marked a failure. He simply had been placed in the wrong position.

This is why the right fit is so critical. You may hire an outstandingly qualified employee, but if you put him in the wrong job, you set him up for failure, and you miss a great opportunity to utilize him in other ways.

A TV Executive Makes a Hiring Mistake

Cora, a recently downsized cable-TV producer with 20 years of experience, applied for an assistant producer position at her local public television station. She clearly excelled in all job requirements, and the HR manager who interviewed her immediately brought her upstairs to meet Tyler, the station's executive producer. Tyler spent five minutes reviewing Cora's impeccable resume and impressive portfolio, and there was no doubt in his mind that she could easily handle the job. But before the interview concluded he informed her that she wasn't right for the position.

"You're overqualified," he said, dismissively. "You'll get bored in a few weeks, and you'll quit, and then I'll have to start the interviewing process all over again. I'm not willing to take that risk."

"No," Cora assured him, "I won't quit. I definitely want to work here. I've always wanted to contribute to public television because the quality of programming is unsurpassed. And frankly, I've been in management for 15 years of my career, and I'd like to work each day without the extra burdens that a management position imposes."

Tyler said, "Why are you so sure you'll stay with us?" His skepticism was obvious to Clara by the tone of his voice.

"Look, I'm at a different stage of my career, and I think we would have a good fit," Cora said, making an honest attempt to assuage the executive producer's fears. "I know the work, and I would be easy to train. I'll accept a cut in pay because the job market is tight. I sincerely think we can make this work. I'm just asking for the chance."

Tyler, however, was unmovable. Clara, frustrated, left the station without the job.

So, did Tyler make the right decision? Not likely, since overqualified candidates can be expected to stay longer and perform better than job applicants with less experience, especially when 10 percent of Americans are unemployed and seeking work. A candidate's willingness to embrace lifestyle changes should not be judged harshly or rejected, so leaders should not impose their personal values on prospective employees and overthink the issue.

It's my guess that Tyler missed hiring what might have been an outstanding TV production executive.

Eight Hiring Guidelines

Since people are the largest factor in your personal on-the-job success or failure, selecting and hiring the right people for the job is critical. In his book, *Selecting Stars*, Word Wright International (Oct. 28 2002) Fred J. Lewis of The Quaker Oats Company identified eight pillars of hiring success:

1. *Lose a good candidate before you rush the process and hire a bad one.* When I first started to hire people, I would gather a group of acceptable candidates, interview them, and then hire the best of the group. However, I learned that someone with great skills only qualifies for your vacancy if their skills match what you need. Before you hire someone, determine the various qualities and characteristics you need. Before you begin the selection process, prioritize those desirable qualities and characteristics. If you interview candidates without a clear idea of what you need, you risk hiring errors. These can cost you dearly in terms of time, money, and productivity.

2. *Ensure that candidates either have or can develop the core competencies you value as drivers of your success.* Explore three distinct sets of factors before you examine candidates. These factors will form the bedrock of your hiring decisions: (1) For this specific assignment, do you want a doer, a manager, or a leader? (2) What core competencies must an individual have to succeed here? What specific technical competencies does the individual need for this assignment? (3) What qualities and characteristics are you looking for in each individual? Developing an ideal candidate profile that describes characteristics for every new hire facilitates hiring successful people in every position. You will know what you want in those who you hire.

3. *Make certain that your criteria for the hiring decision is consist-ent.* Look at internal candidates first and then move to external candidates if no one meets your needs. Internal job placement and promotion motivate your people and make everyone feel they can

participate in the growth and opportunities that come from the hard work and success of the team. When taking this direction, remember you have determined what you want and need in a candidate. Don't compromise just to promote someone internally. Identify great candidates from within and from outside the organization using consistent criteria.

4. *Ask questions.* The only irrelevant question is the one you don't ask. Developing your interviewing process involves deciding the number and type of interviews you plan to use. Determine how often you want to see each candidate and what you want to learn before making a hiring decision. After thinking about what you need to know about your candidate and making an outline for the information you seek, develop questions designed to solicit the information you need, the key to making a decision on their suitability for your position. Never leave an important question unanswered. If the candidate sidesteps the query, ask again at a later point in the interview.

5. **Hire your top candidate, not someone else's top candidate.** After you've reviewed all resumes, met with candidates, and selected your top few, you now need to make your decision. At this point, you've tentatively decided on your top candidates and the strengths of each. Verify their references and seek information from others to validate what you know so far to surface potential red flags. Now you must decide who has the edge. No one else can tell you how to make up your mind. You have to live with the decision, not them. Hire the candidate you think best.

6. **Make the leader's decision, not the manager's.** Managers tend to select people who have the best technical qualifications for a position, those who have excellent credentials and experiences, and backgrounds that indicate they'll succeed. Leaders view the same person differently. They tend to select people who have the spirit and commitment to get the job done. They also seek technical qualifications, but they place a higher value on feelings about job candidates' ability to succeed. They notice those qualities and characteristics that have made employees excel in the past.

Presumably all top candidates are well qualified. What gives one the advantage is the spirit and commitment to get things done. Defer to the leader in you when making the hard choice among good candidates. Before you present your offer, you may stipulate some conditions candidates must fulfill or tests they must pass before the job is theirs.

7. *Make your offer of employment a memorable event.* Prepare the offer to convince each job candidate that your opportunity is superior to all others. To ensure that your applicant views your offer as a career opportunity versus just another job, consider two parts when preparing to make the offer: (1) the formal presentation and (2) the physical setting. Make both of these as memorable as possible. Always present the formal offer in a written form to show the prospect you view this proposal as official recognition of their qualifications for the position, its responsibilities, and compensation package. Where you hold this meeting will say volumes to candidates about how you view them. Pick the best spot you can to make your statement.

8. *Be slow to hire and quick to fire.* You've hired a new employee, and they've spent some time on the job. Despite all your best efforts to identify the perfect candidate, you now realize you've made a mistake. You've worked with the individual to solve the problems, tried training, and allowed for some experience. Your decision did not come lightly, but you know things won't correct themselves. When you're convinced that you must make a change, you need to quickly take action. Don't agonize over letting the person go. Move ahead with it quickly, whether they've been on the job a week or a decade. Prolonging the situation has no benefit. You and they need to move on. If you know they aren't cutting it, and have fairly discussed the issues with them, they, too, should know it.

The best thing you can do for your firm is to admit your mistake, make a change as quickly as possible, and find someone else who is right for the assignment. The best thing you can do for failed employees is to help them move on to a place where they can succeed.

Takeaway from Chapter 12

Describe three hiring mistakes you have made in the past, and define those people you hired not as outright failures, but as three *marginal* employees. The latter are much harder to fire than those who fail outright because it's inherent in human nature to give marginal players a second chance . . . then a third chance . . . then a . . . well, you get it.

Unfortunately it's the marginal players who drag down your performance, not the failures who you have already terminated. Keep that in mind as you hire job candidates, and during the initial on-the-job evaluation period, don't allow so-called marginal players to make excuses because the very definition of marginal players is that they are smooth, eloquent talkers, often quite convincing, but by the time their second marginal performance rolls around that's your cue that you made a mistake and it's time to make the tough decision.

Practice 2: Never Stop Developing People

L et's look at two employees and compare their career paths. Both are the same age, both college graduates, both recent hires with an aircraft company. Lionel works in the company's sales support department, while Mary works in production planning.

Lionel's boss comes from the old school that doesn't believe in the value of training, consequently, Lionel receives the bare minimum dictated by company policy. Mary's boss is just the opposite. He has created a development plan for Mary that includes scheduled training in those areas that both Mary and her supervisor believe will expand her capabilities.

Fast-forward five years. Lionel is languishing in a low level sales support position while Mary has been promoted twice and is now in middle management.

> *Hands-On Advice: Develop every one of your employees, and when their capabilities expand and performance improves so will yours.*

Developing and training is another key to keeping people engaged and motivated. By encouraging and promoting ongoing training and development, you create a pipeline of talented people who are full of ideas, thoughts, and inspiration. This sends a strong, motivating message to each employee: we care and we're willing to invest in you. You'll then be rewarded with tremendous engagement and enthusiasm, positioning your organization as an employer of choice.

Here's an even worse scenario, one that plays out time and time again in business. Jack was hired as a purchasing agent for a large electronic game manufacturer. His boss, Robert, the purchasing manager, took Jack under his wing and trained him the best way he knew. Robert's intentions were good . . . at least as far as bringing Jack along.

Unfortunately, Robert cut corners. In an effort to impress his boss, the vice president of manufacturing, he drove vendors to reduce their prices to the point that vendors' profits declined, often precipitously. Vendors scrambled to meet the pricing structure demanded by Robert. When that happens quality is always the first casualty, and it was no different here.

Jack followed his boss's example with the predictable result. When Robert was fired Jack's future was compromised. He left the company shortly.

The moral of this story is that the wrong kind of training can be disastrous for both a company and employees who had the misfortune to be subjected to it. It's always helpful to have training programs reviewed and bought off by not just an employee's immediate supervisor but also an independent third party, usually a knowledgeable person in human resources or a supervisor of the party conducting the training. That type of oversight prevents problems.

The Necessity of Ongoing Training

Training is crucial to your company's future, as it creates a pipeline of talent that positions your company for success. It motivates employees by sending a strong message about their worth to the organization. It creates enthusiasm and improves work quality and morale. Finally, it boosts productivity. Trained employees are always more productive.

When Jack Welch was CEO of General Electric, he regularly trained employees at the company's training facilities in Crotonville, New York. He shared his knowledge and turned GE into a culture where learning is valued. Andy Grove, former CEO of Intel, also went into the classroom and taught. Before Roger Enrico took the reins at Pepsi, he personally trained many of his people.

Training enables employees to reach their optimum potential. If you fail to take it seriously, your employees won't have any respect for it. Even in tough economic times, you must make training a priority and budget for it. Some managers may balk at your efforts to train staff. They'll say, "We can't take people away from their day-to-day work for training. We'll lose productivity." Nonsense! If managers believe their people cannot benefit from training, perhaps they should be replaced.

Ask people how they learn best. So many companies will hire a new employee and place him or her in front of a computer on his first day of work. They train this unlucky hire by saying, "You're going to go through the slides, do this and then do that, and after the training we'll put you to work." This doesn't qualify as training. Some people can't learn in front of a computer. People have different facilities for learning: oral, visual, perhaps tactile. People learn best through one of these three approaches, but you can't arbitrarily select one over another.

Make training an everyday affair, a day-to-day activity. This is a simple approach that doesn't require a formal classroom setting. Often, all you need to do is ask, "How are things going today?" The employee may give you cues that indicate a training session is required, and it needn't be formal. And keep in mind that in some training sessions, employees may not pick up something they can use immediately, but it's a concept or skill that can help them down the road.

Highly effective leaders train, motivate, build, empower, and retain an optimal high-performing, creative, and innovative team by investing wisely in people. Develop, recognize, reward, and promote from within. Keep on board a high-performing team. Great leaders create more leaders at all levels by nurturing their development. They don't just delegate work, they delegate decision-making powers. When people have the authority to make certain decisions, they feel more responsible and loyal. So, empower your people. Don't micromanage them—turn them loose to perform their jobs. Explain the task, tell them what needs to be done and why, but don't tell them how to do it. Then they'll take ownership, accept accountability, think creatively, and offer ideas. When they feel you value their ideas, they'll find ways to boost performance.

Training: My Story—A Game That Came Down to One Play

As a basketball coach, I had a team of very short players one year, normally the kiss of death for a basketball team. For us to be competitive we had to be the best-conditioned team in the league. This meant going back to basics, so we practiced fundamentals of the game and worked our butts off to become the fiercest team in the city. I wanted the players to react instinctively when they hit the floor, without thinking (or overthinking) their moves. Effective training would help us get there.

Every night, we'd go through grueling three-hour practice sessions. The team would run conditioning drills before and after each training/practice session. And they hated it! They looked at me skeptically and questioned everything I told them to do.

I explained that I wanted them to be the best conditioned team. "When you get tired physically, you get tired mentally," I said. "I don't want that to happen . . . and neither do you. We're the smallest team in the league, and our only advantage is powerhouse conditioning. We also have to excel in the fundamentals of the game because there's little margin for error. So, we're going to work hard."

At the end of every gut-busting practice, when the team was totally exhausted, we diligently trained for end-of-game situations. I'd set up various scenarios by having my managers put different times on the game clock and then run plays that fit the scenarios. For example, we would put five seconds on the clock, and I'd say to my team, "You have five seconds to go. We're down one point. We have the ball at midcourt. What do we do?" Or: "We have the ball at the end line and have to go the length of the court, and we're down two points, with one second to go. What do we do?"

We'd train for these end of game scenarios every day, and they hated it because they were mentally and physically fatigued. All they wanted to do was go home.

"No," I'd say. "I want you to be able to execute when you're tired. I want you to succeed at the end of the game, when the chips are on the line and the game is at stake." So, we worked on these scenarios every day at the end of practice.

One day, I happened to miss practice, and my assistant coach called me to say he had planned on letting the team go home early and not run end-of-game situations. Then he dropped the bombshell: The team had refused to leave until they ran the end-of-game situations, and they said that it was important to be prepared. At that moment I realized they understood the value of our training.

Fortunately, we didn't have to use this training until the end of the season, in one of our most critical games. We were playing a team whose members were, on average, four inches taller. My tallest player was about six feet three inches, but we were fast. With all of those grueling practices under our belts, we were in great shape and fundamentally sound. I knew we could outplay the opposing team in terms of conditioning and thinking ability, but they were physically stronger, bigger, and so much more talented. Nobody gave us a chance. Nobody thought we could keep up with them, let alone win. Everyone said we were going to get blown out.

From the beginning tip-off, it was a close game, back and forth, back and forth. There wasn't more than a three-point difference between us during the entire game. With 30 seconds to go, we were ahead by one point. Our opponents came storming down the court and made a shot with 10 seconds to go, and went up one point. We now had the ball, with only 10 seconds to go, and I called a timeout to set up a last-second shot.

As my players came to the bench, several of them were smiling. "What's so funny?" I asked.

"Coach, we know what we're going to do," one of my players said. "We're going to run 24 West. Tony is going to get the ball, score, and we're going to win the game. We've been practicing this all year long."

Being the brilliant coach that I was, I asked, "Are you sure?"

Everyone looked at me and said yes in unison.

"Okay. Go do it."

Now, we had the ball at the end of the court, with 94 feet to go. We were down 1 point, with 10 seconds to go.

The clock didn't start until a player in bounds touched the ball. We took the ball out of bounds. The first pass came in, and the clock started ticking as we dribbled the ball up court. The second pass was made, and Tony came off a double screen. He caught the ball, went up, and took the shot. As the ball went up in the air, I stood up from the bench and it felt like it was in slow motion, just like in the movies. As the ball reached its apex and started its downward flight, I thought, "Six months worth of training, six months worth of hard work, and it all comes down to this."

The ball continued to come down and down and finally down into the net, and we won the game. It was sheer pandemonium! We were mobbed by fans and carried off the floor. But it all came down to training, training your people so when it's on the line they come through. That's what it's all about in business and sports and life. Train your people for the tough times, and they'll come through. Training brings out the best in them.

Train to Retain

Researchers at the Iowa State University College of Business have confirmed the link between providing professional development opportunities and retaining employees.

Management professors James McElroy, PhD, and Paula Morrow, PhD, studied 961 employees at 176 companies in the People's Republic of China. They found that even the best HR departments must allow employees to further their career goals. Failure to provide such training has a negative impact on employee loyalty and commitment. "Promoting and rewarding skill acquisition," Dr. McElroy says, "results in greater bang for the buck in terms of commitment."

Professional development programs create a psychological contract between an organization's leadership and its employees. "For the latter, it's a mental schema that you carry around in your head concerning the relationship you believe exists between your contributions to your employer and what you're induced to contribute," Dr. McElroy explains. He reminds leaders to make programs available to both new and long-standing employees, as company veterans are often erroneously assumed to be loyal. Offering such opportunities is especially important if your company has experienced a wave of layoffs, downsizing, mergers, or reorganizations. The investment in employee development after these traumas can help restore stability and allay workers' anxieties.

Empowering People

Once you've hired the right people, empower them. If you can't empower effectively, your team, department, and company will never grow. I distinguish between *empowering* and *delegating*. I've seen so many people delegate work to their direct reports and keep piling it on. Anyone can delegate work; an effective leader empowers people with decision-making responsibilities. It doesn't do you any good to surround yourself with great people and then micromanage them. You need to turn them loose to perform the jobs they're capable of doing. Empowering people is one element of effective leadership.

New hires often come fully charged, excited about their new adventure, and filled with energy and potential. By tapping into that energy, knowledge, and wisdom right from the start, you can maximize the new hire's potential, extend the handshake, and fuel that energy well past the beginning of the employment cycle.

While recruitment continues to be one of the most costly HR processes, its long-term effectiveness is being eroded by high attrition. Hiring doesn't stop with the job offer. Today, rerecruiting your best people is as critical as hiring them in the first place. Often new hires leave too early for an organization to enjoy a return on its recruiting investment. And if they stay, are they productive, engaged, loyal, and committed? Have they simply checked in or are they tuned in and turned on as well?

The relationship between manager and new hire is crucial to retention and performance. To increase retention and build loyalty during that critical first year, start by building the relationship between new hires and their managers.

Great leaders realize that in order to be successful they have to create more leaders at all levels. Therefore, empower your people; nurture the development of leaders. Delegating work without delegating the ability to make decisions about their work is ineffective. Your people cannot grow and expand their wings. They must have that authority to feel they are valued members of the organization. You will improve your employees' capabilities as well as motivate them. By empowering your people, you are allowing them to reach their potential. When you fail to empower people, barriers are created that people cannot overcome. If these barriers remain long enough, people give up and leave. Many of those people go on to become great leaders at other organizations.

Another crucial role is nurturing the growth and development of other leaders—creating leaders at every level. Growing leaders at every level by investing in training and developing them enables you to build a much stronger company.

Jonathan Delegates

I was coaching Jonathan, the president of a very successful company, and we were discussing one of his major challenges: time management. When he received feedback from his managers and employees, people complained about how he could never spare enough time to deal with important issues and meet with people on a regular basis to discuss progress. More than one made comments like this: "There's never enough of John to go around, and he never has time for me."

Jonathan had his hands in everything his organization did. He not only made big decisions, he spent an inordinate amount of time on details, which he should have empowered other people to handle. Jonathan told me that managers in the company had to come to him with requests for new smartphones for their direct reports. He believed that he had to be the decision-maker or people would take advantage and cost the company more money.

When I heard this, I had to stop myself from jumping across the table and shaking some sense into Jonathan. "You have projects all over the world, and your business is growing each day," I reminded him. "You are faced with myriad top-level decisions and global clients with distinct cultures. Are you telling me that you're the person who decides which employees are allowed to have a smartphone? Are you serious? You're the person who talks to people about this minutia?"

Just then, there was a knock at the door. A manager wanted Jonathan to review a document. Several minutes later, someone else asked him when his coaching session would be over so a group meeting could be held. After the second person left, I thought it would be a good idea to retrace these events with Jonathan. "Let's take a step back here," I said. "Jonathan, do you trust your people to do the right things?"

"Sure do," he said with obvious pride. "That's why I hired them."

"So, why don't you just let go?"

"How do you mean let go?"

"Who is the most logical person to handle the smartphone matter?"

Jonathan said, "I suppose the IT department would be the best."

"Is the person in IT trustworthy and capable of making this decision?"

"Absolutely," Jonathan said.

"That's Joan, right?"

"It is, and she's doing one hell of a good job."

"So, why don't you let her be responsible for these decisions and then hold her accountable for keeping costs down? Have her set a budget for smartphones. By giving her this responsibility, you're letting Joan know that you trust her to make this decision. Furthermore, you're taking one more small responsibility off of your plate so you can focus on the long-term growth of the company and strategic matters."

Jonathan agreed. Then I asked him what I considered to be the coup de grâce of my coaching lesson: "*Do you understand the consequences of not empowering other people to make decisions?*"

He stared back at me, somewhat apprehensive.

"They'll walk out the door. They'll think they're not trusted, that they're being held back and can't go any further at your company. If you want to prevent that, empower them to make decisions and hold them accountable. Turn them loose, and give them decision-making authority, because if they're great people, they'll make great decisions. That's how you develop and grow people within the team and organization."

Poor Leaders

The characteristics of poor leaders include:

- The need to control and create a climate of negativity, coupled with rare or no praise and recognition.
- The inability to keep their word, poor treatment of people, taking credit for others' successes, and blaming others for their personal failures.
- The habit of covering up mistakes, resulting in high turnover and a lack of engagement by those who stay.
- Failure to delegate or empower people. Instead, they micromanage others' work. Their inability to develop a culture of trust deprives people of opportunities to grow and gain confidence. By controlling people and undermining them in front of their peers, poor leaders damage their companies and destroy productivity.
- Promoting employees based on technical know-how, high performance, or seniority. These individuals are often placed into the leadership role without any basic training. Is it any wonder they tend to underperform? We'd never expect a poorly trained physician to cure us. How, then, can we expect ill-equipped leaders to lead without proper training? We set them up for failure, and a formerly top-notch employee, through no fault of his own, suddenly becomes an albatross.

Effective Leadership Development

While some leaders seem to be born with extraordinary abilities, most develop their skillsets by learning, practicing, and refining them daily.

Just as a competitive athlete trains to win, leaders must commit to work hard, adopt a positive attitude, and demonstrate a desire for constant learning. They must also understand that their leadership style will change over time and, as circumstances dictate, it's imperative to remain flexible.

I encourage aspiring and emerging leaders to create a plan, put it in writing, and then work it. People who put their goals in writing are usually more successful. Read as many books and attend as many training courses as possible, within and outside of the company. Vary courses to experience a broad spectrum of leadership skills.

What Individuals Can Do

Identify areas in which you must improve. We all have blind spots. We see some of our weaknesses, but we can't identify all of them. Working with a coach is a powerful way to improve leadership skills. One-on-one coaching provides more support than other training methods. Coaches are attuned to unique, individual needs.

So, learn what your company looks for in its leaders. Have a competency model that identifies effective leaders' strengths and characteristics. Study this model and practice the competencies. If no such model exists, seek out successful company leaders and talk with them to gain a better understanding of how they became successful.

Volunteer to lead small projects that provide useful leadership experiences. You'll gain confidence and enhance weak skillsets.

Use 360-degree feedback and other assessment tools to identify leadership competencies and skills. This provides a valid measure of the areas that require work. You must understand how your behavior is perceived by others to effectively change your behavior, and 360-degree feedback often solves this problem.

Stay curious. Seek new opportunities and experiences, and always be open to trying something out of your normal comfort zone. Education, assessment, training, and coaching place you in situations that enable you to succeed and gain confidence.

What Organizations Can Do

What steps can organizations take to develop effective leaders? Effective leadership development (LD) programs can be designed, developed, and implemented to teach basic leadership skills and behaviors needed in today's highly competitive landscape. Programs must be driven by business needs and designed to enhance capabilities for current and future leaders. A leadership program should be tied to company values, and the skills and behaviors taught should support them. In addition, the program should build on a set of leadership competencies that are unique to the organization.

Ongoing development for managers and leaders starts at the top with senior-level commitment. Failure to develop current and future leaders (and create a strategic succession plan) results in an inability to compete. Baby Boomers, who account for most upper- and mid-level managers, are transitioning out of the workforce. We will soon face a severe shortage of skilled leaders. Senior management needs to move quickly, with a strategic succession plan, to grow and nurture talent.

Recently, an executive in a Fortune 100 company told me how critical the next few years will be to grow bench strength, as the company anticipates losing 30 percent of its key people to retirement. The company needs a strategic initiative to implement LD programs immediately.

As an example of the type of LD programs required, our firm provides customized LD programs designed not only for senior managers, but also for high-potential individuals and front-line managers. When participants master leadership skills, they're ready to take a quantum leap up the leadership ladder.

We customize these LD programs to fit the needs of organizations and participants. We interview stakeholders and participants before we design the program to understand current leadership knowledge and skill levels. We then integrate the culture, views, and philosophy into the program. We focus on such core areas as creating and driving a vision, building and managing relationships, becoming a strategic thinker, demonstrating deep business knowledge, solving problems, making decisions, achieving results, communicating and listening effectively, coaching, empowering people, developing performance goals and standards, providing performance feedback, building strong teams and team dynamics, executing tasks, managing conflict, leading change, engaging employees, developing talent, and much more.

These LD programs can last from 6 to 18 months. Structure and format depend on an organization's needs, desired outcomes, and participants' skill levels. For example, one company identified 75 high-potential leaders. We designed and developed three programs with 25 participants each. They lasted six months and involved three components: a series of monthly workshops, one-on-one coaching, and a leadership project in which they recruited and led a team to put learned skills into practice in real time. After six months, each participant presented project results to fellow classmates and described in detail the pitfalls, challenges, and rewards faced along the way.

A second program involved upper-level executives. We held a series of biweekly three-hour evening programs that ran for nine months and included one-on-one coaching.

A third program involved 20 participants from the same company, but from different locations. We kicked off the program in person, with all participants in attendance, and we explained the objectives and expectations. Thereafter, every other week for 26 weeks, we held one-hour group teleconferences to learn various leadership skills. I also coached each person during this time to reinforce identified skills.

Each program was unique, depending on the organization's needs. Our LD program includes 12 components:

1. *Leadership framework.* The framework supports high-performing teams and produces results. We provide a balanced approach that equally addresses people/task focus; short-term/long-term time horizon; and internal/external business factors.

2. *Development design.* This includes goals, learning modules, knowledge, skills and behaviors, stories, development strategies, and learning experiences.

3. *Pre-assessment surveys.* Assessment of current knowledge, skills, and behaviors and identification of areas that need development. This boosts self-awareness.

4. *Personal/team goals.* Creating custom personal, team, and orga- nization goals.

5. *Core values and competencies.* The knowledge, skills, and behav- iors tied to core values and best practice core competencies.

6. *Content/curriculum structured around real work scenarios.* The content draws from several disciplines including organi- zational learning, team building, business acumen, and client- relationships.

7. *Learning modules.* Since people tend to learn best in small increments, we deliver most of the content in learning modules. Each chapter has a series of short, focused learning modules. This encourages application of the skills and concepts.

8. *Practice and application.* Since most people learn best by doing, we've designed practice and application of new knowledge and skills into each section to develop effective behaviors (habits, actions, and patterns). Participants put the principles of effective leadership into action via practice and application in their job. To acquaint you with the methodology for accomplishing this, I designed the section titled Takeaway in this book. These are exercises you'll find at the conclusion of every chapter aimed at helping you improve your leadership abilities. They focus on specific aspects of the chapter, but you can apply the same methodology to analyze issues across the board.

9. *Facilitated development (feedback and coaching).* As coaches, we facilitate the learning and development experiences. They develop self-observation, self-awareness, self-responsibility, and self-mastery to keep growing.

10. *Progress reports.* They report on how they're doing in applying the concepts and reaching their goals. They make the concepts part of how they lead every day to achieve sustainability.

11. *Results and outcomes.* They not only learn about effective leadership, they actually achieve business results and outcomes by applying what they learn.

12. *Reflection, review, and evaluation for continued improvement.* Because what constitutes dynamic leadership starts with ingrained

core principles—those beliefs that come from within—I encourage self-examination followed by application of those principles aimed at continual performance improvement.

Nurturing Growth

How can managers and leaders develop the people who report directly to them so these direct reports can assume more responsibility? To develop people to take on more responsibility, a leader must support and coach people so they can cultivate new skills and embrace opportunities for professional development and personal growth. Leaders must guide others to create their own development plans, not do it for them. People are more productive when they take ownership of their plans.

Next, you have to set expectations, encourage people to achieve their goals, praise their successes often, and ensure the flow of open communication. Leaders must challenge, probe, and ask questions to teach decision-making. Learn to ask open-ended questions such as: How does that work? What does that mean? If you do this, what do you think may happen? Why do you think it will work? What's your next step? Which tools do you need? These questions teach people to become analytical and think more strategically. Lastly, you must empower people by giving them ownership, which shows your confidence in their abilities and enables them to succeed or fail on their own.

See that each employee is not just doing a job, but that his reach is also being stretched. Assign people to jobs in much the same way that sports coaches or music teachers choose exercises for their students, to push them just beyond their current capabilities and build the skills that are most important. About two-thirds of people's development comes from carefully chosen job assignments and about one-third from mentoring coaching and classroom training. Put managers into stretch jobs that require and them to learn and grow. For people trying to improve, making real decisions in real time is the central practice activity that produces growth. Your hardest experience—the stretches that most challenge you—are the most helpful.

Find ways to develop leaders in their jobs. You experience tension between your need to develop people by moving them through different jobs and your need to develop their expertise in certain domains by leaving them in jobs. A division has a tough time competing when the boss moves on every 18 to 24 months (a typical pattern). The challenge is to provide the growth benefits of new stretch assignments without moving people into new jobs so often.

Know the critical roles of teachers and constantly provide feedback. Great performance is built through activities designed specifically to improve particular skills. Teachers and coaches are helpful in designing those activities. Yet at most organizations, nobody is assigned the role of teacher or coach. Employees aren't told which skills will be most helpful to them, nor how best to develop them. Top-performing organizations have explicit coaching and mentoring programs. Careful job assignments and other programs determine the direction of an employee's development; mentors provide detailed advice on which subset of skills need attention immediately. And people receive frequent, rapid, and accurate feedback to improve performance.

Identify promising performers early. Working on people's development early creates huge advantages, and yet in most companies, development programs are reserved for an elite group of executives who are several years into their careers. Developing future leaders early creates a competitive advantage that lasts for decades, as their pipelines of high achievers become bigger, better, and more reliable.

Develop people through inspiration, not authority. Deliberate practice activities are so demanding that no one can sustain them for long without strong motivation. The best leaders contribute to that motivation through a sense of mission. Identifying or even creating an inspiring sense of mission requires a journey deep into the corporate soul.

Invest time, money, and energy in developing people. People development is at the center of the CEO's responsibilities. Indeed, the biggest investment may be the time of the CEO and other executives. As they see what the boss is focusing on, they become similarly devoted to developing people. Not that these companies rely solely on the power of example. Virtually all of them evaluate executives partly on how well they're developing people, including themselves.

Make leadership development part of the culture. At the best companies, developing leaders isn't a program, it's a way of life. For example, honest feedback has to be culturally acceptable; at many companies it isn't. Devoting time to mentoring has to be accepted.

Empower—Don't Just Dump

To empower your people, explain the task, tell them what needs to be done, but don't tell them how to do it. When you overexplain or tell people exactly how to complete a task, you remove any creativity from the assignment. It becomes thoroughly boring, and there is no challenge. People needn't develop in any capacity whatsoever, nor do they take ownership and accountability. As General George S. Patton said: "Don't tell people how to do things. Tell them what to do, and let them surprise you with their results."

Empowered employees aren't afraid to think outside the box or offer ideas because they know they have management's support and that senior executives want their ideas and contributions. Employees who feel the company values their ideas strive to devise new ways to help the company perform better. The more empowered your employees are, the greater the rewards your company will reap in terms of higher bottom-line results.

Takeaway from Chapter 13

Here is an exercise that will dredge memories from your past.

Divide a sheet of paper into two columns. Write the names of two former supervisors at the top of each column, one you considered exceptional, and one you considered the worst you ever had. On the left side, write descriptive words such as motivate, instruct, help, teach, trust, and inspire. These words constitute the characteristics that *you* consider had the most impact on you. Evaluate the two supervisors in terms of the way you feel about them, not the way you think you should feel about them.

For each of the traits described, rate the two supervisors as follows, and mark your grades in the respective junctions of row and column: A = Superior, B = Acceptable, C = Below average, F = Failure.

The object of the exercise is to demonstrate that leaders have an *emotional impact* that affects the life and performance of those working for them. Notice the word *life*, because it's not just the job, it's the emotions workers carry home with them in their hearts and stomachs. Those emotions spill over and affect workers' family lives.

Carry this perspective with you wherever you work, and you won't have any problem understanding how the people who work for you feel.

14

Practice 3: Understand the Value of Coaching

Coaching plays a crucial role in keeping people engaged and committed. It brings out the best in them and helps remove obstacles to their success. Coaching is not about telling people what to do or how to do it; rather, you help people discover their own paths by encouraging and questioning. Help eliminate their roadblocks by asking questions like: With which past projects did you struggle? What steps will you take to achieve your goals? What excuses are you making? What's holding you back? What have you tried since the last time we talked? *Open-ended questions make people think through obstacles*. And coaching shows that you care and are willing to share yourself with them.

We include coaching in all of our LD programs because we're trying to change behavior. People attend training programs and learn many new ideas and skills. But as soon as they return to their offices, they're hit from all sides with client issues, personnel problems, and the dozens of other daily matters of urgency. As a result, they have no time to fully digest and practice what they learned, and they frequently lay aside leadership program content.

We seek to accomplish two goals in every LD program: change participants' behavior and make newly learned skills part of their everyday work habits. Changing an old habit and developing a new one takes time. Coaching reinforces training by working one-on-one with each person to abandon bad habits and adopt the more positive ones learned during training. Participants can then discuss what's working, and not working, with their coaches in complete confidence. The coaches hold them accountable and are there for support when needed, which proves extremely valuable.

One study tracked executives who participated in an LD program, followed by eight weeks of one-on-one coaching. Training alone increased leadership productivity by 22.4 percent, while coaching and training increased productivity by 88 percent. The combination of coaching and training is crucial if you want to gain a return on investment from your training dollar.

Use coaching to enhance the capabilities and performance of leaders, high potential employees, and top producers. When leaders coach, people become more confident and motivated, which leads to higher performance and productivity. Leaders build relationships of trust when they support people to be all that they can be.

Organizations with a strong coaching culture develop higher engagement and performance. A coach asks: What are my people's strengths? What are their goals, their ambitions, their technical and managerial limits? A coach works one-on-one with key employees to stop bad habits and start positive ones. Participants can discuss what's working, and not working, in confidence, and the coach holds them accountable and supplies support.

Coaching increases productivity, builds teamwork, motivates employees to elevate performance levels, and helps them overcome obstacles to success. A great leader spends time working with individuals to see the blocks in their performances. A successful leader and effective coach are one and the same. People do not and will not change until they see the need to. A good coach listens to people to find ways to break down the barriers that keep them from reaching their full potential. They work with their people to outline a plan of action that clearly states the goals for improvement and accountability. Coaching helps people learn, grow, and change. It provides a powerful structure through which people can focus on specific outcomes, become more effective, and stay on track.

My Father-in-Law, My Coach

When I was a CEO, I had certain issues that I could not confide to anyone else. I had to deal with these problems on my own. My father-in-law, Ed, was a well-known consultant, and he became my confidant. Every time I had one of these decisions to make, Ed coached me. This went on for an entire year.

One day, a key issue came up, and I needed some help. I picked up the phone and began dialing Ed's number. Before I dialed the last number, I put down the phone. I realized that during the entire year I had been talking with Ed about my problems, he had never given me a direct answer to any of my questions. Suddenly, I felt angry.

I muttered to myself as I picked up the telephone and started dialing his number again. As Ed answered, I had a revelation. "Ed! I just realized that during the whole year I've been asking for your advice, you've never once given me a straight answer."

There was a silence at the other end of the phone. "Jeff," he said, "you have the answers. You know your business. I don't know your business. As your coach, it's my job to ask you the questions that will lead to that 'aha!' moment . . . and you're doing a pretty good job of it."

At that moment, and for the first time, I understood what coaching was all about. It's not about providing answers; it's about guiding the person being coached in the direction of the right answer.

I use Ed's approach in my coaching practice today. I don't give people the answers. A good coach asks great questions to help people move from point A to point B, asking the questions that will cause the proverbial lightbulb to go on in someone's head.

Coaching requires a lot of probing. Ask questions like: What will make the difference here? What have you done to foster change on your team? What did you learn from this process? If you did it over again, what would you do differently? In the bigger scheme of things, where does this fit in? Is this the most effective use of your time?

Three Skills of Effective Coaching

Coaching requires you to master three skills: questioning that leads to understanding, structuring jobs correctly, providing positive reinforcement. Let me explain.

Effective questioning opens the door to understanding what's on people's minds. When you're coaching somebody, ask open-ended questions that cannot be answered with a yes or no. You want the person you're coaching to think about the answer. However, managers need to ask the right questions . . . questions that help employees realize their strengths, their failings, their needs and how they can best contribute to their organizations, and by extension to their abilities. Great coaches know the answers even when employees don't.

Armed with that knowledge, great coaches structure jobs and work environments that allow each individual to flourish. They provide resources and training. They continually monitor progress and provide feedback, knowing when to encourage but also when to be brutally honest.

An "atta boy" for a job well done is often the positive reinforcement that works wonders. Outstanding leaders go out of their way to boost the self-esteem of their employees. If people believe in themselves it's amazing what they can accomplish, so give them well-deserved praise.

Start catching people doing something right. Watch how that inspires your team to greater performance. I guarantee you'll see a difference if you keep it up. But it has to come from you.

The Manager They Call "Coach"

Joe manages the school bus function for a very large school district in a densely populated county. It's a demanding job, one that takes mechanical skills, scheduling skills, cost control skills, and—most important of all   people skills.

Joe's employees call him coach because he behaves like one. They joke that they can almost see the lanyard around his neck with a whistle attached. He somehow manages to touch base with each and every one of his employees every day, asking how things are going and how he can help out. This daily contact allows every one of his crew the opportunity to discuss problems and concerns. Joe's crew is a happy one, indeed.

> *Hands-On Advice: Provide your people with the tools and the encouragement they need to handle their jobs.*

Those things alone will convince them that you're concerned about their welfare, interested in their development, and willing to share their burdens.

Coaching People

Coaching is one of the most important leadership duties and responsibilities. When leaders take the time to coach, people become more confident and motivated, which leads to higher performance and productivity. Leaders build relationships on trust and encouragement, and they need to support people so they can be all they can be. Organizations with a strong coaching culture develop much higher levels of employee engagement and performance.

Coaching helps people overcome obstacles to their success. As a leader, take the time to get to know your people because coaching is based on trust and confidence. The coaching process will bring to the forefront:

- What kind of assignments do they handle best?
- What kind of assignments should they avoid?
- How far can they advance in the organization?
- What are their ambitions?

When leaders have answers to these questions, they can structure jobs within the work environment and provide the feedback required to enhance performance. That allows people to find their road map to success and with the appropriate resources and training.

Coaching is not about providing the answers. It's a process of using questions, active listening, and support to help people achieve a higher level of success. Coaches ask the right questions to move people to what

I call the "aha" moment. This occurs when people being coached figure something out and realize they have found the answer. The leader didn't give them the answers, but asked leading questions to help them find it. This is what makes coaching so powerful.

Active listening means giving your total attention to the person you're coaching. This is vital. You need to hear what the person is saying and not saying. This skill may prove difficult for some leaders because active listening requires them to suspend judgment and carefully tune into what the other person is saying and feeling.

Coaching opens lines of communication to create a comfortable environment where performance issues can be discussed freely and without defensiveness. Leaders who are effective coaches have more successful teams, higher morale, and, in most cases, better bottom-line results. The benefits of coaching include: improved trust and morale, improved performance, skill development, innovation, productivity, confidence, motivation, better customer service, higher retention of key people, less stress, and applied potential.

Organizations are focusing on coaching for several key reasons: People are your key source of competitive advantage. They have to be adaptable and flexible. We have to do more with less. Maintaining a high-performance culture is key to survival. Coaching provides these benefits and many more.

Coaching need not take a lot of time. Coaching doesn't always have to be conducted in formal sessions. It may be as simple as walking to a person's desk and asking how things are going, or having a short chat in the hallway. Organizations invest millions of dollars in equipment, hold weeks and months of meetings, and spend an inordinate amount of time making a decision, but they shortsightedly may not invest the same time and money in coaching their people!

People are your human capital and most valuable assets. If leaders invest the appropriate time and money in coaching, people will be more productive and motivated, and the organization will show better bottom-line results. One University of Pennsylvania study found that spending 10 percent of revenue on capital improvements boosts productivity by 3.9 percent. A similar investment in developing human capital increases productivity by 8.5 percent, more than double the gain.

So, if leaders spend time coaching people, there are obvious benefits to the organization.

Years ago, I followed Tiger Woods for several holes at the Buick Invitational Tournament in San Diego, and I marveled at his concentration and skills. I asked myself: Does Tiger Woods need a coach to be a great golfer? The answer is probably no. But has he become a better golfer by working with a coach? The answer is a resounding yes! In Tiger's case, coaching helped him succeed beyond his then-current level of play and elevated his game. Look at it this way: Coaching is not intended to fix a problem. The same applies to coaching top leaders who cling to bad habits. A qualified coach can turn an excellent leader into a true powerhouse.

I'm often brought in to deal with leadership issues. Providing feedback is one key area. As executives move into greater levels of responsibility, they receive less—perhaps even no—feedback from others on their performance. The unfortunate consequence is stagnation. Critical leadership and interpersonal skills often reach certain levels, and the executive is given no opportunity to become an even better leader. Working one-on-one with an objective third-party coach offers these leaders a trusted advisor who can focus on behavioral changes that organizations are ill equipped to handle.

The most common leadership areas that require improvement include improving poor communication skills, building job-critical competencies, changing executive behavior to create a positive impact, handling indecisiveness, leading a multigenerational workforce, effectively managing stress and burnout, sharpening the skills of high-potential employees, increasing productivity, building strong and effective teams, resolving conflict, making goals congruent with the company mission, handling fear of failure or success, time management skills, lack of assertiveness, imbalance between work and life, stagnation in comfort zones, and insufficient feedback to direct reports.

Dealing with Difficult Employees

Unfortunately, many leaders steer clear of dealing with difficult people in the workplace, thereby contributing to conflict through avoidance.

There will always be difficult employees, regardless of organizational level or the position an employee holds. People problems are often the most challenging parts of a leader's job.

Often, people are difficult because they may not know any other type of behavior or because no one has ever told them their behavior is inappropriate. Either way, when behavior poses a problem, leaders must deal with it quickly. The longer you wait, the worse the situation becomes. Failure to act swiftly can have a devastating effect on other employees. They may become upset, unproductive, and suffer low morale. If one person's negative behavior persists long enough without a resolution, good employees may ultimately get fed up and leave. As a businessperson, you can't afford to risk this.

The leader's goal is to find a solution by staying focused on the problem and not attacking the person causing it. Instead, point out specific examples of the individual's objectionable behavior. Encourage the person to talk and be honest with you by asking open-ended, leading questions. Avoid questions that can be answered with a simple yes or no. Then, listen carefully to what's being said. The more probing you can do, the better your chance of identifying the real source of the problems.

Become an active listener. Paraphrase key points the other person is making. For example, say: "What I hear you saying is—" and repeat what the person has told you. Let the individual acknowledge whether what you heard is right or wrong so you're on the same page. Remember: You want to uncover the reasons for the behavior, so don't interrupt when the person is speaking and remain nonjudgmental.

Once you determine the source of the problem, work together to create opportunities to find solutions that correct behavior. Make sure the person comes up with some of these solutions on his own, which allows ownership in remedying the problem and gives people a vested interest in the outcome. Then, create an action plan that holds the person accountable for future behavior problems. Accountability is vital: If the behavior continues—and depending on its severity—you'll need to determine when and how to handle follow-up counseling. And if the behavioral changes fail to occur, possible termination is the next step.

When dealing with difficult behavior, determine the problem, identify reasons for it, generate options, evaluate these options, create an action plan that focuses on accountability, and follow through on the plan.

Difficult employees should never be surprised if termination occurs. From a legal and HR perspective, you must document every counseling and disciplinary meeting where you outline expected goals and consequences for failing to meet them. After verbal warnings, issue written warnings when negative behavior continues. After several written warnings, make sure employees understand that their jobs are now on the line.

Takeaway from Chapter 14

Take an hour or so away from the fray of daily combat and shut off your smartphone. Find a quiet place like a park bench or a comfortable chair in your study, and conduct this mental exercise.

Search your memory and find an instance or time that coaching helped you succeed when, without a change of course provided by the perspective of an outside and objective viewer, you might have failed.

The person coaching you might have been anybody with the right combination of experience and insight such as a professional coach, a family member with a solid business background, or an executive from your company familiar with your work.

Now, recall that coach's specific advice. Did she identify certain weaknesses such as an abrupt and dismissive manner with your staff, or your tendency to overload the organization with so many assignments that your people were spread too thin to do good jobs? The range of a coach's help obviously varies, but narrow your selection to *one* time or *one* problem for purposes of analysis.

Next, cite the particular recommendations your coach suggested and your response. Try to be as specific as possible. Finally, evaluate the results.

The purpose of this exercise is to sharpen your coaching skills so when you mentor others you will understand what works and what doesn't when helping your people find the solutions to their problems and shortcomings.

Practice 4: Motivate and Inspire People

Leaders and cheerleaders share a common goal: to inspire your team to do well without getting in their way. Successful leaders devote themselves to a bold ideal and channel their teams to fulfilling it.

Inspiration requires you to be a great role model. Members of your team will recall how you led them in previous tasks, and they will often adopt your style. If, however, you have previously failed to command team members' respect, your team may take a more Wild West approach, thereby inviting chaos. Your encouragement and support will help inspire your team to victory, and rewarding team members for a job well done reinforces their achievements. If a project hits a bump in the road, you need to maintain your optimism, according to Marshall Goldsmith, PhD, author of *Mojo* and *What Got you Here Won't Get You There*.

Being the executive optimist means you have to view challenges or problems as opportunities for growth and improvement. As Goldsmith writes: "If we can take the positive spirit inside us toward what we are doing now and extend it to what other people are doing—in other words, make our optimism contagious—then each of us has a better chance of becoming a person who can rise from a setback that might crumble others."

Don't allow a bad apple to spoil your team's motivation. A firmly entrenched pessimist can drag down everyone's spirits, so meet with this team member for an attitude adjustment. If negative behavior continues, you may want to remove this person for the good of the team. Remind each team member that the organization's mission takes precedence over personal agendas.

All Members Have to Pull Their Weight

Pete was the bad apple you read about in the previous paragraph. Despite repeated warnings from his supervisor, Pete tried to wiggle out of every assignment, dodged the boss when he came around, and didn't respond to requests to help his teammates.

Few of his fellow team members wanted anything to do with him. They managed to work around Pete for some time, but eventually they came to the conclusion that Pete just wasn't a team player. When output and quality started to deteriorate, the supervisor took Pete off the crew.

> *Hands-On Advice: Don't wait too long to get rid of a sour apple.*

If you wait too long to remove a problem staff member, your employees might lose their respect for you, and that's going to impinge on your performance as well as the team's. Your reputation as a fair boss is on the line.

Focus on Your People

A company is nothing more nor less than the collective abilities and spirit of its employees. Without highly motivated and inspired employees, you will struggle to survive and thrive. Great leaders motivate people to work together and achieve goals, instill confidence, and earn employees' trust—a commodity that can never be bought.

Leaders and managers must recognize that the downsizing epidemic has created a big pool of underemployed workers who have been forced to take part-time jobs, usually without benefits, to support their families. These workers, now known as involuntary part-timers, are facing unprecedented levels of anxiety and stress, thereby creating a unique human resources challenge for today's leaders.

In 2010, the U.S. ranks of involuntary part-timers had bulged to 9.2 million Americans, a historical record, according to Susan J. Lambert, PhD, and Julia R. Henly, PhD, associate professors at the University of Chicago.

When managing such employees, you must be sensitive to their most common workplace and financial concerns:

- No medical, dental, life, or disability insurance.
- The inability to access public benefits (unemployment insurance, cash assistance, family and medical leave).
- Last-minute changes in job schedules, which disrupt family life. Limited advance notice of work hours, usually dependent on fluctuating business volume.

According to Dr. Lambert, "Unpredictable work schedules can translate into instability in family routines and practices, placing added burdens on already strapped and busy families, their caregivers, and extended family members. We find that hourly retail employees with more predictable work schedules report lower levels of stress, less work/family conflict, and fewer work interferences with nonwork activities, such as scheduling doctors' appointments, socializing with friends, and eating meals together as a family."

When you hire an involuntary part-timer, you essentially transfer risk from the company to the employee, she says, and workers' problems often remain unresolved, even after economic recovery.

Leaders and managers can help these employees by trying to give them as many work hours as possible, with minimal scheduling changes. This not only eases their anxieties, but it allows you to reduce turnover, most common among sales associates, younger workers, and recently hired workers, Dr. Lambert claims. Be flexible when accommodating doctors' appointments and other important family needs.

Leaders Discuss Motivation

How can leaders best motivate employees? Here are some answers, expressed in their own words:

"Great leaders facilitate, they don't command or control like infantry officers in combat. Even under those dire circumstances, great infantry officers understand how to motivate troops. They recognize the need for discipline, but the best of them temper it through motivational techniques. So, why do some business leaders feel the compunction to act as infantry officers (as they see them)? It's ego, pure and simple. And, in the long run, it doesn't work. Great leaders understand that facilitation is the key to motivating employees."

"Continuous learning is the foundation for improvement and the cornerstone of motivation. When employees learn, they grow, and when they grow they are motivated to do better jobs, to engage, to participate, to be part of the team. Learning is an inclusive experience that brings everybody into the fold."

"You'll really see the effects of motivation in periods of crisis. That's when a motivated team pulls together, and their combined strength is mighty powerful. It's equivalent to synergism, where one plus one equals three. Without that motivation you don't have engagement, and when you don't have engagement, results seldom exceed mediocrity."

"Contrary to what some leaders believe, compassionate management isn't for sissies. It doesn't mean abandoning performance standards at the expense of placating employees. It does mean empathizing with people who have problems by driving to the core reasons for those problems and providing employees with the tools to fix those problems. Compassionate management, in that sense, is a potent motivational tool."

"Never underestimate the effect your bearing, your facial expressions, how you walk and behave, has on employees. If you hold yourself erect, maintain a calm demeanor, keep the expression on your face consistent, and walk with a sense of purpose, even under the most stressful circumstances, it will spill over to employees, from workers through executives, and motivate them to face their problems with a sense of purpose and resolve."

"Motivation doesn't work when you have the wrong people working for you. Highly effective leaders hire outstanding performers, place them in the right jobs, empower them, and watch as they accomplish great things."

"Successful leaders never accept the status quo. They continually ask questions and seek answers and alternatives that are thoroughly explored. This is the kind of intellect that identifies hard-thinking employees and gives them the opportunity to excel."

"It's difficult to let go, to assign employees the responsibility to do what you now do. But if you want a highly motivated workforce, that's exactly what you must do. You'll be amazed at what people accomplish when they're given both the authority and responsibility for their work."

"True leaders meet problems head on. They don't evade, delay, avoid, and make excuses. Their ability to see things clearly, to possess the fortitude to accept responsibility, sends a clear message throughout the organization and motivates employees to do the same."

"One of the most destructive influences in a company is politics that flourishes unchecked. When employees see that real achievements take a backseat to fawning, servility, and insincere flattery, their motivation goes into free fall. When you find a successful leader know that he has eliminated that pernicious influence."

"In the successful company, its leaders have curbed the need to extract as much as possible from employees and replaced it with the need to instill value in them."

"One of the greatest tests of any leader is the ability to identify the strengths and weaknesses of employees and find ways to place them in jobs that magnify those strengths and minimizes weaknesses."

Takeaway from Chapter 15

Take a lesson from Richard, an experienced turnaround specialist. Start by guessing what his most difficult task is in *any* turnaround. No, it's not reducing inventory, developing higher quality products and services, improving customer satisfaction, increasing market share, or reducing overhead. Richard explains: "My initial assessment of a company in hot water starts with the effectiveness of its quality, cost, sales levels, and so forth. You know, the surface signs that show that the management is stumbling. But those aren't the reasons the company is in trouble. The reasons go deeper. They inevitably begin and end with how the leaders perform their jobs, how they interact with people, how effective they are at motivating and inspiring other members of the organization.

"By the time I arrive on the scene the top leaders are gone, released by the board, but the problem of ingrained faulty leadership remains in the form of middle managers, those most likely influenced by the departing leaders . . . and that's when the need for true change begins.

"My biggest challenge is to motivate those remaining to accept the new order of things, and inspire them to do better jobs because rapid improvement is a necessity in a troubled company. Unfortunately, some of the remaining middle managers don't have the wherewithal to make the switch to the new way of thinking. They continue to do business in the unsuccessful manner of their former bosses and suffer the same fate."

Richard's story is instructive. Coaching can only take hold when those being coached accept the absolute need for change. In such cases, motivating employees and inspiring them are of paramount importance. Otherwise, the required changes may not work as effectively and as quickly as needed. It's something to keep in mind when you assume a new leadership role in your company and you become the coach or leader being coached. Effective coaching is not automatic. It happens because smart, hard-working leaders make it happen.

16

Practice 5: Master Communication

Burt was production manager of a small machine shop. The company had been going through some rough times and employees were on edge, apprehensive about their jobs.

The company owner had been working on a merger that promised to pump extra cash into the business and increase sales through the addition of a supplemental line of products.

Unfortunately, he failed to let Burt and his employees know in time, and Burt lost most of his highly skilled welding crew to a competitor across town. The company hustled to hire hard-to-find replacements, but not in time to prevent a really bad quarter. The business came close to shutting down.

> *Hands-On Advice: There's no substitute for keeping employees in the information loop.*

As a leader it's your responsibility to show employees that you really care about them by keeping them posted on company plans, results, and problems.

Since the 2008 downturn in the economy, people feel vulnerable and overwhelmed. They are also worried about cutbacks and layoffs. Communicate everything to them by letting them know what is happening in your company, team, or department. Open the lines of communication and let people know that you care about their job performance and about their personal lives. Effective leaders place a high value on human capital.

Another major leadership issue is information sharing, keeping people in the loop so they can perform their jobs efficiently. I always say, "Communicate, communicate, communicate, communicate . . . and then communicate even more!" You must have open lines of communication up and down all levels of the organization. I believe in the KISS principle (keep it simple, stupid or keep it short and sweet). Simple things move through an organization faster, eliminate clutter, and reflect greater clarity.

When communicating, leaders must use different formats to get their message across: newsletters, emails, one-on-one or group meetings, and town halls. The most important goal is clarity. Often, leaders know what they want to communicate, but they fail to communicate clearly. When speaking, our tone of voice or inflection may have different meanings to people from diverse backgrounds and levels of experience. As such, it's incumbent upon leaders to communicate in a way that's clearly understood, without confusion, ambiguity, or misinterpretation.

Poor communication is one reason so many initiatives fail. Think carefully about how you express yourself, and develop a communication plan. How you communicate with people will vary, depending on the recipients and their positions in the organization, the parts of the initiative you want to share with them, and the timing of the communication.

Leaders and organizations can never take communication for granted; they need to think of it as a product. This requires them to take an occasional communication inventory: looking at all current channels, vehicles, systems, and networks to find out who communicates to whom. Then, analyze the communication system and make it as effective as you would any other system in the organization.

Improving Communicating Ability

More than half of what we communicate comes from body language. The way you carry yourself is important. Stand upright. Sit in your chair. Look like a leader. If your body language doesn't match your job title, what message do you send?

What is your tone of voice? How do you project what you say? Are you clear and direct, or do you mumble, with no passion in your voice? What about your vocal quality? Is it even, or do you sound high-pitched and overly excited? Surprisingly, spoken words account for less than 10 percent of communication. How you say it (tone of voice), along with your body language, will determine whether your staff hears what you say.

Effective leaders hold regular team meetings, conduct individual meetings, are accessible, and set SMART goals: specific, measurable, achievable, realistic, and time-based. The SMART system allows you to communicate goals so people can understand them.

Andrew Identifies a Key Issue in Communication

While conducting a leadership development program for a company, a participant named Andrew approached me. He said he wanted to discuss how he could more effectively communicate as a leader. "One thing I find in our organization," he said, "is that leaders often know what they want to do and say, but they have trouble communicating and articulating their thoughts and ideas so everyone clearly understands the directive."

I thought about Andrew's statement and realized how many times I'd witnessed this problem in the past. I, myself, had been in similar situations as an employee, given unclear and confusing directives. And as a leader, I had been conscious of how I came across. This triggered memories of something that happened a few years ago, when I was giving a speech.

Beatriz's Engaging Smile

I was the keynote speaker at a conference whose theme was leadership and team building. As a speaker, I work hard to make sure I'm clearly communicating my thoughts and ideas to the audience. One practice I always apply to make an immediate connection with my audience is to scan the room, making direct eye contact with as many people as possible and drawing positive energy from them.

As I did this, I made eye contact with a woman sitting in the third row. Every time I made a key point, she would nod her head and smile. As I made key point after key point, she kept nodding her head and smiling.

"Wow, this is great!" I thought to myself. "I'm really communicating with her and the rest of the audience. I hope she'll not only take the information I'm providing back to her job and use it to become a better leader, but also share it with her peers to make them better leaders."

As I finished my presentation and made my final key point, I looked at her again. She gave me a giant smile and nod. "I really hit a home run!" I thought. "I really connected with this group! What a wonderful speech I just gave!" When I walked off the platform that day, I was feeling great. I headed to the scheduled group luncheon.

I was standing in the lobby, talking with one of the conference's organizers, when I spotted, out of the corner of my eye, the woman who had given me such great feedback. She was sitting all by herself, so I decided to walk over and thank her for being so attentive.

"Hi. I'm Jeff Wolf, and I want to thank you for being so attentive today. I hope you were able to pick up useful information."

As I reached out to shake Beatriz's hand, she looked up at me, with her great big smile, and said, "No speak English."

Talk about a humbling experience! I felt ridiculous because I thought I was doing such a great job! When communicating, leaders must take responsibility for making sure everyone understands. We know what we want to say. So, how do we communicate it to the team, staff, or company? How do we ensure everyone will understand what we mean and what we say? I mistakenly took Beatriz's understanding for granted.

Just then, another conference planner came over to speak with me. "Hi, Jeff. I'm so glad you've met my niece," she said. "She just flew in from Italy last night and doesn't speak a word of English. I thought I'd bring her here today and let her sit in the audience because we have a family function later tonight, and I didn't want to drive all the way home to pick her up and come back this way again."

I had to remind myself that I'm always communicating, and I can never take this for granted.

Are You Listening?

The second aspect of leadership communication is listening—the receiving end of any conversation or dialogue. Great leaders are great listeners who generate a powerful connectivity among people. As Betsy Sanders, a senior vice president for Nordstrom, once said, "To learn through listening means that you listen openly, ready to learn something, as opposed to listening defensively, ready to rebut. Listening actively means you acknowledge what you heard and act accordingly."

Here are some tips for active listening:

- Be in the moment. Give the person your full attention. Try not to think about how you will respond. Suspend judgment about the person's statements.
- Lubricate the conversation with phrases like "uh-huh," "yes," and "so" to show you're listening. As for body language, be sure to nod your head and lean forward.
- Periodically paraphrase. Restate what you've heard to test your understanding.
- Avoid interruptions. Don't interrupt and try to finish their statements or interject your thoughts before they finish.
- Periodically clarify the other person's meaning by using open-ended, probing questions.
- Slow down. Leaders are sometimes moving at such a fast pace that they don't slow down to take the time to listen to their people.

When people feel listened to and heard, they become energized, which generates connectivity between people and leads to powerful conversations!

Write down three things you learned from your employees last week. It could be a process, an idea for improvement, a customer challenge, or a team issue.

If you can't list three things, you probably haven't been listening carefully enough to your employees.

The average speaker can deliver 140 words per minute. The average listener can comprehend 300 words per minute. We fill in the dead space in our conversations with distractions: looking out the window, talking to ourselves, anticipating the speaker's intent.

Nuances of Nonverbal Communication

In human interactions, communication is not limited to verbal interchanges or the use of language. Nonverbal communication is extraordinarily powerful and has been the subject of study by many social scientists, philosophers, and psychologists. It is defined as all wordless communication, including hand gestures, posture, facial expressions, and eye contact. Additional components of body language include vocal intonation, speaking style, speed, and tone, each of which affects how you communicate in the workplace.

Nonverbal communication is thought to be more unconscious than verbal communication. While you have to think about language before using words, nonverbal communication, whether we're talking about a smile, laugh, facial expression, or hand movement, is usually unplanned.

While vocabularies and languages are considerably different across cultures, nonverbal communication remains universal, understood globally. People from Massachusetts to Morocco will understand a smile or a frown.

Kinesics, the science of interpreting body language, was first introduced in 1952 by American anthropologist Ray Birdwhistell. He studied how people communicate in social situations, to include posture, stance, movement, and gestures.

In both your personal and professional life, your posture is defined by how you lean, your body's orientation, arm position, and degree of relaxation. Gestures are the movements and signals you use to communicate, such as waving, winking, rolling the eyes, nodding, and pointing. Some gestures can be interpreted in more than one way. Wink at a colleague who's a good friend, and it's a tacit acknowledgment of your relationship. Wink at a secretary on her first day of work, and she may be offended.

Zachary Wings It and Loses His Audience

Zachary, a professor of geology, was nationally recognized for his scientific expertise. His research on mineralogy had been published in numerous journals.

As an academic, Zachary was old school. Picture clichéd representations of Ivy League–educated scholars: a graying beard, a tweed jacket with well-worn patches, a bowtie worn with a button-down Oxford shirt— and you'll have an accurate mental snapshot of Zachary's appearance.

In the classroom, Zachary was not the most charismatic speaker, but he was a virtual geological encyclopedia. He could respond to students' questions with lightning speed and toss off bits of mineralogical trivia that maintained their interest. His colleagues respected his breadth of knowledge and often consulted him when they needed an interesting statistic, anecdote, or citation.

Sophia, dean of the geology department, asked Zachary to speak at the upcoming annual continuing education conference, a weekend series of seminars that drew scientists, high school teachers, college professors, research fellows, and graduate students from across the country. Zachary had lectured at this event numerous times, but this year there was a catch: Sophia asked him to speak on a topic he had never before covered in depth, one that would require a decent amount of new research.

Zachary brainstormed fresh topics and gave Sophia a perfunctory description of his lecture, which she accepted without complaint. She trusted him fully and assumed he would rise to the challenge.

Zachary, however, was always swamped, and he waited until the last minute to prepare his lecture. He assumed his body of knowledge would carry him through the presentation. But three months after he filed his synopsis with Sophia, all he had were some notes on a few pages of legal paper, with no photographic slides or PowerPoint graphics. Busy grading final exams, Zachary decided he would wing it at the conference, now just three days away. This would prove to be a bad decision.

On the first day of the conference, almost 1,200 attendees flocked to the campus to hear 12 nationally recognized experts lecture on new geologic trends. Zachary, the only professor to represent his university, was scheduled to speak after the lunch break, and he felt a knot in his stomach.

Reality was setting in: the highly experienced lecturer, with more than 15 years of teaching under his belt, had failed to prepare adequately. He tried to stay calm by reminding himself that he had given hundreds of lectures in his lifetime. This one, he reasoned, shouldn't be any different.

When Sophia introduced Zachary, he rose from his chair and placed his notes on the lectern. What happened next could only be called a debacle: Zachary spoke into the microphone, but his normally confident voice came out as a scratchy whisper. He began to follow his notes, but soon realized they were disjointed and disorganized.

As Zachary became increasingly uncomfortable and self-conscious, he felt beads of sweat form on his forehead and noticed that his shirt was also becoming damp. This caused him to lose focus and stumble over his words. His eyebrows were knitted together, he became pale, and his hands looked shaky as he gestured a bit too wildly. His eyes, fixated on the notes he had scribbled, seldom made contact with his audience.

How will I get through this? Zachary said to himself, realizing with dismay that he had minimized the importance of practicing his presentation. He rambled on, pulling tidbits of basic information from his undergraduate lectures and hiding behind the glasses he repeatedly pushed up his nose. The material was old hat to his audience, and he saw people shifting in their chairs and growing restless. Those who knew him were exchanging puzzled glances, wondering why one of the most prepared professors in the department was off topic and fumbling so badly.

Zachary filled all 60 minutes of his speech, but he and everyone else knew it was a disaster. Afterward, Zachary tried to slip out the door, but Sophia confronted him, hands on hips. "What happened?" she asked.

"I had a script and stuck to it," Zachary replied defensively. For Sophia, this was a nonanswer, and she worried that attendees who had never seen Zachary at his best would write him off as an addled, absent-minded professor who was ill-prepared, monotonous, and academically unsound. She told Zachary she was disappointed in his performance and worried attendees would lose respect for the department.

Zachary replied in anger: "Listen Sophie, you're overreacting."

Sophia's mouth tightened. "I'm sorry, but I don't think you understand the ramifications of what just happened. People paid a lot of money for this conference, and they may not return for future programs."

Zachary nodded curtly but remained silent. His jaw muscles rippled.

"Zachary, you of all people know how prospective graduate students judge the quality of the department based on its professors' performance. This performance, if that's what you want to call it, may steer high school teachers to recommend different colleges. Working geologists and professors from other universities will have a laugh at your expense, wondering why you lost it up there. I'm sorry, Zachary, but today's showing was an embarrassment—and it was bad for business."

Zachary was fuming as he left the room, but deep down he knew Sophia was right. He'd blown it, and his frantic body language had exposed his anxiety, disorganization, and poor preparation.

Functions of Nonverbal Communication

It's vital to understand how we communicate, not just the meaning of the words we speak. As a leader or manager, you should explore how nonverbal communication serves many functions:

- Repetition. Gestures, such as nodding, serve to reinforce what's being said. A nod of the head is, in fact, one of the most universal gestures, understood across many cultures as an agreement or understanding between two people.

- Substitution. Substitution involves replacing a spoken word with a nonverbal cue. You can nod your head without saying a word or wave your hand instead of saying good-bye. You haven't uttered a word, yet you have communicated effectively.
- Complement. A smile or pat on the back can complement words of enthusiasm or praise.
- Accenting. You may accent a particular word in a sentence, such as "I am *very* disappointed in you!" A strong tone of voice dramatizes the message.
- Misleading or deceiving. Can you tell when an employee is lying? Detecting deception is usually based on nonverbal cues. Facial expressions, body movements, and tone of voice will often expose the truth versus lies in criminal investigations.

Improving Nonverbal Communication

Workplace communication, whether verbal or nonverbal, drives all activity between you and your vendors, customers, and coworkers.

So, how do you improve it as you listen to and speak with others?

Step 1: Watch yourself . . . and others. When communicating, focus on the use of your body. The goal is to increase the expressive nature of your body, when appropriate, without being overdramatic. Be aware that gestures are often more useful with groups such as in meetings and presentations. If a person's words fail to match his nonverbal cues, it's best to trust the nonverbal messages. Listen with your eyes. In most cases, the nonverbal message is more accurate.

Step 2: Maintain eye contact. Eye contact is crucial when speaking with anyone, particularly coworkers, superiors, or direct reports. It promotes trust and understanding. Try to increase eye contact when speaking with others, and see if they're making and maintaining eye contact with you. If someone avoids eye contact, you'll likely sense the person's discomfort or dishonesty. You can ease another's discomfort by asking questions that enhance communication.

Step 3: Work on your posture. Your mother emphasized the need to stand up straight and avoid slouching in your chair. As it turns out, Mom was giving you your first lesson in nonverbal communication. Posture is a nonverbal indicator of confidence level.

A gesture conveys a message by using one part of the body, whereas a postural shift involves the movement of the body as a whole. A closed posture (folded arms and crossed legs) indicates a closed personality and a lack of confidence. Open posture (arms spread in a relaxed manner) is a much more confident pose. Posture should also be in sync with conversations so you avoid sending mixed messages. When you're sitting behind your desk or at a meeting table, sit up straight. Don't slump; it conveys disinterest and inattention. Leaning back, or rocking back and forth in your chair, tells others you're bored. In contrast, leaning forward in your chair when listening to someone speak demonstrates active interest in both the person and conversation.

Step 4: Straighten your desk. A sloppy desk or office sends the message that you're disorganized and careless. Messy desks may be a symptom of a larger problem such as inefficiency, which stems from an inability to find files or other important papers. Disorganization creates stress and limits productivity. Instead of creating vertical piles on your desk, rely on to-do files that can be stored inside a drawer.

Step 5: Read your audience. If you're making a presentation, be aware of your audience's nonverbal communication. As your presentation progresses, watch for signs of slouching, yawning, or dozing off; this means you've lost their attention. If, on the other hand, the group is energized and interested, participants' body language may convey that they want you to ask for their thoughts and input. Learning to read a group's mood enhances your abilities as both a speaker and manager.

Step 6: Listen to your voice. Paralanguage, or paralinguistics, involves the various fluctuations in one's voice, such as tone, pitch, rhythm, inflection, and volume. These cues can have a powerful effect on communication. A loud or very forceful tone, for example, may convey a stronger and more serious message, as compared to softer tones. Sarcasm can also cause problems in the workplace. A manager's sarcastic tone creates stress because his tone (joking) is meant to contradict his words (hurtful or biting).

Step 7: Question yourself. Throughout the day, monitor your progress. Ask yourself the following questions about your performance: How was I perceived at the meeting? Could I have done something differently? Were people really interested and paying attention to what I was saying? Did I listen well to others? As you answer these questions, your self-awareness will increase.

Lucille Slams the Door

At age 49, Lucille was the marketing director for a nonprofit legal clinic. She had come aboard five years earlier, having handled marketing efforts for a small real estate firm. At the previous job, she was a one-woman band, and she had limited experience in managing employees.

Lucille was not well liked by her colleagues. Even Rodney, the clinic's affable CEO, merely seemed to tolerate her. Many of Lucille's peers and direct reports sensed she was unhappy in her personal and professional life, and they detected an underlying insecurity that tainted her efforts to communicate with others. Far from shy, Lucille had no qualms about blasting those around her when she was frustrated or didn't get her way.

To complicate matters, Lucille seemed to have only one facial expression: sour, with the occasional scowl thrown in. Colleagues and potential clients never saw her smile or laugh, and they were puzzled by the stark incongruence between her job responsibilities, which were heavy on personal interactions, and her attitude, which was considerably low on warmth and expression of even the most basic emotions.

Clients had mixed reactions to Lucille's humorless persona. Some would complain to the higher-ups that she lacked empathy and didn't seem to care about them. For others, Lucille's lack of warmth didn't seem to pose a problem, but no one had ever raved about interactions with her.

Lucille's direct reports were in a constant state of flux. They often complained about her, and turnover was much higher in her department, as compared to other departments within the organization. She simply couldn't retain employees, many of whom showed great competence, as her managerial style matched her uninspired and cheerless visage.

While Lucille's job description required her to regularly produce glossy brochures and other marketing materials that featured happy client testimonials and photos, her somber communication style and facial expressions often put people off.

Why, exactly, did the legal clinic put up with Lucille's dour persona? As it turned out, CEO Rodney, 67, had developed cardiovascular problems over the past few years and was in the office fewer than two days a week. He trusted his department heads to run the show, for better or for worse, and annual employee reviews were essentially rubber-stamped. The truly effective department heads were loyal to the legal clinic because they enjoyed their work and were passionate about supporting the nonprofit's mission, but they winced every time they were forced to deal with Lucille.

Five years into Lucille's tenure, Rodney was facing heart surgery and finally decided to retire. The legal clinic's board of directors screened about a dozen candidates and soon hired Caleb, a younger, more ambitious, and very hands-on leader. The clinic's most successful, respected, and well-liked department heads relished the opportunity to work with such a dynamic, collaborative, and passionate leader.

Predictably, Lucille took a dislike to Caleb shortly after his arrival. Each day, the amiable and people-focused Caleb would stop by and chat with department heads. This was bad news for Lucille, who considered herself a lone wolf and avoided contact with others whenever possible.

It didn't take long for friction to develop between Caleb and Lucille. He was upbeat; she was grim. He smiled and gave people pats on the back; she never returned the favor. As Caleb completed his first month, he began to grow weary of Lucille's gloomy facial expressions, not to mention her listless tone of voice and generally unfriendly vibe. He called her into his office for a counseling session and told her she would need to change her approach to her work relationships.

Unfazed, Lucille continued to behave in her ingrained ways, and she was now carrying one of the world's largest chips on her shoulder. Her interactions with colleagues became even more contentious, bordering on tortuous. Lucille resorted to slamming her office door when she wanted to express her displeasure, a hostile act that proved, yet again, the power of nonverbal communication.

Caleb had just about all he could take. He issued a written warning to Lucille about her attitude and behavior, wherein he described potential consequences if Lucille continued to exhibit her status-quo behavior. Over the next month, the butting of heads never ceased, and the whole office was soon succumbing to the strain. People were jumpy, and nerves were becoming frayed. The actions of one person were creating a hostile work environment, and Caleb knew the war would have to end ASAP. He fired Lucille, who was shocked by his betrayal of her loyalty to the organization.

And, yes, Lucille slammed the door on her way out.

About Face

In their book, *Toy Box Leadership* (Thomas Nelson, 2009), communication experts Ron Hunter Jr. and Michael E. Waddell note that people have six universal facial expressions: happiness, sadness, fear, anger, disgust, and surprise. They describe the face as an "extension of emotions" and "interpreter of intent" and urge leaders to bring eight faces to work: (1) empathetic, (2) confident, (3) intense, (4) attentive, (5) happy, (6) sincere, (7) optimistic, (8) disappointed.

Such expressions are vital factors in workplace communication.

Empathy. Defined as identification with, and understanding of, another's situation, feelings, and motives, empathy allows you to put yourself in others' shoes. It fosters connectedness with your boss, colleagues, direct reports, and clients, embodying your ability to listen—and really hear—what others are feeling, experiencing, and trying to say. Your facial expressions communicate whether you do or don't understand others' situations, revealing more about your true inner feelings than words ever could. Academy Award–winning actress Susan Sarandon, known for fully inhabiting the characters she plays by placing herself in their shoes, once said: "When you start to develop your powers of empathy and imagination, the whole world opens up to you." Managers and leaders can experience a similar payoff.

Confidence. Your confidence level depends on belief in yourself and your inner strength, as well as your ability to handle life's ups and downs without chastising yourself. Psychoanalyst Sigmund Freud believed confidence and our sense of self are initially imbued in us by our parents. "If a man has been his mother's undisputed darling, he retains throughout life the triumphant feeling, the confidence in success, which not seldom brings actual success along with it."

This confidence, or lack thereof, ultimately follows us into our adult years, which can have a direct impact on our ability to build and retain workplace relationships.

Our bosses, colleagues, and direct reports want to see our confidence, which we convey through facial expressions and other forms of nonverbal communication. According to Hunter and Waddell, confidence shows others whether we have a positive sense of identity (knowing who we are), purpose (comfort with our goals), and competence (whether we can lead and get the job done).

A lack of confidence is contagious. If you're feeling wobbly, your staff will pick up on your nonverbal cues and begin to feel anxious. Your boss may start to question your ability, even if you've had a terrific track record. And your colleagues will gather at the water cooler to discuss whether you've lost your edge.

Joe Paterno, one of the best college football coaches, believed his team could not win without feeling and exhibiting confidence. Losing, he noted, was inevitable if his team failed to play with "supreme confidence," and he warned that self-doubt could become a habit that seriously impacts performance. Paterno also believed in a shared sense of confidence, in which "a team outgrows individual performance and learns team performance," thereby setting the stage for collective excellence. Perhaps this explains Paterno's ability to win more football games than any other collegiate coach.

Intensity. Your level of intensity determines how passionate you are about your job, and your face will communicate to your boss, colleagues, team members, and direct reports exactly where you stand. "Success as a leader is defined by your ability to persuade with clarity and passion," writes body language and motivation expert John Boe in *Principles of Persuasion*. "Leadership is synonymous with effective communication."

When you gather your team for a meeting or give a presentation, it will take your audience all of five seconds to determine whether you have the right intensity and passion required to motivate them. Your words won't be the giveaway; chalk it up to your facial expressions, body language, and other forms of nonverbal communication—all of which reveal your true feelings.

Facial expressions will out you if you're a phoning-it-in type of leader. Media mogul Oprah Winfrey has described passion as energy and advises others to "feel the power that comes from focusing on what excites you." Only then will your team members mirror your behavior.

Attentiveness. Paying close attention to others requires that you look into their eyes as they're speaking and show them the respect they deserve when listening. Humility is crucial. You must be willing to focus on others' needs and temporarily put yours on the back burner. Think back to your childhood: How did you behave when you failed to get your parents' attention? Odds are you acted out, provoking them to respond with negative attention, an unpleasant outcome, but something you emotionally craved over their seemingly intolerable inattention. Now, the bigger question: Have you ever watched yourself do something similar at work?

Each of us, at some point or another, will react as we did as children and play out a scene that may have taken place more than 30 years ago, when we were still living under our parents' roof. The circumstances at work may be different, but the response is the same, and it's not pretty when you inadvertently blow off a colleague's or direct report's comments or concerns. If they act out, probe into what caused their reaction. Often, a manager's inattentiveness is the prime suspect.

Attentiveness also requires you to make the person (or people) with whom you're speaking the center of this moment's universe. Your face will either encourage or discourage others from honestly communicating with you. Unfortunately, many leaders are too immersed in their own priorities and deadlines, so they fail in the attentiveness department. All interactions require leaders to promote confidence and put others at ease.

Happiness. Happiness may seem like an obvious requirement for establishing relationships with others, but as Lucille's story demonstrates, it's not obvious to everyone. For Lucille, it was her Achilles' heel. Miserable people share the wealth with those around them, and it's the proverbial gift that keeps on giving. If we're happy, we create an invigorating culture. If we're unhappy, others will feel down, even anxious, when dealing with us. Still, no one expects you to skip through hallways and plaster a smile on your face 24/7. Think of happiness as a measure of satisfaction—the pleasure you take in collaborating with others, accomplishing tasks, meeting goals, and motivating your team.

Susan Brooks, cofounder of Cookies From Home, describes a visit to a new restaurant. Her attempt to enjoy a nice dinner turned into a comedy of errors. The family-style restaurant boasted signs and menu descriptions that focused on customer satisfaction. Actions, however, always trump words, and nothing about the eatery offered a happy dining experience:

- The hostess barely made eye contact, and her body language was stiff. She ignored Brooks and focused on her seating chart, which led the restaurant's newest customer to wonder why workers seem to get more attached to the process rather than the human connection.
- When Brooks was finally seated and able to place her order, her server brought a delicious-looking chicken casserole. As Brooks enthusiastically took her first bite, the entrée scalded her mouth, and the server was nowhere to be found.
- Brooks also had to repeatedly ask for silverware, beverage refills, and the check, and she was consistently kept waiting—all signs of inattention to customers.
- The ultimate slight was the manager's response to Brooks' request to bring the check and pack up her leftovers. When he returned, he silently placed two takeout containers in front of her, demonstrating absolutely no intention of wrapping up the remnants of her less-than-satisfactory meal.

The restaurant staff and manager seemed to live in a customer service abyss, guilty of inattention and unhappiness with their jobs. All aspects of their nonverbal communication did them in, and they were apparently too busy to form words. If you're dissatisfied with your job, there's no effective way to mask your feelings. Your facial expressions, nonverbal communication, and resultant actions will show you're simply not there. Dissatisfy a customer, and word-of-mouth will put you out of business.

In contrast, facial expressions that convey your satisfaction set the stage for a productive business environment.

Sincerity. Many of us have had a boss tell us to keep talking while she checked her smartphone or listen to a team leader who pronounces our name wrong. Insensitivity is the hallmark of tone-deaf managers. They have no problem checking their messages or emails while others are talking, or cutting off people in the middle of a thought to summarily dismiss their ideas. The condition is epidemic, leading many companies to hire executive coaches to provide sensitivity training. Facial expressions convey sincerity or insincerity, honesty or dishonesty. Instinctively, we know when someone is being insincere. Don't make this mistake with your colleagues, as it will undermine trust and foster ill will.

Dave was an area manager for a large retail chain. Every month he would visit each store in his territory and spend two hours with the manager of each store. The purpose of Dave's visit was to build a deeper relationship with each manager through face-to-face meetings, since most of his communication was by phone, instant message, and email.

The problem, highlighted in his 360 feedback, was that when Dave made his visit, he paid more attention to incoming emails and phone calls then he did to his managers. Hence, they felt unimportant and unheard!

Upon receiving this feedback, I suggested that Dave leave his phone in the car so he could spend quality time with each one of his managers. As a result, morale improved and his meetings became highly successful.

This is a common problem. All of us feel tethered to our smartphones. It's great to stay up-to-date but it can interfere with relationships. We can't allow our voice communication via smartphone to detract from face-to-face communications.

Optimism. Optimism is more complex than viewing yourself and others as glass-half-full versus glass-half-empty kind of people. Optimism can give companies a competitive edge. Employees are more engaged, so productivity soars. Companies grow, even in tough times, and reap higher profits. Leaders need to be optimism ministers; their facial expressions must convey optimism. You need to monitor yourself for smirking, pouting, glaring, eye-rolling, and other nonverbal signs of displeasure. Make a choice to express optimism by smiling and maintaining eye contact.

Disappointment. Bad news, including product failures, a drop in profit, and employee layoffs can't be conveyed with a smile. It requires empathy and sincerity, which serve as testaments to legitimate disappointment. Disappointment is also appropriate when an employee's work fails to meet your standards. I'm not talking about scorn, hostility, insults, or anger. Remember: You're unhappy with the project's outcome or employee's behavior, not the individual. You can express disappointment with facial expressions that mirror your words, without making matters personal and annihilating an individual's spirit and future commitment. And when the employee does rally to complete the task and ultimately succeeds, offer verbal praise and nonverbal reinforcement: a pat on the back, handshake, huge smile, even a fist bump.

Technology Conundrum

Because we rely so heavily on our ability to decode facial expressions, technology has the potential to create problems for us. Telephone communication, for example, sends your words across a network of wires or cellular towers, but it lacks facial expressions. The same applies to e-mail, texting, and voice messages, which may explain why some people prefer these communication modes, particularly leaders who aren't as personally invested in their business relationships. Introverts also like to rely on these forms of communication to remove themselves from personal interactions.

Email and texting have been shown to be a less reliable means of communicating and probably less accurate, particularly if the content is sensitive and we lack the ability to see others' facial expressions.

Videoconferencing has replaced the need for many in-person business meetings, but it can also be frustrating: the image on the screen is often delayed as your computer processes it.

Videoconferencing also limits simultaneous natural exchanges, as many of the nonverbal signals that accompany our words are missing.

Should we therefore abandon these technologies? No. But we should use them appropriately, with routine matters, and never for disciplinary hearings, terminations, performance reviews, and other highly personal and potentially combustible interactions. As George Clooney's character proved in the hit film *Up in the Air*, firing someone via videoconference isn't the optimal way to handle such sensitive issues.

Takeaway from Chapter 16

In the following multipart exercise, I don't want you to evaluate your performance; instead you're going to evaluate your boss's nonverbal communication skills. Use these eight factors to complete your evaluation: (1) empathy, (2) confidence, (3) intensity, (4) attentiveness, (5) happiness, (6) sincerity, (7) optimism, and (8) disappointment. For each of the eight factors, write a short description of how well or how poorly your boss performs.

Now have a trusted associate familiar with your boss's work perform the same evaluation, but don't allow her to read your evaluation.

When you're done, compare evaluations. Chances are you'll both agree on some factors . . . but not on others. Whoa, you say, what gives?

What gives is that perception is everything. We all react in somewhat different ways to our bosses, depending on our psychological makeup and experiences, and the least skilled bosses tend to react in different ways to each of the employees working for them. This is especially true in nonverbal communications where people are often guilty of revealing their true feelings. As a leader you need to treat everybody equally, especially those who work for you if you want to avoid being accused of playing favorites, and nowhere is it as easy to slip up as in nonverbal communications.

Practice 6: Build an Optimal Team

Strong teams have defined expectations, clear goals, and a shared vision, and the personal and team discipline to achieve them. This discipline is built into the team structure, systems, processes, strategy, philosophies, values, policies, and plans. People want to work in a culture of high values, ethics, honesty, and discipline. They will sacrifice some degree, even a high degree, of personal freedom in exchange for team wins. Great leaders attract the best and brightest, and then turn them loose. They create a pipeline of talented and creative people. A leader's upbeat attitude becomes contagious, lifting the morale of all. Without highly motivated, inspired, and disciplined people, teams and organizations struggle.

Effective leaders are team builders. They understand that bringing people together creates harmony and allows them to work collaboratively toward achieving successes they never could accomplish alone. In truth, strong teams will make or break an organization.

A valuable team focuses on the same priorities and sees the big picture. The group learns to communicate better and respect one another, forging strong relationships and trust. Team building improves accountability and fosters rapport. When you're working on a team, there's no place to hide. If Mary and Lester don't get their jobs done, then I can't do my job, which means we're personally accountable to each other. When team members function well, they develop a satisfying camaraderie.

There are several key components to highly effective teams:

- Goals—a sense of purpose and direction.
- Roles—who does what, when, and where.
- Processes and procedures—how things get done and how decisions are made.
- Relationships—how people get along.
- Leadership—providing inspiration and guidance.

To Build a Strong Team, Trade "Me" for "We"

"Talent wins games, but teamwork and intelligence wins championships," basketball great Michael Jordan once said.

Each of us should embrace this profound bit of wisdom from the superstar who won five MVP awards over the span of his career, the man who was also named the greatest North American athlete of the twentieth century by ESPN. You will face unnecessary challenges and certain defeats if you fail to build a strong team. Why, then, do so many leaders and managers flounder when they are charged with leading a team?

In many cases, leaders limit their focus to their own performance: how they will be judged by their CEOs or shareholders, whether completion of a specific task will garner the admiration of others, or how they will be compensated personally for their achievements. Just like toddlers, they want to be the center of attention at all times, and everyone else is supposed to orbit their sun.

Remember the old axiom about checking your ego at the door? Adopt it as a mantra, to be repeated as you arrive at your office each day. In its most basic form, team building requires you to trade *me* and *my* for *we* and *our*. Great leaders understand that their ultimate success depends on the combined forces of a highly skilled group.

Scott Snair, author of *West Point Leadership Lessons: Duty, Honor, and Other Management Principles* (Sourcebooks, September 2, 2005), refers to a team's cooperative efforts as being part of something bigger than any individual. As president of his 1988 West Point class, a platoon leader during Operation Desert Storm and now a respected business consultant, he realizes that the team that builds on the individual strengths of its members eventually becomes a whole that's much greater than the sum of its parts.

Duke University basketball coach Mike Krzyzewski would agree: "To me, teamwork is the beauty of our sport, where you have five acting as one. You become selfless. Your job, as a leader, is to build team morale and effectiveness by determining what motivates those you supervise. You must, therefore, build one-on-one relationships with each member of your team, a strategy that will allow you to identify each member's core strengths and weaknesses. You can then play to each employee's strengths during team meetings and projects, setting up each individual to succeed."

Kelley Holland, a former *New York Times* contributing business columnist, says building optimal teams is even more important during tumultuous economic times. The good news, she wrote, "is that what works is often fairly simple and inexpensive."

Six Essential Leadership Responsibilities That Build Effective Teams

To create a fully functional team, the leader needs to exhibit six leadership traits.

1. *Build trust.* Trust is a three-way street: A. You must be able to trust each member of your team. B. They, in turn, must be able to trust you. C. Team members need to trust one another. Trust is earned, so set the stage for success by creating regular and ongoing team building opportunities. You can start with small projects involving two- and three-person teams. In due course, you'll want to expand team size and

the scope of assigned projects. Never compromise your team's trust in you by assigning a task that is well beyond their skills level. This managerial mistake sets them up for failure, and it can irreparably damage your relationship.

In their book *Leadership Styles: A Powerful Model,* professors Pierre Casse (Moscow School of Management) and Paul Claudel (Institut d'Administration des Entreprises, at Jean Moulin University) advise leaders to ask these questions before assigning a team project: Are my team members prepared to complete the task? Am I sure they have the required skills and experience? Do they understand the stated goal as well as how it fits into our departmental or company mission? Are they reliable and committed? Will they perform ethically? "The leader will have to make sure that team members want to be empowered and take the corresponding risks," write Casse and Claudel. "According to how much competence the team member demonstrates and how much the leader can trust him, different degrees of empowerment will be devolved."

2. *Communicate.* Watch any police drama on television, from TNT's gritty *Southland* to NBC's wildly successful *Law & Order* franchise, and you will notice how law enforcement officers remain in constant communication during tactical operations. Their lives depend on it.

You can't expect your team to understand and execute a task without clearly communicating your goals and objectives. In some cases, you will be a hands-on leader, participating in the task and offering close supervision. In other instances, you may assign a team leader, who will be charged with keeping you up-to-date on the task's progress.

This may sound easy, but communication remains "one of the greatest challenges in life, to say nothing of business life," writes business consultant and former U.S. Marine Corps reservist Dan Carrison in his book, *From the Bureau to the Boardroom,* (AMACOM, January 14, 2009).

Communication must flow in several directions: How you articulate your message. How others hear your words (the takeaway message). How well you listen to—and hear—what team members say.

Any glitch in these communication channels can lead to a major disconnect, even project failure. And if you rush through communication efforts, rattling off details without ensuring clear messaging or ending a meeting with "Got it? Okay, let's do it," you discourage team members from asking crucial questions that may make or break their endeavor.

As Carrison explains: When an FBI supervisor parts company with one of his or her street agents after discussing an upcoming operation, the supervisor does not walk away wondering if "Jones gets it," nor does Agent Jones ask himself, "What was I supposed to do?" Both the supervisor and the agent are of one mind.

Disney Communication: This is included in both the formal communication that is generated by the cast communications department of the Disney University as well as the informal communication delivered by line management. A weekly newsletter called *Eyes & Ears* is produced in-house to keep the 36,000 cast members informed of business updates. There are also divisional newsletters specific to the different work units to keep cast members informed about their location.

Communication goes beyond formal needs. Line managers keep the front-line cast members informed of new happenings, changes to schedules, and key events by holding informal talks before the shift starts at each location. Front-line managers take the log from the previous shift, check the staffing schedules, then get out in the area and manage by walking around. In fact, up to 75 percent of their day is spent out in the areas. This allows immediate attention to concerns around the parks and resorts and accessibility of cast members to management representatives.

3. *Offer sufficient resources and autonomy.* Teams fail when members lack the time and resources required to complete their assignment. Perform a reality check. Ask yourself how much time and how many tangible resources you would need to fulfill the project's demands. Next, determine whether your team, based on members' experience levels, requires more, less, or the same amount of time. Seek input from team members, asking them to honestly assess how long specific components of the task will take. Your goal is to develop an accurate, realistic timeline.

If you have chosen a team captain to lead a task, allow this person to delegate responsibilities as she sees fit. Make sure the captain knows the difference between delegation and abdication. The team captain's job is to set the vision, delineate strategies (often with the help of other team members), and provide the conditions and support needed for success.

As for autonomy, don't micromanage your team (or team captain). Give members an attainable goal and enough autonomy to complete it. Monitor progress, but avoid being overly intrusive. You're a manager—not a babysitter. Let team members feel empowered enough to embrace responsibilities and enjoy a sense of ownership. Remind the team that you are available if anyone needs a consultation.

Recognition programs exist at all the different locations at the Walt Disney World Resort. They are there to recognize those cast members who go above and beyond what is expected to help the company exceed guests' expectations. Guest comments and letters sent in are often used in recognizing this exemplary service. Cast members recognized for their exemplary service can receive anything from lunch with their boss to a stay in a Walt Disney World Resort hotel with their family. While these awards are appreciated, often favorite rewards include a reserved parking space close to the cast member's work location for a month or an "Applause-O-Gram" posted on a bulletin board describing the exemplary performance.

Disney rewards long-term cast members with promotions from within. They typically look internally to fill promotional opportunities before going outside to hire. Beginning with their 10-year anniversary, cast members are recognized every five years at a lavish service awards activity. In addition to a social event that includes bringing a guest, cast members also receive a plaque, a gold ring, or other distinctively Disney recognition awards for their longevity.

Disney has found that if it casts correctly for roles in its shows, provides initial orientation and on-the-job training, communicates effectively, and takes care of its cast members, it helps maintain the corporate culture that continues to lead to pride in the organization. This is why so many cast members smile and say,

"I am proud to work for Walt Disney World Co." This is what leads guests to say excitedly, "I am going to the Walt Disney World Resort!"

4. *Build self-efficacy.* Team members must know that you have confidence in their abilities to complete a task. They, in turn, must feel secure in meeting your goal.

If an employee feels uneasy about his role on the team, consider pairing him with a high-performing peer. This strategy can help boost the self-assurance of an employee who has not yet achieved self-efficacy—an individual's judgment of his ability to successfully complete a chosen task. Team members' self-efficacy will affect the choices they make when working on a task, as well as their doggedness when setbacks occur. It's your job as the leader to uncover employees' fears and barriers to success and alleviate their concerns, including shyness; self-consciousness; poor communication skills; fear of conflict; impatience with, or dislike of, other members of the team; and bias (gender, racial, ethnic).

5. *Hold team members accountable.* Every team member should be held to the same standard of excellence, regardless of training or years of experience on the job. While each person's precise task will vary, all team members' commitment to completing the job should be unwavering.

6. *Conduct routine debriefings.* FBI agents always debrief after a mission, Carrison notes, but the corporate world often reserves critiques for negative outcomes (fault-finding sessions). Small mistakes in an otherwise successful project may go overlooked, which tacitly implies they can be repeated in the future. Wildly successful efforts may be greeted with a mere "Nice job. Here's your next task . . . ," a true motivation killer.

Debriefings should focus on high and low points during the project's run. When you review your team's completed work, note individual performance and provide meaningful praise. Team members should be rewarded when they cooperate, coordinate, and share knowledge with coworkers. And when a team member fails to cooperate or complete his task, speak with him in your office. The meeting should be private, but team members should know that it is taking place—and that there are consequences for failing to pull one's weight or working well with others.

Before ending a debriefing, ask each team member to share thoughts on improving performance in the future: What would they change? Which steps could have been streamlined? Were any of the steps unnecessary? Were any steps overlooked? Are any procedures archaic . . . performed simply because they've always done it that way? Is a technology update in order? Was there any overlap or redundancy among team members' jobs?

You may be surprised at the constructive feedback you receive. Employees also appreciate that you value their opinions and suggestions, and that you're willing to make changes that solidify future team efforts.

Fuzzy Focus

If every member of your team has failed to complete assigned tasks, they may have fallen victim to fuzzy focus, according to Gayle Lantz, founder of the leadership consulting firm WorkMatters and author of the article (in *HR Planning*, 2007) "Team Building Blocks and Breakthroughs." Fuzzy focus occurs when teams have lost focus on results or members had never been clear about their goals in the first place, she writes. "Instead, they have become too internally fixated on other team members: judging what they are doing, making assumptions, back-stabbing, finger-pointing, etc."

Before blaming team members for an unsuccessful outcome, assess whether you, as their leader, fulfilled your responsibilities. Did you clearly explain your goals and expectations? Did you communicate effectively? Did you ask team members to describe, in their own words, their perceived role in completion of the task? Did you regularly check in with team members to ensure they were on the right course? Did you follow up, as necessary? Did you inspire them?

Building high-performing teams requires open communication, constructive dialogue, cooperation, and appreciation of what each person brings to the team.

High-performing teams have operating guidelines. They speak honestly and make direct requests, disagree respectfully, display a "we're all in this together attitude," and support team decisions.

To build a motivated team, leaders must create a culture where people are allowed to be heard, empower people to make decisions, encourage and welcome new ideas, and create positive energy.

Teamwork and Strong Teams

Effective leaders know that their organizations will realize substantial benefits by building strong teams to reach their objectives and strategic goals. Bringing people together on the same page is highly effective because people can accomplish more collectively than individually.

Every participant brings a unique skillset to the team. Some may be highly creative at coming up with new ideas, others may excel at details, and some have the ability to move the group's ideas forward and follow through to completion. It's very rare to find one person who has all of these skills. By working together and combining what everyone brings to the table, the group's goals will be realized much faster.

Teamwork also builds camaraderie and encourages open communication. When every member is focused on a single outcome, strong relationships and trust are built, one of the most important aspects of teamwork, if not the most important. Every team member must have complete trust in fellow participants as well as faith in others' desire to work in the best interests of the team and company.

When building a strong team, leaders should look at each member's strengths and abilities to determine whether the group can gel. When there's a good fit, teams combine their strengths to achieve the group's overall goals. Leaders should also nurture team growth and development to ensure everyone contributes in a positive way.

To build strong teams, develop a team culture that includes:

- Defined expectations, clear goals, objectives, and shared vision.
- An established timeline with individual and team accountability.

- A clearly articulated purpose for the team's existence.
- Team members' complete acknowledgment of the roles they play.
- Well-defined processes/procedures on how work will be done.
- Team access to all available resources required to reach the goal.
- A diverse team composed of members with complementary skills.
- Individual and group commitment to the work to be performed.
- The shared knowledge that each team member is valued and will be rewarded for hard work and effort.
- Clear, honest, and open communication among all team members.
- Rules of conduct, including steps to resolve any emerging conflicts.

As companies struggle to become more innovative, teams will become more important. Bringing together people with multiple skills and competencies leads to innovative products, services, and strategies.

Learning Teams

If you have trouble motivating your troops or working with your counterparts in other functions, then you'll probably agree that traditional top-down management has outlived its usefulness. The world is too complex for one leader to figure it all out and impose her views on the rest of the organization. The organizations that will excel in years to come will be those that understand how to gain the commitment of employees at all levels and continually expand their capacity to learn.

In the new learning organization, your people will aim high, learn to create the results they desire, and reap the bottom-line benefits necessary to sustain success in the global marketplace. Says Arie de Geus, head of planning for Royal Dutch Shell, "The ability to learn faster than your competitors may be the only sustainable competitive advantage." The learning organization is my view of what a corporation can and should be.

We Are Not the Enemy

Lois took over a team that had been run in the traditional top-down management style, with orders coming from the boss and trickling down to individual workers.

She never forgot her first day on the job when a worker told her, "Our last boss scowled at us, issued orders, and then checked our progress every step of the way. I had to tell him, 'Hey, we're not the enemy.'"

Lois never forgot that. It was like a mantra, stuck in the back of her mind. She made every effort to include her crew in decisions, and she succeeded.

> *Hands-On Advice: Treat employees with the same respect you would pay to your mother or father or somebody else influential in your life.*

Treating your staff with respect will keep you from slipping into the traditional command and control mode, something that's easy to do.

Six Learning Disabilities

Though we may see and think in straight lines, reality is made up of circles. Linear thinkers are always looking for a thing or person who is responsible. Systems thinkers take on greater responsibility for events, because their perspective suggests that everyone shares responsibility for problems generated by a system. The following six learning disabilities arise when we view the world in linear, not systematic, ways.

1. *I am my position.* Most people confuse their jobs with their identities ("I'm an accountant"). While they understand their daily tasks, they may not understand the purpose of the enterprises they take part in. Instead, they see themselves in a system in which they have little power and no need to take responsibility for poor results.

2. *The enemy is out there.* Some organizations and people find an external agent to blame when problems arise, a result of looking at the world in nonsystematic ways. Focused on our positions, we can't see how our actions have an effect beyond their boundaries.

Focusing on an external enemy is almost always a mistake. Usually "out there" and "in here" are part of the same system.

3. *Illusion of taking charge.* Proactive managers are encouraged and admired when they tackle problems fast. But is taking action against an enemy on the outside really proactive? This brand of proactive is reactive in disguise. Being truly proactive means seeing how we contribute to our own problems and solving those first.

4. *Fixation on events.* We're dominated by events: last month's sales, the new budget cuts, who got fired, product introductions, and so on. Events distract us from seeing long-term patterns of change that lie behind them, and that, of course, inhibits us from understanding these patterns. Slow, gradual processes like environmental decay, the erosion of the education system, or a decline in product quality are more destructive than sudden events.

5. *Delusion of learning best from experience.* We may learn best from experiences, but people often never experience the consequences of many of their most important decisions directly. It may take years, for instance, to see the consequences of R&D decisions.

6. *Myth of the management team.* In most organizations, a valiant, experienced, and savvy management team stands ready to do battle with problems and dilemmas. Nevertheless, teams in the business world tend to fight for turf and avoid anything that will make them look bad. To keep up the appearance of a cohesive team, they may hide disagreement and come up with watered-down decisions that everyone can live with.

Solution: Team Learning Discipline

The antidote to these learning disabilities and to the high mortality rate among companies is to practice the discipline of team learning.

Have you ever been involved with a team that functioned superbly? It may have been in business, school, or sports. People trusted each other, complemented each other's strengths, compensated for each other's weaknesses, aimed for goals higher than anyone might have dared individually, and, as a result, produced an extraordinary outcome. In such teams, each member is committed to continual improvement, each suspends judgment as to what's possible and removes mental limitations, each shares a vision of greatness, and the team's collective competence is far greater than any individual's. Team members recognize and understand the system in which they operate and how they can influence it.

These characteristics describe the essence of a learning organization. As with any team, the organization doesn't start off great, it learns to be great. Team learning is the process of aligning a team to avoid wasted energy and to create the results its members want. Team learning builds on the disciplines of shared vision and personal mastery because talented teams are, necessarily, made up of talented individuals. Because the IQ of a team can be much higher than that of any of its members, teams are becoming the key learning unit in organizations.

The discipline of team learning involves mastering the practices of dialogue and discussion. In discussion (a word with the same roots as percussion and concussion) views are presented and defended, and the team searches for the best view to support decisions. Participants in a discussion often want to win and see their view prevail. While dialogue and discussion can be complementary, most teams can't distinguish between them. The original meaning of the word dialogue, according to physicist David Bohm, suggests a free flow of meaning between people. Bohm contends that in dialogue a group accesses a "larger pool of common meaning" that can't be accessed by individuals alone. The purpose of dialogue, then, is to go beyond the understanding held by each team member, and to explore complex issues creatively from many points of view. After dialogue, decisions can be made and thus comes the need for discussion, where action is the focus.

Team Health

All the competitive advantages—strategy, technology, finance, marketing—that we've pursued in the past are gone. The disciplines haven't disappeared, but they have lost their power as meaningful competitive advantages, as real differentiators that can set your company apart. Why? Virtually every organization has access to the best thinking and practices on those topics. As information has become ubiquitous, it's almost impossible to sustain an advantage based on intellectual ideas.

However, one simple, reliable, and virtually free competitive advantage remains—team health. Healthy teams all but eliminate politics and confusion from their cultures. As a result, productivity and morale soar, and good people almost never leave. For those leaders who are a bit skeptical, rest assured that none of this is touchy-feely or soft. It is as tangible and practical as anything else . . . and even more important.

Even the smartest team will eventually fail if it is unhealthy. But a healthy team will find a way to succeed. Without politics and confusion, it will become smarter and tap into all of the intelligence and talent it has.

Team health requires real work and discipline, maintained over time, and the courage to objectively confront problems hindering true team achievement. Leaders must confront themselves, their peers, and the dysfunction within their teams with honesty and persistence. Persistent leaders walk into uncomfortable situations and address issues that prevent them from realizing the potential that eludes them.

Four Disciplines

To get healthy, leaders need to take four simple, but difficult, steps:

1. ***Build a cohesive leadership team.*** Get the leaders of the organization to behave in a functional, cohesive way. If the people responsible for running a team, department, or organization are behaving in dysfunctional ways, then that dysfunction will cascade down and prevent organizational health. And yes, there are concrete steps a leadership team can take to prevent this.

2. ***Create clarity.*** Ensure that the members of that leadership team are intellectually aligned around simple but critical questions. Leaders need to be clear on topics such as why the organization

exists and what the most important priority is for the next few months, and eliminate any gaps between them. Then people who work one, two, or three levels below have clarity about what they should do to make the organization successful.

3. *Overcommunicate clarity*. After the first two steps (behavioral and intellectual alignment), leaders can take the third step: over-communicating. Leaders of healthy organizations constantly repeat themselves and reinforce what is true and important. They err on the side of saying too much, rather than too little.

4. *Reinforce clarity*. Leaders use simple human systems to reinforce clarity in answering critical questions. They *custom* design any process that involves people from hiring and firing to performance management and decision-making to support and emphasize the uniqueness of the organization.

Healthy teams get better at meetings. Without making a few simple changes to the way meetings happen, a team will struggle to maintain its health. Healthy teams rarely fail. When politics, ambiguity, dysfunction, and confusion are reduced to a minimum, people are empowered to design products, serve customers, solve problems, and help one another. Healthy teams recover from setbacks, attract the best people, and create exciting opportunities. People are happier, the bottom line is stronger, and executives are at peace when they know they've fulfilled their most important responsibility: creating a culture of success.

Applying the principles of great performance is hard, but the effects of deliberate practice are cumulative. The more of a head start you get in developing people, the more difficult it will be for competitors to catch you.

Takeaway from Chapter 17

The following team-building exercise fortifies the strengths of teamwork while exposing the team's weaknesses and setting the stage for establishing improved performance.

You give the team, normally a small group of four to six people, several bags of balloons and a few rolls of tape and instruct them to build the tallest freestanding tower they can with the material on hand and within a short period of time, say 20 minutes. Then turn them loose. Normally this is done in competition with other teams, and at the conclusion of the exercise the team with the tallest structure wins the exercise.

Such a project, under the pressure of limited time and materials, demonstrates both the effectiveness and shortcomings of teams. For example, some teams lose precious minutes squabbling over who leads the project, then lose time as some team members begin constructing the structure independently, without regard to their limited building materials. Others fail to listen to instructions. Others collapse under time constraints.

This exercise shows how important it is for the team to establish procedures and roles. When every member of the team acts independently of one another, little or nothing gets done. When they act in concert, with each team member understanding his role, things get done.

At the conclusion of this exercise you will gain a better understanding into the complexities of establishing workable and effective teams.

18

Practice 7: Deliver Excellence and Satisfy Customers

C ustomers are vital to your success. As a leader, you must continually enhance and reinforce the ideals of customer satisfaction. Anyone, or any organization, can serve a customer, but meeting their needs so they become loyal customers falls into the leader's jurisdiction. You must also inspire your people to provide outstanding service. The happier your customers, the more they return.

Competition is tough today. Why should I buy from your company when I can get something similar from your competition? An effective leader drives customer satisfaction through the entire organization, from top to bottom. Whether we're talking about the maintenance crew or the CEO, it's everyone's job to understand that customers/clients come first.

The Car of My Dreams

I had worked very hard and had reached a point early in my career where I could afford a certain luxury automobile. I was excited about beginning the hunt for the one that was right for my family and me. I had read and talked to current owners about what great cars the automaker I selected produced and how shopping for one was a very pleasant experience.

My wife and I, along with our four-year-old daughter, visited only three dealerships, having decided on the model and color of our choice. At the first dealership, the salesperson we encountered was extremely nice and offered first-class service. Unfortunately, she didn't have the color or model we wanted, and we proceeded to the next dealership, eager to find the car of our dreams.

We walked into the dealership—our preferred choice, as it was very close to our home—at 4:45 P.M. on a Friday. We were approached by the salesperson and, after the introductions and exchange of business cards, I said, "If you have a black model with a tan interior in stock, and if the price is right, we will buy it tonight."

He looked at his watch. "Yes, we do," he replied. "But do you think you can come back in the morning, as I have to leave at 5 P.M. today. I have early dinner plans."

I looked at my wife and then back at the salesman. "Do you understand what I just said?" I asked him.

He said he was sorry to inconvenience us but still repeated that he had to leave and asked us to return in the morning to buy the car. Then, he turned and walked away.

We stood there in utter disbelief. After several speechless moments, we shook our heads and began walking out of the showroom. Before we could reach the door, the general manager stopped us and asked if he could help us. I told him what had just occurred. "No problem," he said. "We have the car in stock, so just come back in the morning and we can take care of everything."

The next morning, we went to a third dealership and bought our car. We drove around the neighborhood and were very pleased as we headed home a few hours later.

As we walked into the house, the phone rang. It was the salesman and general manager from the second dealership. They asked what time I was coming to the showroom to buy the car. They apparently expected us to return.

I explained, as nicely as I could, that we had bought the car from another dealer because "you couldn't be bothered with us last night," and that we were very happy with our new car. I thanked them for their time.

I was about to hang up, but the pair began to chastise me for not coming back to their showroom. They also said I was making a mistake buying the car from the other dealer because their service was poor. I hung up the phone and vowed never to deal with these people again.

How effectively was that general manager in instilling leadership and driving customer satisfaction? My experience was a lesson in how *not* to serve a customer. I don't know what he was thinking and how many other salespeople at that dealership acted in the same way. He certainly wasn't demonstrating effective leadership skills or driving customer satisfaction.

For the next few years, whenever a friend, colleague, or acquaintance was looking to purchase this particular car, I always told them my story and discouraged them from visiting that particular dealer. I urged them instead to buy from the highly professional salesperson at the third dealership. I've estimated that the lousy customer service and poor judgment of that second dealership have cost them lost sales of 15 cars.

But the story doesn't end there. Six years later, when I wanted to trade in my car, I returned to the scene of the customer-service crime. I gave them first chance because the dealership was the closest to my home and I thought things might have changed. I was met by a nice salesperson. I explained what had happened six years earlier, and he grimaced and apologized profusely for the experience. He told me both the salesman and general manager were no longer there and that he would make sure I was taken care of.

I said I was shopping on price only, and that I was visiting two dealerships: the one I had bought the last two cars from and this one. I said the dealer offering the lowest price would get my business today. He gave me his price, and off I went to the dealership from which I had purchased my last car. I got a price that was $450 lower than the first dealership. I called the salesman at the first dealership and told him I'd come back and buy the car today if he could match the price. He said he would get back to me in an hour and let me know. One hour later, he called back to say there was no way the other dealership could sell the car for that price. I offered to fax him the quote, and said he couldn't match the price.

Once again, I drove to the dealership from which I had purchased my last two cars and bought the car at the quoted price. Because this was the third car I had purchased from them over the years, they threw in several additional items for free, as well as a gift certificate for dinner for two at a nearby restaurant. In addition, the general manager called a few days later to thank me for being such a loyal customer, and he said that if there was anything I ever needed, I should personally contact him. He added that he looked forward to seeing me again when I brought the car in for service.

When my car hit the 3,000-mile mark, I brought it in for its first service. True to his word, the general manager came into the waiting area and invited me into his office. As we spoke, I looked around and noticed several framed letters hanging on his wall from satisfied customers. I began asking him several questions about his customer-service philosophy. He told me that a dealership is only as good as the people who work there. One of his leadership responsibilities was to make sure every person who worked at the company understood the value of satisfying the needs of every customer who walked through the door. Part of being a good general manager, he said, is making sure that every employee understood this concept and practiced it daily. He said he spent a great deal of time working with his staff on this principle.

In our quest to become effective leaders, we must realize that one of our goals is to always remember the customer. More importantly, we must remember to work with every member of our staff, team, department, or organization to make sure they have the proper mindset for dealing with customers. In business, we talk about satisfying the needs of the customer, but in many instances it's all talk and no action.

Highly effective leaders create a quality product, brand it, sell it well, and satisfy and retain customers and clients to achieve desired results. They seek to continuously improve their quality products and services and have high employee engagement and customer satisfaction. They use their drive and ambition to make things happen, to make a difference daily. They're excited about their role, always seeking ways to improve and motivate and inspire their people. They get things done in ways that maintain relationships and sustain results. When people believe in themselves, they achieve amazing things.

Inspire your people to provide outstanding customer service. The happier your customers, the more they return.

M. Anthony Burns, the CEO of Ryder Systems, says that successful leaders today are driven by three priorities: creating shareholder value, a laser beam focus on their customer, and competing in a global environment. Those who best meet these challenges understand that those three priorities are interdependent. Often companies with the best integrated logistics have a strong competitive edge. As the market leader in integrated logistics, Ryder helps its customers achieve the goals of shareholder value, customer satisfaction, and global opportunity. "I believe that integrated logistics—having the right product in the right place at the right time—is the new battleground in global competitiveness."

Product delivery, availability, and service are as important as the quality of the product being delivered. If your product isn't prominently displayed on the retail store shelf when the customer is ready to buy, your competitor's brand may very well beat you to the punch.

In marketing terminology, there are four Ps: product, price, promotion, and place. Traditionally, most companies have concentrated on the first three Ps, leaving the fourth P, place, as a competitive frontier where a genuine edge can be gained. Place refers both to where the product is ultimately sold—often the store shelf—and to the entire process of how products are brought to market.

Ted Opens a New Market

Ted, a new salesman for a travel accessory company (toiletry kits, carry-on bags, and packing organizers), expanded sales in his region by persuading travel agents to sell his line of products. It was an unusual outlet and so successful that the company included sales pitches to travel agents in all other regions of the country.

> *Hands-On Advice: Open your mind and consider new (even outrageous) possibilities for your job, whatever that job might be.*

The outrageous part helps you think outside the box. If you're in sales, consider unusual outlets for your product or service. If you're in operations consider new avenues for cutting costs. If you're in customer service imagine new ways to satisfy customers. Open your mind and consider all manner of possibilities.

The Disciplines of Excellence

Although leaders vary in their definitions of excellence and how best to achieve it, most agree that excellence is a never-ending pursuit and that whatever their challenges and opportunities are today, they'll change tomorrow. Leaders often face nine challenges:

1. *Communication.* People lack clarity and direction, limiting innovation.
2. *Accountability.* Measurements of and responsibility for results are insufficient.
3. *Engagement.* People don't seem to care as much or aren't sure of their individual roles.
4. *Alignment.* Activities aren't connected with the company's mission and strategy.
5. *Direction.* There's a disconnect between planning, strategy, and execution.
6. *Transition.* People feel a desire to "pass the torch" successfully but have trouble doing it.
7. *Control.* Events feel out of sync.
8. *Frustration.* There's excess friction at work.
9. *Risk management.* There's a need, often unaddressed, for determining profit variability versus the projected growth rate.

An excellence program is an organized approach to grow leaders' ability to deal with an ever-changing and challenging environment. The program needs to grow with the business and enable leaders and their employees to align plans and activities to support the strategies and achieve goals. An excellence program will address the nine issues mentioned above.

Innovate, measure, learn. Innovate purposefully. Innovation means problem-solving, and everyone has the ability to solve problems. This discipline provides principles and measurement tools that are used in the other disciplines to help leaders set clear goals and align daily activities to meet them. These goals should align with company priorities, and employees should use their innate creativity to meet or beat goals.

Learning. First, step back. Gain perspective on the factors that affect performance. It is achieved through a series of discovery exercises, exploring externals (competitors, industry, economics) and internals such as goal performance, stakeholder feedback, corrective measures, and SWOT (strengths, weaknesses, opportunities, and threats) analysis. All team members provide input on performance by completing a 360-degree feedback survey and annual performance appraisal.

Enduring excellence has: (1) a repeatable methodology to drive leadership, (2) external coaching for accountability, (3) a system to align the activities of team members, and (4) a community of like-minded people to accelerate learning. When these elements come together, leaders expect to see enduring change.

Customer Intimacy

The first commandment of marketing is *Know thy customer*! Customer research is the key to knowing your customers, whether they are people or a set of data in a computerized order-fulfillment database. And the better you know your customers, the more successful you are likely to be in meeting their needs—along with your own.

Four concepts capture what today's customers want: faster, better, cheaper, and *their way*. There is no mistaking the message. The company that can shave delivery and turnaround time, provide better quality, and tailor its products and services to the customer's precise needs is a company to be reckoned with.

To gain an insurmountable edge on the competition, add one more dimension: first-class customer care. It pays to provide outstanding customer service as a part of the package you present to customers.

In today's service-sensitive, service-focused, service-centered economy, companies that offer high-quality customer service keep customers 50 percent longer, have 30 percent lower sales and marketing costs, experience a 10 percent higher return on sales, and have about 12 percent higher net profits.

When customers are pleased, employees are frequently more satisfied with their jobs and more likely to stay. Who wants to work for an organization that customers hate? And who isn't motivated by a customer's thanks and a manager's "well done!"?

In concept, delivering quality service is simple: Make sure you know what customers want and expect of you, be flexible in meeting these demands, treat customers like partners rather than adversaries or end users, and make it easy for them to do business with you. This mission is easier to talk than walk. But you can make a go of it if you listen and understand your customers' wants and needs, respond effectively to customers' evaluations of their experiences with you, and discern what your customers will want in the future, which calls for an intimate knowledge of your customers' wants, needs, and expectations.

Knowing your customers intimately means more than market research. It means listening to, understanding, and responding to your customers' evolving needs and shifting expectations, and often in unique ways. It means knowing each other's businesses so well that you can anticipate each other's problems and opportunities, and work together on solutions and strategies. So, listening and responding to customers must become everyone's business.

How can you foster the kind of intimacy that creates long-term loyalty among customers? Start by seeing customer transactions not as a random collection of experiences, but as relationships built on knowledge, caring, and experience.

Customers are no longer shapeless, featureless, mass markets. They are specific, narrow groups with their own unique personalities and views of what constitutes quality service. What customers want, how they want it, and how they do or don't get it, add up to a service-satisfaction index that determines whether they'll continue doing business with you. You need a rich, constant flow of fresh, timely information about your customers and how they view your products and services today.

Excellence in Customer Service

In an era in which customers demand high-speed information, the role of the customer service function and the employees who deliver this service are pivotal. Customer service has become communication central for day-to-day information on customer satisfaction, customer relations, and customer intentions. The customer service frontline has become not only your first line of defense but, increasingly, your vital early-warning system. Today's customer service managers must be experts not only in customer relations, problem-solving, and core products and services, but also experts in gathering, synthesizing, assessing, and distributing data. Every customer contact is a critical data point, a chance to learn something important about a valued customer.

Today's customer service function is a profit center through its impact on customer retention and future plans. We all need to learn new ways to listen to customers and expand the parameters of what we listen for. Customers with strong feelings—positive or negative—are the customers most likely and least likely to do business with us again.

Service quality is recognized as the marketing edge that can differentiate one commodity from another. The service imperative means that we must pay increasing attention to whatever it takes, one-on-one and one-by-one, to earn the love and loyalty and respect of our customers.

Effective customer service starts with a comprehensive definition of customer service. Current definitions are based on meeting or exceeding customer expectations, satisfying or delighting customers, or delivering in full on time. While these are necessary conditions, they are insufficient to guarantee success.

I define customer service as the process of building customer trust in the delivery of selected goods and services. Trust forms partnership. Satisfaction at a transactional level is insufficient. Trustworthiness is needed to become a partner and to remain a partner. Without trust, no customer would enter into such a relationship.

I view customer service as a series of well-defined tasks that focus on building the customer's trust. To execute this process, every person needs to be trained until behavior that builds trust becomes habitual. The reward system needs to be aligned toward developing the habit and reinforced to ensure that it is sustained over time.

The psychology of buying is the psychology of trust. So, use every opportunity to build trust. Fine-tune the customer service process to build trust. Continuously building trust assures continued success.

Trust is a function of competence and character. Competence is understanding needs and arriving at solutions that work in the customer's context and constraints. Character is using the competence to propose a solution that is in the customer's best interest. Customers need to believe that you have the character to use that competence in their best interests.

While initial perceptions of character and competence help land new customers, keeping customers is a function of the customers' expectations, the actual service delivery performance, and what the organization does to close gaps between expectations and outcomes. Train your people to use the gaps as a way to build trust. The question to ask is "Where can I invest the next dollar to build the most trust?" The most effective way to build trust is to focus on delivering those services where there is vibrant synergy between the organization's core competencies and the customers' needs.

Cal Darden, VP of operations for UPS, asks, "What is your formula for success? In 1886, an Atlanta pharmacist named John Pemberton concocted the formula for Coca-Cola. Today, the secret formula for Coke is locked away in a secure vault in Atlanta. Only a select few have access to this recipe that has given longevity to one of America's landmark companies and strongest brands. At UPS, our formula for success is not locked away in a secret vault or hidden from view with restricted access. Our formula is out in the open for every employee to see and to provide the guidance we need to respond to business needs.

"UPS was started in 1907 by a determined 19-year-old, Jim Casey, with $100 in his pocket. His idea for a bicycle messenger service would turn into one of the most successful enterprises in the world. Today, his entrepreneurial spirit lives on in the 360,000 UPS customers who are reinventing the business to synchronize global commerce.

"In our drive to keep our success formula fresh, one thing remains constant. That is a culture built on the timeless values of integrity, excellence, quality, and the human spirit. It's about doing the right thing each day to manage our reputation. We maintain the values that have served us well. At UPS, everyone is a steward of the brand.

"We must ask: 'Where will our next generation of leaders come from?' Many leaders are putting their budgets where their priorities are. And those priorities include leadership development. For most executives, leadership development is a major priority. In most cases, senior executives are committed to funding leadership programs. Indeed, investment in the bench strength of 'high potentials' is not faltering. Investing in our people for a life-long career has been a big plus for UPS and its people. For UPS leaders, employment longevity enables them to get experience across many different parts of the business. I've worked in many jobs in many places—and that experience and training delivers continuity. When a new chairman takes the reins at UPS, the leadership transition is seamless, logical, and strategic. Our experienced leaders are trusted to perform their roles without disruption."

In their book, *Built to Last* (HarperBusiness; 3rd edition, 1990), authors Jim Collins and Jerry Porras explore what makes up a great company. A great company has a strong vision that encompasses both an immutable core ideology and envisioned future. That vision transcends the current leader because it has been institutionalized. A visionary company religiously preserves its core ideology—changing it seldom, if ever. From this adherence to a set of beliefs comes the discipline and drive that enables a company to succeed in rapidly changing environments. The fact is, culture matters. It takes more than charismatic, visionary leaders to build visionary companies. It requires a core ideology.

Takeaway from Chapter 18

You can discover how well you know your customers by conducting this exercise: Select one of your major customers. List all of the major services you provide to maintain the trust of that customer. Include benefits you consider over and above the norm. Include pricing, quality, quantity discounts, delivery, problem solving . . . list everything.

In a column adjoining the services you've described write how well or how poorly your main competitor provides the same services for that account. If you're unaware of what services your chief competitor provides, especially extra benefits over and above the norm, you're at a decided competitive disadvantage, because when times get rough and the customer cuts back orders, yours may be the first to go or get cut.

Add to the list, services your main competitor has that you don't. You shouldn't be surprised what they are, but you might be.

Now rethink what you need to stay or become that customer's favored supplier. Think in terms of reinvigorating the relationship. And always remember that trust is the keyword. When your customer trusts you, he has faith in you, and that's the most crucial benefit you can provide.

Practice 8: Balance Your Work and Personal Life

It Will Help You Find the Right Perspective

A proper work and personal life balance continues to be a key issue for most leaders today. With the pressure placed on leaders to execute and perform, what steps can they take to extract the most joy from their work?

Leaders are working longer hours, making work-life balance a critical issue that won't go away soon. Certainly, technology has a huge impact on our lives. Immediate access and availability through smartphones, instant messaging, and email, put great pressure on leaders to respond quickly to both large and inconsequential problems.

When I coach executives, I find that many are tethered to their devices. As a result, they tend to experience a loss of focus, lack of energy, and decline in decision-making ability, leading to job burnout, high stress, divorce, and even alcohol or drug dependency.

One effective way to combat work-life balance issues is through time management. When you efficiently manage your time, you have a more balanced life, higher productivity, less stress, and greater job satisfaction. I recommend several key steps:

- Learn to say no. As leaders, we are always asked to take on more responsibilities, deadlines, and commitments. It's human nature to try to please everyone and expect more from ourselves, but we can easily accept more work than we're realistically capable of completing. Saying no in a professional way prevents you from overloading your schedule and accepting more than you can handle.
- Determine when you're at the peak of your day. People have peak and low periods during a workday. Find your peak, and tackle the most important issues during that time.
- Create a not-to-do list composed of activities that need to be completed, but needn't be personally handled by you. Decide who you can empower to complete these tasks and delegate.
- Empower others. Surround yourself with great people and empower them with decision-making responsibilities.
- Establish a no-contact time. Close your office door for 15 to 30 minutes each day. Let everyone know that you're not to be disturbed. Don't answer the phone or emails or reply to smartphone messages; instead, choose to work on issues that require your most immediate attention.
- Maintain your energy and exercise regularly. Stay hydrated by drinking plenty of water and eat balanced meals. Go for five-minute walks two to three times a day.
- Implement periodic stand-up meetings. Much of what's achieved in a one-hour meeting can be handled in 15- to 30-minute gatherings where everyone stands. This keeps people on track and focused on resolving key issues quickly.

Work-life balance involves more than time management. Leaders must recognize the need to slow down, enjoy life, and replenish their energy supply daily. Having a balanced life takes into account all your needs, including family, friends, work, play, private time, exercise, and spiritual time. It's a matter of getting your priorities straight.

We often say we're working long hours for our families, but if we ask our families they'll say they would like to have us around more. Think about the impact you have on family by working long hours. Then take a few minutes out of your busy day and try to figure out how to cut back and rearrange your priorities.

The key to achieving a balanced life is building it into your schedule like anything else and then making it a habit. Start by making an action plan: Look at your schedule two to three weeks in advance and block out time for things you enjoy doing and people you enjoy being with. It takes discipline to do this, and discipline is what leaders have.

Making a commitment to work-life balance makes leaders more productive and better prepared to handle the daily tasks, while providing the time to enjoy life.

Jack Finds the Way

After Jack's wife died he truly regretted his inordinate focus on work—the term workaholic is apt—and not spending enough time with his wife and family. But that horrible experience was a wake-up call. He reordered his life to achieve a balance between work and family, now determined to give his children the attention he had failed to give his wife.

> Hands-On Advice: Don't fool yourself into thinking that work comes first, family second.

Spending a disproportionate amount of your time on work will deprive your family and yourself of untold joy. Strike a balance between the two.

Work/Life Balance

About 30 years ago, Americans were perceived to be slackers by major industrialized nations, especially efficiency-obsessed Japan. But much has changed, as Juliet B. Schor, PhD, writes in her book, *The Over-worked American: The Unexpected Decline of Leisure* (Basic Books; Reprint edition, 1993), "In the last 20 years, the amount of time Americans have spent at their jobs has risen steadily," she writes. "Each year the change is small, amounting to about nine hours, or slightly more than one additional day of work."

In truth, the productivity of American workers has doubled since 1948, leaving us on average only 16.5 hours of leisure time per week after completing job and household responsibilities, statistics that have led Dr. Schor to call the United States the workaholic nation. Our work hours, she notes, increased 12 percent between 1973 and 2000. Slacking is a term that can no longer be applied when you consider how many hours we work each year, as compared to breadwinners in other nations.

Currently, the U.S. worker puts in more hours than his or her counterpart in other industrialized countries, and leads the way in terms of productivity. But we don't seem to be rewarded for this productivity. We paradoxically trail the world in average allotted vacation days per year. Americans now comprise the most depressed and mood-disordered workforce in the world.

Psychiatrist Edward M. Hallowell, MD, who specializes in diagnosing and treating attention deficit disorder (ADD), believes each of us needs strategies for coping in a world gone ADD. In his book *CrazyBusy*, he writes: "Many people are excessively busy because they allow themselves to respond to every magnet: tracking too much data, processing too much information, answering to too many people, taking on too many tasks, all out of a sense that this is the way they must live in order to keep up and stay in control."

But control is a myth. The more you try to control everything around you, the more exhausted you'll become. So, how can you achieve work-life balance when the deck seems to be stacked against you? And is this goal even possible? Pause and take a long, deep breath. Close your eyes and rest for a few minutes before we explore the ways in which you can juggle the demands of your personal and professional universe without winding up in a padded cell.

Barbara Burns Out

Barbara was known for apologizing on the job. She was a meticulous and industrious worker, and her employers had always valued her, but Barbara carried with her a fear of being fired.

Even though Barbara had never lost a job, her fears stemmed from a feeling of inferiority because she had never attended college. Nonetheless, hard work had allowed her to advance to a middle-management career. As production manager for a large New York City magazine publishing company, Barbara was charged with ensuring that all advertising film and digital files made it to the printer on deadline. The job could be grueling, as Barbara had to deal with tardy clients, demanding editors, and rushed printers.

After 12 years on the job, Barbara's company had begun downsizing, even though the well-established publisher was simultaneously adding new magazine titles to its portfolio. Barbara found herself in a position familiar to many managers: She was forced to do more with less. Her workday became a 10-hour affair, five days a week, and she occasionally had to go into the office on Saturdays to keep up with her workload. None of this extra time was compensated.

Barbara talked with John, her boss, about the finite number of hours in a day, but she found him to be unsympathetic. John was focused on the bottom line, and he didn't care that Barbara's workload had expanded to what had been the workload of two people. No additional hires would be approved, he told her, so she needed to find a way to pull off her responsibilities. Each day, Barbara would cry on her way to work. She was earning about $41,000 a year, and she knew she was both underpaid and overworked. The job became so debilitating and stressful that Barbara was diagnosed with clinical depression. Her doctor prescribed antidepressants, which left her feeling unfocused and tired. Something had to give.

Barbara decided to quit her job. She needed a break, and she couldn't keep pace with the publishing company's demands. Even though she was low on savings, she gave notice and began searching for a new job.

In today's hypercompetitive environment, she landed a part-time job that paid fairly well, and she temporarily moved in with an aunt so she could build up her bank account. It wasn't the ideal situation for Barbara, but a profit-driven, inflexible boss drove her to choose her health and sanity over a paycheck. Barbara has since taken a second part-time job, but she worries about her lack of health insurance benefits. If her situation doesn't improve, she has decided that she will relocate to a city with lower overhead expenses and, if necessary, begin work in a new industry.

Get a Life

Anna Quindlen, the Pulitzer Prize–winning *Newsweek* columnist, advised graduates at Villanova University to "get a life." Quindlen, who at 19 lost her mother to breast cancer, meant a real life, "not a manic pursuit of the next promotion, bigger paycheck, or larger house. Do you think you'd care so much about those things if you blew an aneurysm one afternoon, or found a lump in your breast? Get a life in which you notice the smell of saltwater pushing itself on a breeze over Seaside Heights, a life in which you stop and watch how a red-tailed hawk circles over the water gap, or the way a baby scowls with concentration when she tries to pick up a Cheerio with her thumb and first finger." Getting a life requires that you reexamine your priorities and definition of success. And what mattered to you in your 20s may no longer be your *raison d'être* in your 40s or 50s.

What's Important to You?

Do you live to work or work to live? It's a simple, yet critical, question. Working to live should pay the bills while bringing you satisfaction. Living to work, however, means you are likely making sacrifices in other areas of your life: marriage, family time, going out with friends, hobbies, recreation, exercise, and other aspects of healthful living.

For many of us, the term *workaholic* has become a badge of honor. This misguided approach places work at the top of our priority hierarchy . . . and then we wonder why our spouses serve us with divorce papers, our kids are alienated because we're never home, and we're too tired to enjoy the activities that have historically given us pleasure. Since our society places high value on work and lauds individuals for their strong work ethic, recognizing workaholism as a dangerous problem is an uphill battle. Bryan Robinson, PhD, a professor emeritus at the University of North Carolina at Charlotte and author of *Chained to the Desk* (NYU Press; Second edition, November 1, 2007), says that he is "appalled at how society, and the media extol workaholism—a syndrome that affects 25 percent of our population and causes people to fall apart." He speaks about the dangers of workaholism from first-hand experience. A self-confessed former workaholic, he compares his addiction to his father's alcoholism. Since childhood, work defined his self-worth and sense of stability.

Gayle Porter, PhD, a professor of management at the Rutgers University School of Business, asserts that "excessive work can be viewed as an addictive behavior" with "dysfunctional behavior patterns that interfere with operations." The workaholic lifestyle is detrimental to your ability to function and to organizational health.

Health Implications

As Barbara can attest, psychological studies across the decades have found that workaholics are more stressed, depressed, anxious, and angry. They have an unrelenting fear of failure, are generally perfectionists, have an overriding sense of inferiority, and expect more of themselves than they can realistically deliver. They also tend to talk about their work obsessively, work even when they're sick, refuse to take vacations, and lack any kind of separation or boundaries between their home and work lives.

Workaholism is positively associated with ill-health (psychological distress and physical complaints) and negatively associated with life satisfaction (job and family satisfaction) and job performance. The need to work compulsively hard also contributes to insufficient sleep and workplace sleepiness. Tired nurses make more errors, while drowsiness and sleepiness are major causes of accidents for professional drivers.

Solution 1: Learn to delegate. Trying to do everything yourself, coupled with viewing others as not up to the task, will put you on the fast track to workaholism. Gary Duehring, PhD, compliance officer for the MRI Diagnostic Center of Michigan, acknowledges that many managers don't delegate because something could go wrong. Yes, this is indeed a possibility, even a probability. But how else can you test whether a person is ready, willing, and able to assume new challenges? Failure to delegate locks you into an irrational and self-destructive "I can do everything myself" mode. And "while some failure is to be expected, it can be minimized by proper evaluation of the situation and proper communication." Dr. Duehring writes, "Delegation is a calculated risk," leading to "development of an effective and efficient staff and department."

Solution 2: Take your allotted time. Do you skip your daily lunch break or eat at your desk? Are you guilty of eating breakfast at your desk (deskfast)? If so, you're not taking the time you need to replenish your body's energy. It may surprise you to learn that you'll be even more productive if you grab a healthful lunch outside your office's four walls, followed by a 10-minute invigorating walk. Sick leave and vacation time were also invented for a reason. If you're sick, you're not supposed to go to work. If you break this rule, you'll become even more run down, and you'll selfishly risk infecting your coworkers. Trust me; they won't appreciate your ill-advised gallantry. Vacation time is also earned, so be sure to use it . . . and I mean all of it.

Workers who take their vacation days have a lower incidence of cardiovascular problems. Taking much-needed vacation breaks is not only good for you—it is also good for your business. So, don't feel guilty about taking vacation time.

Solution 3: Unplug yourself. In her book, *Coming Up for Air* (Hyperion; First edition, March 15, 2000) Charles Schwab Executive Vice President Beth Sawi reminds us why we need to unplug ourselves occasionally from email, cell phones, instant messages, pagers, Black-Berrys, and iPhones. These devices leave you connected 24/7/365, with little time to enjoy a pleasurable, relaxing, uninterrupted life. Sawi asserts, ". . . but nothing interrupts that sense of control like the rhythmic beep-beeping of some electronic device demanding your immediate attention."

Solution 4: Manage human interruptions. Don't be afraid to close your door or put your phone on voice mail when you're busy. You can't concentrate when a steady stream of humans enters your office or calls you. Some offices may frown on closed doors, so you'll need to talk to your boss about finding a happy medium. Keeping doors closed all day sends the wrong message, but trying times call for self-protective measures.

Solution 5: Decline with gratitude. It can be difficult to say no to colleagues and bosses. But survival depends on what physician Richard A. Swenson, MD, calls "declining with gratitude." In his book, *In Search of Balance* (NavPress, 2010), Dr. Swenson describes a common situation: Someone comes into our office, asks us to do something, and we automatically say yes. "Five minutes later," he writes, "we run into the bathroom, stare at the mirror, and say: What did I just do? Habit, work ethic, and the desire to be a team player have trapped us once again. Most people overestimate the repercussions of an appropriate no, fearing wrongly that it might represent the end of a friendship or job." The old adage "think before you speak" is relevant when you're asked to take on more responsibility.

Are We Having Fun Yet?

If you aren't excited and energized about going to work, you must change. After all, you spend one-third of your time at work. Fun must be part of an organization's strategy. Look at the list of companies that make fun part of their strategy and culture: Southwest Airlines, Starbucks, Disney, Nordstrom, Walmart, Trader Joe's, Land's End. What else do these organizations have in common? They are all very profitable!

I can think of four specific benefits for businesses that encourage fun:

1. Fun is a healer. When people are having fun, the brain releases chemicals called endorphins, which help heal the body. It reduces absenteeism and helps keep people healthy and happy each day.

2. Fun breeds creativity and new ideas. As people enjoy their jobs and have fun, they become more creative and imaginative. They begin to think outside the box and don't fear failure.

3. Fun helps maintain workplace relations. America has the most diverse workforce in its history. People come to work every day with different cultural backgrounds. We also have a multigenerational workforce: people in their 20s to those in their 60s. And when they're having fun at work, it breaks down barriers. They enjoy being with each other, can discuss their differences openly, and share new ideas.

4. When you have fun at work, it makes training and teaching easier. In fact, fun is an excellent teaching tool. Whenever our company holds workshops or conducts training, we make sure to include strategically placed activities that focus on fun. The feedback we always receive is positive. Participants say they learned a lot and had fun doing it!

Having fun at work also impacts the bottom line: Fun prompts energy levels to rise. Energy is contagious, and productivity soars. As the company enjoys increased productivity, there's greater innovation. New ideas and concepts take flight, and the bottom line improves considerably.

The first time I flew on Southwest Airlines I was amazed by every employee's high energy and enthusiasm, without exception. All of them were having fun and enjoying their work, from the baggage handlers, reservation agents, and gate attendants, all the way up to and including the pilot. As I waited for my flight, I observed how the employees' positive attitudes and infectious enthusiasm spread to the passengers. Everyone was smiling, upbeat, and having a good time. No wonder Southwest is so profitable when many airlines struggle. Having fun at work makes a huge difference.

Takeaway from Chapter 19

Jody Urquhart, a motivational speaker, has a test for determining the fun factor in a workplace. In her article "Creating a Fun Workplace: 13 Ways to Have Fun at Work!," Judy has a test for whether your staff is suffering from "terminal seriousness." Scan your workplace and take note of the five key elements of Judy's test:

Do you regularly catch people laughing or smiling at work? YES NO

When something funny happens do people stop and appreciate it? YES NO

Does your organization have fun activities at least monthly? YES NO

Do you have tools (fun giveaways, draws) to invite employees to participate in having fun in your environment? YES NO

Are managers usually optimistic and smiling at work? YES NO

If you answer *no* to two or more of these questions, your staff likely suffers from terminal seriousness, which negatively affects morale and productivity. The remedy is injecting a greater measure of fun and humor into the workplace.

20

Practice 9: Nurture New Leaders and Retain High Performers

Linda was a nurse in an assisted living facility for seniors. She had been tutored by a nursing supervisor who was a taskmaster and had no understanding or appreciation for those unfortunate nurses she supervised. Because she had suffered from it, Linda knew and understood firsthand the lasting effect of bad leadership. She remembered her lessons well when she was promoted into the job of nursing supervisor and applied her considerable skills to motivate and inspire those who worked with her guidance.

> *Hands-On Advice: You must understand—as Linda did—that figuratively beating people up produces substandard results.*

Unhappy employees produce inferior results. It's as simple as that.

Retain your best people. Keep them focused, reduce anxieties and fears, reduce turnover, and make employees feel loyal and positive about the company they work for.

People don't leave companies; they ditch bad bosses. You can work at the best organization in the world, one that has the reputation of employer of choice, but you'll lose people if you're not a good leader. The relationships employees have with their leaders determines how long they stay at their companies. At least half of people's job satisfaction is determined by their relationship with their bosses. A manager's behavior is the main reason people quit. So, how can you retain your workforce?

Ask questions. Good leaders are always asking questions, and they're never happy with the status quo. They ask: "What if we tried it this way? Our competitors are doing it this way. Did you ever think about doing it that way?" Good leaders challenge the status quo on a continual basis.

Be adaptable and flexible. Leadership requires reinvention . . . of yourself, your team, and the organization as a whole. Circumstances continually change, so you must be adaptable and flexible. Don't stay in the same old mode of operations, as situations and personnel changes will keep your work life in flux.

Identifying and Grooming High-Potential Employees

How do you identify high-potential new leaders? Leaders must be proficient in both hard and soft skills. For years, organizations looked at only hard skills or technical knowledge, such as expertise in strategy or finance. They viewed these hard skills as the most important characteristics of high-potential leaders. However, the soft skills (people or interpersonal skills) are key for the next generation of leaders.

Look for these soft skills: effective communication, coaching ability, listening skills, team-building capability, facility for building relationships with their staffs and teams and with cross-functional areas to achieve goals and get work done, a sense of inquisitiveness, a willingness to improve, a tendency to ask a lot of questions, and an understanding of how their actions affect themselves and others.

Leadership is difficult and demanding because leaders must help drive results, inspire, guide people and teams, and make tough decisions. Clearly, not everyone has the desire to lead, so the first question appears to be: Does the person want to be a leader? What are his goals and aspirations? Does she see the big picture versus having a silo mentality? Is the candidate a problem solver? Does the candidate have the ability to strategically navigate complicated issues? What types of real-life experiences does he have? Is the candidate honest and ethical?

Leaders need to be positive and have a great attitude because they can either impart or sap energy. A leader's upbeat attitude becomes contagious, lifting the morale of those around her. You can always teach skills, but you cannot always teach people how to be positive; they either have a great attitude or they don't.

Observe firsthand how potential leaders work with others and how other people view them. When they stand up to speak in front of a group, do they exude confidence, present articulate, clear messages, and carry themselves well? They should also have good judgment skills in three discrete areas: (1) People. Can they make sound judgments about people, such as anticipating the need for key personnel changes and aligning people to make the right call? (2) Strategy. Are they flexible and adaptable? Can they make changes when a current strategy isn't working? (3) Grace under pressure. When they're in crisis situations, do they remain calm, focused on their goals, think clearly, and develop new alternative strategies? When they make a mistake, do they admit it, let others know about it, and move forward, or do they try to hide it? By admitting mistakes, they serve as role models, communicating that it's okay to fail and make a mistake.

Lastly, employ a series of tests and assessments to further measure their hard and soft skills.

Retaining High-Potential Employees

Once you identify, groom, and promote your most talented performers, you need to retain them—a challenge where there's a war for talent. Most organizations are losing this war as headhunters and competitors vie for the best candidates. What makes retention even more challenging is our mobile society: Top performers may not even think twice about leaving.

Great organizations view employee retention as a competitive advantage and work hard to retain their most talented people, knowing that talented people are their most important asset.

Retention starts with culture. If you want to keep your top talent, you must create an inspiring and energizing culture wherein they can thrive. This means having an organization with shared values, openness, and honesty, thereby creating trust and allowing talented people to voice their opinions and share ideas.

You must empower and encourage people to aspire to do great things and be innovative, and then you reward their successes. High performers want to be challenged, provided with interesting work, and have the ability to make a difference. Leaders must recognize that everyone is motivated in different ways, and they should take the time to find out what motivates each person. If you can pinpoint these motivators, you can work with your staff to achieve extraordinary results.

Continually praise and recognize individual achievements, and make people feel good about themselves and their accomplishments. Be accessible, listen to their suggestions and ideas, and keep them informed of everything that affects them.

People want to work for a company that has a culture of high values, ethics, and honesty. The culture should include open communication. And be certain you place them in the right positions. All too often we place people in jobs for which they're not suited. A specific job may not be challenging enough or individuals may lack the required skillsets. We always want to make sure the fit is correct.

Turnover of top-grade employees is a reflection of failing leadership. If you see a pattern of turnover under a specific leader, a red flag should go up. Talented people will not put up with ineffective leaders.

Lastly, provide continual education and training so leaders can grow and learn new ideas. Then provide a career path with opportunities for growth and advancement.

The Right Work Culture Helps Retain Your Best People

Retaining high performers is a major challenge in today's changing business environment. As the economy continues to improve, studies show top performers may not even think twice about leaving. Great organizations view employee retention as a competitive advantage and work hard to retain their most talented people. Retention starts with culture. To keep your top talent, create an inspiring and energizing culture where they can thrive. This means having an organization with shared values, openness, and honesty, thereby creating trust and allowing talented people to voice their opinions and share ideas.

Empower and encourage people to aspire to do great things and be innovative, and then reward their successes. High performers want to be challenged, provided with interesting work, and make a difference. Recognize that everyone is motivated in different ways and take time to find out what motivates each person. If you can pinpoint these motivators, you can work with your staff to achieve extraordinary results.

Make every leader responsible for keeping talented employees. Continually look for signs of dissatisfaction. Asking questions and receiving feedback are great ways to find out if people's needs are being met. Ask your high performers: What can we do to make you happier here? If the organization could stop doing one thing, what would it be? What's challenging about your work? What motivates you to work harder? What are the greatest obstacles to getting your work done? What resources do you need that you currently lack?

These questions open a constructive dialogue that allows you to discover talented people's needs. Once you gain awareness, work quickly to fulfill these needs. Provide continual education and learn new ideas. Then provide a career path with opportunities for growth and advancement.

Appreciating Human Behavior at Work

One early study of human behavior at work, done at AT&T's Western Electric Hawthorne Works plant in the 1920s by Harvard's Elton Mayo, concluded: "When workers contribute their thinking and learning to workplace issues, their job performance improves."

The initial study set out to discover how lighting affects performance and fatigue of workers. The findings revealed that it is not so much physical conditions that matter. People are motivated to perform well when someone takes the time to pay attention to what they are doing. They are also encouraged to interact socially and to contribute ideas.

Their social needs have a powerful impact on their behavior at work. To tap into the potential of human capital, leaders must pay attention to their employees on a level that respects their human nature and individual differences.

A Promising Sales Manager Leaves Her Company

Skyler, as a young salesperson in the luggage business, managed to top all individual sales records within her first two years of employment after grad school. She did so well that her company promoted her to district sales manager for the states of Arizona, Nevada, and Utah.

She set record sales levels there, too. Within a year of taking over the district, sales jumped 60 percent. It was obvious to the executives of her company that Skyler was a high-potential employee, one the company intended to groom for bigger and better things.

Then, as routinely happens, company management changed. The board of directors felt the current president was inexcusably losing market share in an expanding market. The board hired the president of a competing company, an executive with a hard-nosed reputation.

The new president came in and immediately demanded that each district and regional sales manager increase sales by 20 percent within the next six months. He arbitrarily imposed quotas without including the company's sales managers in the planning process. It was a top-down decision that left the sales force enraged, frustrated, and in panic.

Skyler told her boss that while she felt she could increase sales by 20 percent in certain product areas, she wouldn't be able to in others.

However, her boss was adamant: Do it!

It was apparent to Skyler that the new approach of top-down-command-management was unworkable. She thought the board would eventually recognize the new president's failings, but until then the new regime would be busy firing, demoting, and transferring salespeople, and constantly reorganizing the sales department (the latter often a sign of a weak, insecure executive), embroiling it in perpetual turmoil.

As much as Skyler disliked the thought of running away from a problem, she was convinced that sales not only would not increase, but that it would actually drop. And the final indignity would be that her performance would be tainted by the company's sales failure. She left as soon as she found a position with a competitor.

Workplace Harassment: The Real Deal

Ask your managers and employees: Are any of your employees harassing others? Could it have been prevented? How? Should other employees in the break room do anything after witnessing a harassment encounter? When supervisors witness the scene, what's their legal responsibility as agents of the company? *Are there any warning signs of potential violence?* Who should employees talk to if there's harassment or a threat of violence? What should the employees' supervisor do when employees return from their break angry and upset? If they tell their supervisor what happened, then ask to keep it confidential, fearing retaliation, what should the supervisor do?

These are questions that need answering, followed by a well-thought-out written procedure and employee training emphasizing their individual roles when encountering or witnessing harassment. Keep this well in mind: You can lose your most talented employees if they have to operate in an environment of harassment, and even when they're not specifically involved in a case. Talented people do not want to work in a company that looks the other way when fellow employees are being treated unfairly.

Creating Positive Energy

As a consultant, speaker, and executive coach, I've done business with hundreds of organizations and observed firsthand the state of the workforce. Company success depends on a workforce of highly motivated individuals who are excited about their work. To achieve this state, employees need a strong leader with a positive attitude and enthusiasm.

You don't have to look far to find capable employees; they're everywhere. But, unfortunately, you can't say the same for leaders who understand how to inspire their employees. Leaders either boost the spirits of their people and invigorate them or turn them off.

To create positive energy, catch people doing something right. Heap praise and recognition, instead of finding fault. Leaders can make a big difference in the motivation of every employee. Try to recall the last time you told someone:

- "You really made a difference by . . ."
- "I'm impressed with . . ."
- "You got my attention with . . ."
- "You're doing top-quality work on . . ."
- "You're right on the mark with . . ."
- "We couldn't have done it without your . . ."
- "You can be proud of yourself for . . ."
- "You've made my day because of . . ."

Sharing positive feedback is contagious. Motivated employees feel better about their work and workplace and contribute more to the success of their departments and, ultimately, to their organizations. And motivated employees improve the organization's bottom line. You can take that to the bank! If you are a leader or aspiring leader, keep this tool at the top of your tool kit. It will serve you well.

Homegrown Leaders

One major leadership responsibility is the growth and development of other leaders. They are a company's foundation, and we must provide them with the knowledge and leadership skills needed to move up in the company. We can take advantage of leadership or development programs, as well as supervisory programs.

Jack Welch realized this years ago, and I often refer to his tenure at GE because the company made so many business breakthroughs. Welch believed that developing leaders at every level of the organization, from the person who worked on the assembly line to the CEO, was critical, and that the more leaders a company has, the better it could empower people to make decisions. As Welch once said, "Before you're a leader, success is all about growing yourself. When you become a leader, success is all about growing others."

Takeaway from Chapter 20

From the past 10 years of your career, list three or four high potential employees who worked for you and either left the company for opportunities elsewhere or were transferred to another part of the company, in all instances for either a lateral or lesser position.

Your first order of business is to accept that losing several good people is unacceptable and clearly speaks to your need to probe into the circumstances and find out why in each instance. Chances are that *you* are the core reason. Not that you're a bad person or that you do a poor job. But some behavior pattern of yours may be the reason for the exodus.

Seek objective coaching—some executive outside your organization who can dispassionately analyze the root of the problem and suggest ways to eradicate the problem. Often, your company HR director has this ability, but since she is enmeshed in the politics of the company, it may be difficult and impolitic for her to speak the truth.

Also, take advantage of exit interviews. Departing employees speak the truth. This is a great opportunity to identify your own problems and take corrective action before somebody else . . . somebody higher than you in the company hierarchy . . . takes the matter into his own hands.

Now, let's return to how many losses of high potential employees is acceptable. Is it four, three, two, one? *The answer is none.* Anytime you lose a high potential employee you've got to unleash your own internal Sherlock Holmes and find out why.

Practice 10: Lead Desired Change

Change is the only constant in life. It will never go away. Leaders can look at change in two ways: (1) It's something good that creates opportunities; or (2) change is horrible, something that frightens them.

I urge you to think of change as a wonderful opportunity to think differently. It encourages everyone to move past their comfort zones, try new ways of doing things, and embrace their creativity. Change happens every single day. Nothing stays the same. Business changes and people change. Theories and ideas change, as well. It's your job to adapt and change with them. Accept that change can be positive and convince your people to follow your lead.

Embracing Change

How can leaders inaugurate change initiatives without upsetting morale? Look at it this way: Today, change is necessary (and it has always been so). Business conditions are constantly changing, and yesterday's practices may no longer work. Leaders have to be flexible and adaptable to adjust to shifting business climates, but it's very important for them to understand that leading change is more than just a process.

We often forget that the most important aspects of change are people and their morale. It's often very easy to strategically manage the process and erroneously believe that when we have the correct process in place, change will automatically work. We frequently forget that change is very emotional for the average employee. As leaders, we need to understand that emotional process and the impact it has on morale. One of the most natural human instincts is to resist change, even if it's beneficial.

There are two ways to look at change: (1) change is constant; and (2) change is upsetting. When any significant change occurs in an organization, stress is a given. Expect to see plenty of discomfort and even resentment, even under the best of circumstances when people accept changes.

If not properly led, change can negatively affect individual and organizational performance. Consequences may include a negative work environment as well as decreased performance and increased stress. Even when it's clearly evident that change is working, it's often difficult to keep morale at a healthy level.

As Hard to Move as a Boulder

The creative team of an advertising agency in New York City was tasked with the job of changing the way a soap manufacturer advertised its product. As the saying goes, a funny thing happened on the way . . . the team stalled. It found itself repeating variations on old themes, somehow unable to break the mold and come up with fresh thinking. The account manager was forced to switch the assignment to an outside creative team.

If this can happen in an advertising agency where change is not only a constant but a requirement of success, imagine how it could stall the changes you want to implement in your business.

The more radical the change the greater the resistance. It takes careful planning, not only for the

> *Hands-On Advice: Never underestimate the resistance you're likely to encounter when you attempt to make changes.*

changes you want, but equally important, how the changes will be presented to employees and the indoctrination they will need to accept changes.

Four Phases of Change

Leaders must understand the four phases described by John Kotter that most people go through when attempting to adapt to change:

1. *Resistance.* We are all creatures of habit, and the very fact of change forces people out of their comfort zones. As such, they will usually fight it. They may feel their needs were already being met and that changes make it difficult to fulfill their needs. They may also fear the change will ultimately fail. At this point, people will probably do just enough to get by.

   People also have a very difficult time leaving the past behind them. They are so invested and have often been extremely successful in the old ways of doing things. They're being asked to move out of their comfort zones and learn new ways. Leaders must, therefore, understand that people need time to mourn and let go of the past. They should listen carefully to what people are saying—and, more importantly, to what they're not saying. You need to read between the lines, to understand that what people say isn't necessarily what they feel. They may feel constrained because you're the boss, and they're afraid you'll think less of them if they share their true feelings.

   Leaders must be highly visible and available to answer questions, offer support, and be consistent in their messages. And in this resistance stage, leaders must be optimistic and serve as role models for change.

2. *Confusion.* Many people enjoy being the bearer of bad news. During this phase, rumors run rampant. People feel things are happening too fast and they don't know where to focus their energy. They have problems learning new skills and start finger-pointing at management. It was management who created the

mess, right? So, expect people to be highly stressed, with some even coming close to burning out.

As leaders, we must again be consistent in our messages and communications and set short-term goals that can be accomplished and celebrated. Create incentives to maintain momentum as change occurs, and regularly restate the vision of where the team, department, or company is headed.

3. *Integration.* People will begin taking ownership; there is more positive and less negative energy. People start to experience a sense of control, and there's some blossoming optimism. Leaders need to provide encouragement and keep the lines of communication open. Encourage people to be creative, focused, and share their ideas and feedback.

4. *Commitment.* There is now much less stress and increased productivity. People begin to take ownership, and there's acceptance of the change. Everyone appears to be on the same page, there is an increase in productivity, and the lines of communication are wide open. People feel good about themselves and the accomplishments they have achieved during the difficult change process.

Always respect the past. It served you well over the years. But you don't want to continually look in the rearview mirror. Focus on moving forward.

Resisting Change

People often resist change. It's human nature; no one initially likes change. You've probably been in a situation where you moved somebody's desk around, and it takes him three months to get used to facing a new direction. It's not that surprising; we're all creatures of habit. We get up in the morning, and we embark on the same routines. We get dressed the same way. When we put on our socks, some of us put the right one on first; others put the left one on first—all the time, without fail. When we put on our pants, some of us put our right foot in first, while others put the left foot in first. We do this for our entire lives, and the prospect of change is very uncomfortable.

But if you ignore change or avoid thinking about it, you'll miss out on amazing opportunities to grow and improve. Change is an opportunity to think differently; be adaptable and flexible, and create better systems, products, people, teams, and organizations.

As a leader, you must provide consistent messages on a regular basis. You can't say one thing one day, and then switch your message on another day. Be consistent in messages regarding change, as people are looking to you for leadership. If you're consistent, they'll feel much more secure about impending changes.

Celebrate small successes. For those of you who have children, remember when your child took that first step? You were so excited that you celebrated the event, right? Well, it's the same thing with change. It must be celebrated. Use baby steps to measure success, and be sure to celebrate small successes. When even the smallest positive experience happens, make a big deal about it.

Be patient. Throughout the years, I've coached many leaders who have gone through change initiatives. The one common denominator that effective leaders possess is the ability to be patient and let the change initiative run its course. As a young leader, I did not have the patience to let many change initiatives play out. Early in my career as an executive, I'd often change things up while we were already in the middle of a change initiative, which meant I totally confused people. As I gained more experience, I became more patient. I watched as well-thought-out initiatives took hold and came to fruition. The patient leader will ultimately be rewarded with the desired results.

Pay attention to people's emotions. Don't act shocked or lash out when people initially have a negative reaction to change. When you make changes, be prepared for them to have strong reactions and feel uncomfortable and scared. An effective leader understands that emotions need to be dealt with on both an individual and group level. Once you address people's needs, they will begin to feel more comfortable and accept a change initiative. You can have all the strategy in the world in place, but if you can't handle people's emotions, change will never work.

Get input from your people. One of the best ways to encourage people to buy into your changes is to seek their help and opinions. Let them be part of the initiative. Let them, in essence, touch it, taste it, smell it, and feel it. Then, let them provide as much input as they want. Once they begin to participate, they will start to take ownership of the change, which leads to acceptance. In our consulting practice, we do a lot of strategic planning, which often brings about drastic changes. We start the planning at the top of the organization, and we then let it trickle down to every level. We allow people to poke holes, make changes, agree with it, disagree with it, and provide their own thoughts. Once this happens, most people buy into the change. Their participation in the process helps them feel as though they've had a hand in the results, and they're invested in making it work. They feel proud of what they now own.

Don't look back; look forward and show people the future. I once worked with a company on a change initiative, and management became stuck. Leaders kept looking back at the way things had always been done, instead of focusing on the way things would be managed in the future. This was a serious error. In the end, they couldn't let go of old habits and entrenched ways of thinking, and their change initiative turned into a disaster. Their company almost went out of business.

An effective leader looks forward, showing people how change benefits individuals and the organization. Leaders must focus on the future. They should paint a picture and motivate people by sketching them into the scenic landscape. We want to learn from history, and respect the past, but we must put it in the proper perspective.

It's a team effort. We're only as good as the teams we put together. Effective leaders understand that nothing happens when individuals work in a vacuum. Collective efforts, with ideas and insights and thoughts from all team members, are the ones that succeed—with the added and essential ingredients of determination and hard work.

Expect bumps in the road. When you begin a change initiative, things will happen, and not all of them will be good. In fact, you and your team will encounter many hurdles along the way. As an effective leader, you require the courage and savvy to face these speed bumps, while maintaining a positive outlook. If you're a doom-and-gloom leader, others will mirror your behaviors and emotions. Effective leaders stay strong, exude positivity, and remain calm, even when chaos erupts.

A leader doesn't have all the answers. Instead, effective leaders surround themselves with the smartest and brightest people they can find. Once your team is in place, members will be the drivers and leaders of many organizational change initiatives. It's okay not to have all the answers. Your job is to have all the right questions and challenge people to their fullest capabilities. In other words, make them shine!

When you're leading or involved in a change initiative, you must be a hands-on player and remain approachable. Don't close the door and hide in your office. Be out there, leading the charge. Encourage people to come to you with problems so they feel comfortable and know you have their backs.

Communicate, communicate, communicate. Whenever change is occurring, and it's happening all the time, make sure there's open communication. Encourage people to talk about the change, and make sure you communicate with people at every organizational level.

Be resourceful. Encourage resourcefulness by involving others in innovation, soliciting their ideas, and then using that input to foster teamwork. Encourage your people to brainstorm and share ideas, no matter how wacky. Such free-form thinking often leads to the best new products or services. Never mock an idea or allow employees to do so. You never want to stifle creativity and outside-the-box thinking. Teach your people that it's okay to try a new idea and fail. This will make them even more committed, dedicated, and excited about coming up with a better plan.

Franklin D. Roosevelt said, "It's common sense to take a method and try it. If it fails, admit it frankly and try another. But above all, try something." This is the hallmark of highly effective leadership.

When you do fail, admit it openly. You'll be a role model for your staff, sending the message that it's okay to try and not get the results you intended. Say, "I failed. We all make mistakes. If this idea didn't work out, so be it. It was worth pursuing."

Sadly, many leaders who are self-centered and narcissistic deny their failures. They would prefer to say that everything they do is perfect. That sends a terrible message to the rest of the organization.

Success Story

Alfredo, a native-born Italian, was senior vice president and general manager for a plastics extrusion company in Rimini, Italy, a division of a U.S.-owned multinational plastics company. Alfredo had taken an operation on the verge of collapse and turned it around into a highly profitable venture, thus becoming a star performer in the eyes of the company's leaders. He was promoted to executive vice president and brought to the States.

Alfredo faced a similar situation in his new job. The company was going through a bad period: worldwide sales had flattened, costs had risen beyond expectations, profits had tumbled, and employee disengagement was at a peak. The performance of company managers and workers had plummeted as everybody was afraid of what the future held.

Then suddenly, the CEO died from a heart attack, and the board appointed Alfredo as interim CEO to fill the void and prevent panic. Alfredo rose to the challenge. Using the principles espoused in our Leadership Development Course, he took these steps:

First, Alfredo insisted on absolute integrity from himself and the employees of his company. He set the example by telling the truth, even when it hurt (as it so often does when prior leaders concealed unpleasant truths), and he "walked the walk."

He focused his attention on the people who worked for him, and on managers, supervisors, and workers—everyone. Alfredo understood that great things can only be accomplished by great people, and he set an example that earned the trust of the people in his company.

He knew where he wanted to bring the company and he clearly articulated his vision and ensured that every employee in the company, from workers on the firing line right through his executive staff, understood what their roles were.

Knowing that capable employees leave the company when they lose faith in their leaders, he conducted assessments that enabled every employee to be heard. Alfredo went to great pains to listen to employees and assure that problems hindering employees were corrected.

Alfredo realized that constant training and learning better ways to achieve his goals were key to not falling behind his company's competition, and he extended that philosophy to the rest of the organization by implementing training programs for employees, both in hard and soft skills.

Alfredo personally coached his direct reports to help them overcome obstacles and improve their leadership abilities. He also assured that high potential leaders throughout the company were identified and received personal coaching. He understood that the company's lifeblood and future was invested in high potential leaders and that he could lose them if they didn't receive the grooming they needed and deserved.

He went out of his way to ensure that employees worked in an environment that encouraged people not only to work hard but to enjoy what they were doing. Accordingly, he appointed two CFOs, the traditional chief financial officer and a *chief fun officer* whose duty was to create ways for employees to have fun at work.

Within a few months of Alfredo taking the helm of the parent company, improvements were noticeable across the board in every function of the company. By the end of the year, the company's fortunes had improved dramatically.

Takeaway from Chapter 21

Recall two radically different incidents of change that you experienced in your career, one that was successful, and one that was not.

Write down the characteristics of the unsuccessful change incident: what the change was, its stated qualitative and quantitative goals, how it was implemented, how it was introduced to the organization, who introduced it, what people were responsible for its implementation, the problems it faced, how the change was evaluated, who conducted the evaluation, and your interpretation of why it failed.

Now write down the characteristics of the successful change incident: what the change was, its stated qualitative and quantitative goals, how it was implemented, how it was introduced to the organization, who introduced it, what people were responsible for its implementation, the problems it faced, how the change was evaluated, who conducted the evaluation, and your interpretation of why it succeeded.

Now sit back in a place where you can think. Analyze the differences between the successful and unsuccessful incidents of change. Ask yourself why one worked and the other didn't.

Now write down the reasons for the successful implementation and the reasons for the unsuccessful implementation as you see it. In this way you will expand your ability to avoid the problems and construct successful future change implementations.

Practice 11: Manage a Multigenerational Workforce

A large medical laboratory had employees ranging in age from 21 to 65 working side by side. Clashes occurred daily. Company managers were unprepared to handle a multigenerational workforce, because they didn't take into account the cultural differences that exist between different generations. By the time the company's leaders recognized the cause of the problem, resistance to management had hardened. It took a long time to restore equilibrium.

> *Hands-On Advice: Prepare well for the difficulties you're likely to encounter when you supervise a multigenerational workforce.*

Walk down any typical office corridor, and you're likely to find a 25-year-old working next to a 48-year-old, who's right across from a 67-year-old. Today's workplace has, indeed, become multigenerational, with workers representing four distinct age groups:

1. World War II Generation (those born before 1946).
2. Baby Boomers (born between 1946 and 1964).
3. Generation X (born between 1965 and 1980).
4. Millennials/Generation Y (born between 1980 and 2000).

Each generation, defined as a group of people who have experienced the same trends and events, over the same historical period, has a similar worldview.

In the workplace, their sometimes divergent values and belief systems may become apparent and lead to conflict. Leaders must learn how to manage each generation based on its core values, life experiences, and professional needs.

Shifting Demographics

Over the past 30 years, the workforce has been aging, and workers age 65 and older have increased by over 100 percent in the last decade. What accounts for this shift? Lower birth rates, an increasing retirement age, changes in life expectancy, and tough economic conditions have created a workplace where many Americans choose to remain in their jobs or seek new jobs past the age of 70. This has altered workplace dynamics.

The Baby Boomers are becoming the biggest segment of the labor force, and they will often hold onto their jobs until health issues arise or they're ready to retire on their own terms. In contrast, The Bureau of Labor Statistics (BLS) projects a decline in workers between the ages of 16 and 24 between 2006 and 2016.

As a result, the greatest workplace growth will involve the two oldest age groups: workers ages 55 to 64 and 65 to 74. In fact, the oldest group of workers is expected to grow considerably, as many cannot afford to retire in difficult economic times. Consequently, younger workers will have a harder time landing good jobs as companies downsize.

World War II Generation

The WWII Generation has experienced momentous and tragic historical events, including the rise of Adolph Hitler, the Great Depression, the bombing of Pearl Harbor, and U.S. involvement in WWII and Korea. Journalist Tom Brokaw notably dubbed this group "the Greatest

Generation," as the Depression and two major wars forced them to make innumerable sacrifices. Most families struggled through adversity in everyday life.

Compared to today, the family unit was much stronger, and the extended family was a greater part of American life. The Depression instilled a firsthand understanding of deprivation and scarcity. With high unemployment rates, holding a job was considered a true privilege.

These factors meshed to create a cadre of very dedicated, reliable workers. In the face of their superior work ethic, they have little patience for what they perceive to be lazy or clock-watching younger workers.

In the workplace, the WWII Generation tends to be loyal, committed, and experienced. But this group is also more uncomfortable with conflict and more easily intimidated by authority. This more traditional generation wants to be respected and valued with recognition of its age and experience. Workers can accept being paired with other employees, as long as they are regarded as mentors (and not the other way around).

From a technology standpoint, the WWII Generation may be less comfortable with email and other forms of technology. Memos and letters may have a greater impact.

Managers who reframe goals based on the organization's best interests will have greater success in motivating these workers.

Baby Boom Generation

Born between 1946 and 1964, Baby Boomers represent the largest pool of workers in the labor force today, and they also hold the most powerful jobs. Between 1945 and 1964, 76 million Americans were born, and many key events shaped their lives: the introduction of the birth control pill, the Civil Rights Movement, the assassination of President John F. Kennedy (followed by the assassinations of the Rev. Martin Luther King Jr. and Robert F. Kennedy), Woodstock, the Vietnam War, and the Women's Liberation movement.

Many of these events ushered in significant societal changes, and the 1960s came to represent an age of new independence. The antiestablishment movement and beginning of the drug culture prompted younger workers to question the values their parents embraced.

The Baby Boomers were, and still are, in many cases, more free-spirited, focused on individualism, and devoted to social causes. They redefined traditional values and felt no qualms about questioning the status quo. Parenting also changed, shaping this generation's personal development. No mom in the 1960s was without a copy of Dr. Benjamin Spock's child-rearing guides, which focused on instilling self-worth and optimism. Rules were more flexible, and discipline was less rigid.

As a result, Boomers usually have a more positive outlook than their parents and operate with more confidence. They aren't afraid to challenge existing beliefs, and they're much more vocal than the WWII generation. Boomers are comfortable with taking a strong leadership role, which explains why most of today's CEOs fall into this generational group. They're focused on success, driven to achieve, work well in teams, and work toward assuring effective communication. Baby Boomers prefer face-to-face contact and try to avoid conflict, and they don't respond well to strict managers. They often prefer group (democratic) decisions, and they're more comfortable with infrequent feedback. They value the concept of loyalty and are less likely to change jobs.

Generation X

Born between 1965 and 1980, Gen X (often called 20-somethings), comprise about one-third of the American workforce (50 million employees). This group is also referred to as the Baby Bust generation, as birth rates decreased during this period.

The major events that have shaped their lives include the invention and marketing of the personal computer, the Jonestown mass suicide, corporate turmoil and layoffs, John Lennon's death, the rise of AIDS, a stock market crash, and the *Challenger* disaster.

Increasing numbers of women joined the workforce during the Boomer years and after. In 1950, only 12 percent of married women with young children (younger than six) were part of the workforce, as compared to 45 percent by 1980. The BLS reports that mothers with children younger than 18 entered the workplace in record numbers. Between 1975 and 2000, their employment rate climbed from 47 to 73 percent. By 2004, the rate seemed to have stabilized at about 70 percent.

With moms at work and divorce rates on the rise, more children attended daycare or were left at home to care for themselves; hence, the term "latchkey kid." Gen X learned to be increasingly self-reliant and more resilient as adults.

Gen X is technologically savvy, and the computer is an integral part of their daily lives. This group is less loyal in the sense that Gen Xers are comfortable changing jobs.

Managers can retain them by offering greater independence, as well as a coaching style of leadership. Gen X prefers more frequent feedback from their bosses.

Millennial Generation

The term *Millennial* was coined by William Strauss and Neil How in their book *Generations: The History of America's Future, 1584 to 2069* (Quill; Reprint edition, 1992). Also called Generation Y or the Nintendo Generation, this group was born between 1980 and 2000. Historical events that shaped the Millennials' worldview include the World Trade Center attacks, the Iraq War, threats of terrorism, various corporate scandals (like Enron), and the Oklahoma City bombing.

The group is greatly influenced by technological advances and, most importantly, the explosion of the Internet and computer technology. Having grown up with these tools, Gen Y became tech savvy as children, and they are the most computer literate of any generation. Paper is out, and instant communication, emailing, texting, social networking, and fast results are in.

Millennials were reared in child-centered homes, with parents who were very focused on their children's development, success, well being, and happiness. These parents also had very high expectations in academics, extracurricular activities, social concerns, and community service. For these reasons, Gen Y has learned to multitask, works well in teams, and focuses on achievement-oriented goals.

The Trophy Generation refers to Millennials who were encouraged to participate in sports and other activities that awarded them trophies for mere participation, *not winning*. Some critics have complained that this group has an unrealistic sense of entitlement.

In his book, *The Trophy Kids Grow Up* (Jossey-Bass; First edition, October 13, 2008), Ron Alsop asserts that this phenomenon leads to idealized and impractical job expectations.

In a CareerBuilder.com poll, 85 percent of surveyed managers and executives reported that Millennials had a stronger sense of entitlement, expecting higher salaries, more frequent promotions, and extra vacation time. Alsop criticizes teachers and parents for lavishing Gen Y with unconditional attention and praise for every achievement, regardless of how narrow it may be.

Interestingly, Goldman Sachs launched a training program to deal with this issue. Actors play the role of Millennials who ask for feedback and more responsibility. After the performance, employees discuss the generational issues presented. Expect Millennials to be independent, hopeful, and ambitious. They crave individualized on-the-job training, as well as frequent, positive reinforcement. They're team-oriented and enjoy collaborative efforts and networking.

Unfortunately, America's recent college graduates and employed students are receiving unsatisfactory performance reviews in their new workplaces. A 2009 study of 400 business and HR managers, conducted by the Center for Professional Excellence at York College of Pennsylvania, revealed that 37 percent of this young workforce lacked professionalism, with 25 percent of their bosses complaining that professionalism in this demographic has decreased over the years. Common deficiencies cited include failure to accept personal responsibility (the greatest problem), the inability to accept constructive criticism, and poor etiquette.

Meanwhile, students and recent graduates believed they demonstrate more professionalism than employers actually experience, says David T. Polk, PhD, a professor of behavioral sciences and sociology. "Some of these problems in the workplace are the same things we are seeing in the classroom," he explains. "Students and employees alike are text messaging, surfing the Internet, and responding to cell phone calls at inappropriate times. It appears that, for many, the need to be in constant contact with friends and family has become an addiction. The addicted no longer see it as rude to be obsessively responding to calls or text messages."

Leaders polled also chided younger workers for their sense of entitlement, another barrier to professional behavior. More than 55 percent said these employees feel more entitled than do the young workers they hired just five years ago. Other negative behaviors included needing instant gratification, wanting to be coddled, exhibiting a lackluster work ethic, displaying a poor attitude or demeanor, and expecting the same treatment and rewards afforded to mid-career employees.

The leaders surveyed hold today's universities responsible for students' and graduates' lack of preparation for the real world, regardless of academic major. They urge institutions of higher learning to provide more internships and hands-on experiences, basic etiquette classes, and didactic instruction in common courtesy and personal responsibility.

Bridging the Generation Gap

At age 64, Georgia was the accounting manager for a private art museum, where she had worked for more than 30 years. She had seldom missed a day of work, racking up dozens of unused sick and vacation days over the course of her employment. Georgia was, as an associate said, a contained presence, and her relationship with her three-member support staff was strictly professional. Anyone who entered the department noticed how quiet the area was. The only sounds one could hear were fingers tapping on keyboards and file drawers opening and closing.

Georgia ran a tight ship and expected her younger staff to follow her rules. She was brusque and defensive when questioned, as she perceived any inquiries to be a challenge to her authority. The same applied to her interactions with other departments, as Georgia's famous hallway sign proved. It read: "Your failure to plan is not my emergency." Pity any department head that needed an emergency check or budget printout.

Georgia expected her staff to follow her lead without exception, and anyone who deviated from departmental routines received a sharp rebuke. Breaks and lunch hours were carefully monitored. But working in an art museum posed numerous challenges for Georgia. While the administrative work area was formal, some departments handled more creative pursuits in a more relaxed fashion. These departments were run by Baby Boomer managers, and Georgia disapproved of their more casual approach to work.

Georgia dressed in suits, while the Boomers dressed more bohemian. In contrast to Georgia's rigidity, Boomers could be boisterous and raucous, and they believed no job was worth their time if they weren't having fun.

Conflict often erupted between Georgia and Nikki, the curator who nurtured young artists and mounted the museum's exhibitions. Nikki, 45, was a fine artist who prized the artistic process over Georgia's firmly entrenched administrative procedures. She had set up numerous new programs, including an Art in the Schools project, interactive art displays, and an expanded "please touch" gift shop. These attractions had increased museum attendance, and profits, by 140 percent.

The changes had also increased Georgia's workload, which she resented. Even though the museum's board of directors had approved the hiring of an extra accounting assistant to ease the burden, Georgia didn't want to be bothered with training another employee. She also wasn't ready to admit that her systems were antiquated. Even though her staff relied on computers for data entry, Georgia thought the machines were unreliable, so she insisted on a redundant system using handwritten ledger cards. This doubled the workload, but Georgia threatened to quit every time the board asked her to streamline her systems.

The proverbial camel's back broke when Nikki introduced plans for a new traveling exhibit. The museum would receive increased revenue and national visibility if it took its show on the road, Nikki informed her fellow department heads during a management meeting. Georgia began to fume.

"You people keep making work for us," Georgia said, stiff lipped.

"*You people?*" Nikki asked, "What does that mean?"

"We're stretched to the limits with all of the ticket sales, shop purchases, and program budgets," Georgia said.

"That's insane!" Nikki said. "It's my job to boost traffic and maintain a steady stream of revenue, which is exactly what my department has been doing. Are you saying that we should refuse to grow because you're still bogged down with those damned 1920 ledger cards?"

Georgia stormed out of the meeting, walked to her office, and slammed the door. She was *so* tired of these so-called creative types who thought they owned the place. She called Gordon, chairman of the board of directors, and told him that she was incredibly upset.

Gordon found himself in a familiar, uncomfortable place. He supported Nikki's efforts to expand museum programs. Anything that brought people into the museum should take priority, he reasoned, and Nikki's track record was solid. But Gordon also knew that Georgia hated change and recoiled at even the most profitable new projects because her old systems couldn't keep up with current demands. Georgia's ledger cards had served her well 20 years ago, but her insistence on sticking to them, no matter how obsolete, would likely be her undoing.

Gordon asked Georgia to meet with Tim, the museum's IT director, to discuss how computer backup systems and a powerful network could solve the problem. Georgia balked at the suggestion, but Gordon was firm.

"Georgia, we won't have an accounting department if we don't have a museum," Gordon told her. "I know you're a longtime employee, and I value your dedication, commitment to accuracy, and integrity. But we have to upgrade our systems to accommodate critical changes. I know this is difficult for you, but I don't see any other way to get things done."

Georgia was devastated, and she took several vacation days to mull over her choices. She was only a year away from retirement age, but she had planned to keep on working until her 70th birthday. She enjoyed her work, wanted to stay busy, and was afraid of losing her identity.

The following Monday, Georgia returned to the office and approached Tim. "Let's look at the computer options," she said, sighing. Over the next few weeks, she and Tim examined different programs, and he customized them to fit her specific needs. Whenever Georgia had a problem or question, she called him, and he would come to her office.

While Georgia and Nikki would never be best friends, they dealt with each other professionally, albeit occasionally curtly. Gordon decided he could live with that arrangement and told Nikki she had the board's go-ahead to launch the traveling exhibit program. He reminded her that Georgia had been a loyal employee for three decades and needed some TLC.

"She's really doing her best," he told Nikki. "Change throws her."

"I know, and I don't hold any animosity toward her," Nikki said. "I know she shuts down when we want to try something new. Perhaps we can work on ways to reduce her fears." Gordon had bridged the generation gap.

Basic Leadership Techniques

Despite such conflicts, there are many advantages to having a multigenerational workplace. A multigenerational team encourages more flexibility and higher quality. Having employees from different generations also broadens a company's viewpoint and perspective, leading to more creativity and greater representation of the population as a whole.

In their book *Generations at Work* (AMACOM; first edition, 1999), authors Ron Zemke, Claire Raines, and Bob Filipczak suggest leaders follow five steps when managing a multigenerational workplace:

1. Be accommodating to each employee's unique generational needs, learning styles, and values. This requires an understanding of fundamental differences and preferences, as presented in this chapter.

2. Avoid a one-size-fits-all management style. Play to and respect each employee's strengths, and don't rely on a cookie-cutter approach when building teams and solving problems.

3. Have a sophisticated, fair management style, one that offers feedback and recognition that are tailored to each employee's needs.

4. Offer continuous training and encourage advancement.

5. Don't forget to nurture your experienced employees. It's easy to focus on younger workers' needs, so don't neglect your duty to monitor older workers' progress and needs.

If you're tempted to ignore generational differences, you can count on culture clashes, which manifest themselves as breakdowns in staff motivation, engagement, and retention, according to Claire Simmers, PhD, professor of management at Saint Joseph's University. During a recent panel discussion sponsored by the Greater Philadelphia Chamber of Commerce, she offered the following advice on bridging generational gaps:

1. Focus on outcomes. Different generations may take different approaches, and each may be equally effective.

2. Embrace differences. Be tolerant when seeking common ground, and teach tolerance to team members. When working with teams, encourage members to present the entire marketplace of ideas. Never make assumptions or display biases based on age.

3. Be flexible. "The employment contract of the twenty-first century is different from when Baby Boomers first entered the workforce," Simmers says. "The relationship is more fluid for both employer and employee. Younger employees may be more mobile and appear less loyal, but the same is true of most organizations."

4. Strive for an age-neutral workplace. Managers who recognize and successfully deal with intergenerational differences will "have a more pleasant and more productive business," Simmers says. Communication improves, and recruitment practices and systems

are redesigned for the twenty-first century. Employees are more engaged, motivated, and productive, which ultimately improves the organization's bottom line.

Work Arrangements and Benefits

IBM Global Business Services takes into account the unique needs of each generation through life-staged benefits and rewards.

As each generation's values are distinct, so are their life-cycle-based needs, with specific benefits appealing to different groups. For example:

- Workers in their 20s appreciate auto insurance, extra vacations, gym memberships, and continuing education.
- Those in their 30s could use mortgage assistance, parenting and childcare services, college savings plans, and retirement education.
- For workers in their 40s, benefits like a savings plan and retirement education may be most needed.
- For the 50-plus group, workers will value college tuition assistance, retirement planning, health care, and vacations.
- For workers age 60 and above, life insurance, retirement planning, and more flexible hours are most appealing.
- Tailor benefits to specific groups' needs, and they will appreciate your efforts to reward them for a job well done.

Takeaway from Chapter 22

Assume you're managing a department of 100 employees for a large electronics manufacturer. You have workers from many age groups representing four generations: World War II Generation, Baby Boomers, Generation X, and Millennials. Next, assume a problem arises regarding overtime distribution. Apparently, some employees have been getting more overtime work than others, and since overtime pays time and one-half, employees have been squabbling . . . and rightfully so.

The system your department uses is using supervisors to post overtime hours on a large whiteboard hung near the break room. This system, once adequate for a small department with 25 employees is now cumbersome for a department employing 100 people. Also, only some employees can handle specialized jobs, and the overtime in this case is restricted to a small number of employees.

Your reputation as a fair boss is in danger of being shredded, unless you do something quickly to restore the overtime system's equitability.

Your IT department has a solution. It will print daily reports that contain the overtime hours worked for all of the department's employees. This seems like an effective solution and your job is to sell it to the department's employees. But already some of them are griping about: (1) loss of the posted overtime board that all employees can see, (2) knowledge that IT has been known to make mistakes, (3) accusations that one supervisor plays favorites, and (4) complaints that you are making a simple system complicated.

Your job is to sell the new IT-proposed system, which you know is going to do the job. How do you handle the employees representing the four different generations working for you? Think this one out carefully because your reputation for fairness is on the line, as well as your ability to motivate four disparate groups of people. Describe how you will resolve the problems and especially how you will approach the employees from the four different generational groups.

Congratulations

Now that you have finished reading the book and completing the takeaway exercises, please apply the leadership lessons you have learned to the problems and opportunities you face. By applying the takeaway lessons, you can become a highly effective leader. I wish you the greatest success in both your work and personal lives.

About the Author

Jeff Wolf is recognized as one of the top executive coaches in the country and is a dynamic and engaging speaker. A highly sought-after business consultant, his strategic focus in solving corporate and human issues has earned him continuing raves from national firms.

Leadership Excellence magazine named him one of America's Top 100 Thought Leaders for his accomplishments in leadership development, managerial effectiveness, and organizational productivity.

He is currently president of Wolf Management Consultants, one of the most comprehensive consulting, coaching, and training firms in the world. The firm specializes in helping people, teams, and organizations achieve maximum effectiveness.

Throughout the years, he has been a recognized authority on leadership, and his principles, strategies, and inspiration have influenced dramatic growth and changes in countless organizations.

He may be reached at www.wolfmotivation.com.

Ken Shelton is CEO of Authentic Leadership and founding editor/publisher of *Leadership Excellence* magazine. He collaborated with Stephen R. Covey on *The 7 Habits of Highly Effective People* and is editor/publisher of 128 others books on personal and leadership development.

Index